John Henry Newman
and His Age

John Henry Newman and His Age

OWEN F. CUMMINGS

Foreword by John C. Wester

CASCADE Books · Eugene, Oregon

JOHN HENRY NEWMAN AND HIS AGE

Copyright © 2019 Owen F. Cummings. All rights reserved. Except for brief quotations in critical publications or reviews, no part of this book may be reproduced in any manner without prior written permission from the publisher. Write: Permissions, Wipf and Stock Publishers, 199 W. 8th Ave., Suite 3, Eugene, OR 97401.

Cascade Books
An Imprint of Wipf and Stock Publishers
199 W. 8th Ave., Suite 3
Eugene, OR 97401

www.wipfandstock.com

PAPERBACK ISBN: 978-1-5326-6009-2
HARDCOVER ISBN: 978-1-5326-6010-8
EBOOK ISBN: 978-1-5326-6011-5

Cataloging-in-Publication data:

Names: Cummings, Owen F., author. | Wester, John C., foreword

Title: John Henry Newman and his age / by Owen C. Cummings, with a foreword by Archbishop John C. Wester.

Description: Eugene, OR : Cascade Books, 2019 | Includes bibliographical references.

Identifiers: ISBN 978-1-5326-6009-2 (paperback) | ISBN 978-1-5326-6010-8 (hardcover) | ISBN 978-1-5326-6011-5 (ebook)

Subjects: LCSH: Newman, John Henry, 1801–1890. | Catholicism—Great Britain—History—19th century. | Catholic converts—Great Britain—History. | Oxford movement. | High Church movement.

Classification: LCC BX4705.N5 C85 2019 (print) | LCC BX4705.N5 (ebook)

Manufactured in the U.S.A.   12/13/18

With grateful thanks
Dedicated to
Abbot Peter McCarthy, OCSO
And the Trappist Community of Oregon

Contents

Foreword by John C. Wester | ix
Acknowledgements | xiii
Introduction | xv

1. Newman's Pope: Pope Pius IX (1846–78) | 1
2. The Oxford Movement | 22
3. John Henry Newman (1801–90) | 33
4. In Newman's Circle from Oxford: John Keble, Hurrell Froude, Edward Bouverie Pusey | 61
5. In Newman's Circle from the Oratory: Ambrose St. John, Frederick William Faber, Edward Caswall | 88
6. Newman's Women! | 99
7. Vatican I, 1869–70 | 107
8. Newman the Poet | 133
9. Newman the Preacher | 151
10. Looking Back | 162

Appendix: Going Further | 171

Bibliography | 173

Foreword

THE INSPIRATION FOR THE title of Robert Bolt's famous play, "A Man for All Seasons," came from Robert Whittington, a contemporary of St. Thomas More. Bolt gave this English saint a compliment that has endured through the ages, one that very few can claim. With this latest of his many fine works, Deacon Owen Cummings persuades the reader that Cardinal John Henry Newman is one of those few who deserves such a grand accolade. With his usual gift for thorough research and rich insight, Deacon Cummings explores Newman the man, as well as his theology, his preaching, his poetry, his contemporaries, and the challenges that helped to forge one of the greatest churchmen of the nineteenth century.

Deacon Cummings reveals in the pages that follow that Newman transcended the seasons of time, possessing a solid understanding of the Fathers of the Church as well as early Christian dogmas and at the same time exhibiting a creative spirit that allowed those dogmas to breathe and find new life in the "signs of the times." He was a lens that brought doctrine, tradition, and creativity into sharp focus. His important book, *An Essay on the Development of Christian Doctrine*, published in 1845, has had a profound impact on Church life, and its influence can be seen in the writings of the Second Vatican Council and beyond. Little wonder that Newman was invited to be a theological expert at the First Vatican Council.

The seasons of a man's life are also comprised of the people who influence him, whether intimate friends or ideological adversaries. Newman had both and he never ceased to benefit from and contribute to them all. Cummings has a keen eye for singling out crucial relationships and weaves together a rich tapestry of those people who were part of Newman's life: from Pius IX to those who were part of Newman's inner circle in the Oxford Movement, like John Keble, Hurrell Froude, and Edward Pusey. He also explores Newman's friends from the Oratory in Birmingham and some of the women who played a role in his long life. It is through these relationships that Deacon Cummings gives the reader a peek into the heart of Newman. He was a real gentleman and he cherished his friendships. As the late Archbishop John R. Quinn stated in his book, *Revered and Reviled: A Reexamination of Vatican I*, "Newman had a profound concern for people and was acutely sensitive to what might be injurious or hurtful to them. He had a highly developed pastoral sense." Such concern and care for the feelings of others is something that speaks eloquently to our time. Little wonder that Newman chose for his motto *cor ad cor loquitur*. When it comes to friendships and matters of the heart, Newman left us an imitable legacy, clearly outlined in this marvelous introduction to his life and thought.

The seasons of Newman's life can certainly be chronicled by the liturgical seasons in which he preached so eloquently. In his hundreds and hundreds of carefully composed sermons (each of which were certainly beyond the recommended five to eight minutes for today's homilies!) we see the maturity of his thinking. What his preaching lacked in drama it compensated for in substance. For Newman, the pulpit was truly what the poet George Herbert, in his poem *The Windows*, called that "glorious and transcendent place" where God's love and mercy could shine brightly through the window of his preaching. Cummings does justice to this body of Newman's work, allowing the Word of God to continue to reverberate in our hearts as it did in Newman's.

All of the seasons in one's life are colored and textured by beauty. In this regard, Deacon Cummings underscores the beauty that emanates from Newman's heart in his poetry. Cardinal Newman chose many themes for his poems, from dreams to solitude to the kindly light. In all of them, we glimpse the heart of the man as Deacon Cummings allows us to savor and taste the richness found in Newman's poetry, a poetry that expresses meaning that can only be found in verse.

In all of the seasons that make up Newman's life, one thing is perfectly clear from reading this delightful new book: Newman fixed himself on the heart of Christ. Whether in his theology, his friendships, his pastoral ministry, his preaching, or his poetry, Newman's love for Jesus Christ is at the center of it all. Erasmo Leiva-Merikakis tells us that Cardinal Newman gave us a "most practical clue to Christian contemplation" when he wrote: "Scripture has set [Jesus] before us in His actual sojourn on earth, in His gestures, words, and deeds, in order that we may have that on which to fix our eyes." In season and out, Newman fixed his eyes on Christ, trusting in

Foreword

his "kindly light," to lead him one step at a time through all the seasons of life. I believe that Deacon Cummings has succeeded in persuading us that Cardinal John Henry Newman is a "man for all seasons." Furthermore, he also leads us to trust that this pastor and preacher, theologian, and poet, is now with Christ the Light, where all seasons and all time are one, and where "the night is gone; And with the morn those angel faces smile."

Archbishop John C. Wester
Archbishop of Santa Fe
4000 St. Joseph's Place NW
Albuquerque, NM 87120

Acknowledgements

IN PUTTING TOGETHER THIS little book on John Henry Newman the author has incurred many debts, too many to mention by name. But because of the great labor involved, the meticulous care to detail, and our friendship in Christ, I must mention with great gratitude the Most Rev. John C. Wester, Archbishop of Santa Fe, who graciously wrote an introduction, the Rev. Dr. Robin Parry of Worcester, academic editor for Wipf and Stock and a fine theologian in his own right, and Susan Ferguson of Portland, Oregon, my copy-editor on this side of the world. Thank you so much.

Introduction

THE NEWMAN SCHOLAR RODERICK Strange entitles the first chapter in his book on Newman "Have You Read Any Newman?" It is a great way to begin a book on John Henry Newman. Most people have never read anything by him, and perhaps that is true even of students of theology. Yet, this nineteenth century thinker has so much to offer the contemporary student of theology or even the interested layman, not only in terms of his ideas and his thinking but also through his life. Autobiographies and biographies make compelling reading because we often see something of our own lives and their complexity in the lives of others. Newman is one of those theologians about whose life we know a great deal through his own writings, journals, and letters.

As well as those writings that come from Newman's own pen, there is a massive number of studies about his life and his theology, and there seems to be no end to them. Newman continues to fascinate. This popularizing little book is written to introduce Newman and his age to those who know little or nothing about him. The first chapter deals with Pope Pius IX, the Pope who served during most of Newman's life. This chapter provides the background to those issues in the wider church that form the backdrop to Newman. It is followed by a chapter on the Oxford Movement. This is the great movement in the Church of England in which Newman found himself and ultimately from which he moved on when he was received into the Catholic Church. It is important to have some understanding of the richness of this movement. The third chapter is given over to the life of John Henry Newman himself. It tries to capture something of the richness of the man from a variety of viewpoints. Chapters 4, 5, and 6 are taken up with Newman's friends. He had a great capacity for friendship and we can see something of how he relates to them and how they relate to him throughout his journey both in the Church of England and to the Church

INTRODUCTION

of Rome. Chapter 6 describes some of the women in Newman's life. It owes a lot to the scholarship of Joyce Sugg, who was once my colleague at Newman University Birmingham, and who has been studying and publishing on Newman for decades. Chapter 7 considers the First Vatican Council, 1869–70. Newman did not participate in the Council and, while he accepted its decree on papal infallibility, he knew some of the bishops and theologians who attended the Council and he had some important things to add by way of clarification. Chapters 8 and 9 consider Newman as both poet and preacher. Finally, chapter 10 attempts to look back over Newman's life and what he stood for and to find lessons for the present day.

This is not intended to be a work of high scholarship but rather a modest introduction to John Henry Newman, his times—essentially the long nineteenth century, and some of the people and events whose lives intersected with his. It weaves together history, theology, and spirituality, and my hope is that it will lead the interested reader to Newman himself and to the many fine studies of Newman scholars whose works are cited in the bibliography.

1

Newman's Pope
Pope Pius IX (1846–78)

Pius was the first pope to identify himself wholeheartedly with ultramontanism, i.e., the tendency to centralize authority in church government and doctrine and the Holy See.

John Norman Davidson Kelly[1]

The pontificate of Pius IX . . . witnessed the victory of Ultramontanism over Gallicanism.

Ciaran O'Carroll[2]

FROM GIOVANNI MARIA MASTAI-FERRETI TO POPE PIUS IX

FOR THE FIRST HALF of his life John Henry Newman was an Anglican, and for the second half a Roman Catholic. The nineteenth-century Catholicism to which he was drawn was marked by an increasing centralization on the papacy. This papal-centric emphasis is known as "ultramontanism," a movement to which Newman found himself increasingly opposed. Pope

---

1. Kelly, *Oxford Dictionary of Popes*, 310.
2. See O'Carroll, "Pius IX: Pastor and Prince," 125.

Pius IX, who was pope during most of Newman's life, and who was born in 1792, nine years before Newman, identified himself with ultramontanism, both consciously and unconsciously, and that identification spelled the end of Gallicanism—a kind of independence movement in the French Catholic Church—not only in its French form but in any kind of thinking that might be considered critical of the papacy. Pope Pius IX with his ultramontane perspective shaped the excessive papal-centrism of modern times, not only in respect of church governance but also in terms of ecclesiology. His predecessor, Pope Gregory XVI, a known strict conservative in virtually everything, viewed Cardinal Giovanni Maria Mastai-Ferretti as something of an ecclesiastical liberal and said that even Mastai-Ferretti's cats were liberals. Mastai-Ferretti was elected pope as Gregory's successor in 1846, taking the name of Pius IX, and he served the church as pope until his death in 1878. It would be fair to say that he moved from a moderate liberalism to an extreme ultramontanism.

Although concerns were raised about his suspected epileptic seizures, he was ordained to the priesthood in 1819, and was sent by Pope Pius VII to Chile and Peru, accompanying Msgr. Giovanni Muzi, the apostolic delegate to those countries from 1823 until 1825. He was the first pope ever to have an experience of South America, although this was his only prolonged trip outside Italy, and arguably his informed awareness of social and political issues was too closely identified throughout his career with Italy and Europe, particularly Catholic Europe. The South American experience, however, stimulated his interest in the missions.[3] After he returned from this extended visit to South America, he showed no particular interest in pursuing a papal diplomatic career.

He became Archbishop of Spoleto in 1827, was transferred to Imola in 1832, and was made a cardinal in 1840. While in Imola, Mastai-Ferretti was very popular with the poor, and his charitable activity constantly reduced him to straitened financial circumstances. "Far from courting an easy popularity amongst the propertied classes, or the higher clergy, he continued to show, even after he had received the red hat, an independence and liberality of outlook which often cost him the friendship of the larger landholders in his diocese as well as that of the senior government officials."[4] With this sense of commitment to the poor it is not difficult to understand his attitude to the reformers and progressives of his day, an attitude much less

3. Coppa, *Pope Pius IX*, 30.
4. Hales, *Pio Nono*, 35.

suspicious than many of his peers. He sided with the progressive cohort in the church and was an advocate for political reform. His views had been influenced by the work of the priest-philosopher and politician Vincenzo Gioberti (1801–52), and he was sympathetic to Gioberti's liberalizing ideas, but E. E. Y. Hales is right to issue this caution: "It would be difficult to imagine anything more erroneous than the supposition that Pius was sailing with the wind in adopting liberal policies. He was not a great political thinker . . . but he was certainly not so foolish as to suppose that a liberal policy was going to be easy."[5] Pius was a moderate liberal, not an extremist reformer politically. And theologically? He would have had a basic awareness of theology—what Owen Chadwick calls "[theology] in outline," but also a theology "without subtleties."[6]

POPE PIUS IX

In 1846, the somewhat liberalizing Mastai-Ferretti was elected Pope as Pope Pius IX. "The election of Count Giuseppe Mastai Ferretti as Pope Pius IX in the spring of 1846, after the draconian years of Gregory XVI's rule, raised the sorts of hopes and expectations aroused in 1978 by the election of Karol Wojtyla after the fraught and depressing final years of Paul VI."[7] One of the first things he did as pope was to issue an amnesty for political refugees/revolutionaries from the Papal States—that section of Italy that fell under the jurisdiction of the popes—who had been living outside of Italy. They returned in their hundreds. This generous political gesture would create a climate expectant of rapid social and political change in the direction of a unified Italy. The dream of Italian unification had begun to grow towards the end of the eighteenth century, in part stimulated by the French Revolution and the Italian conquests of Napoleon Bonaparte.[8] Italian unification was everywhere in the air, not only in political circles, so that, for example, it had become the passion of the immensely popular dramatist and poet Vittori Alfieri (1749–1803). Allied to these Italian nationalist aspirations were the constant criticisms of political commentators in Europe. "They

---

5. Hales, *Pio Nono*, 57. David G. Schultenover questions the common view that Pius IX was even initially a liberal (*A View from Rome*, 28).

6. Chadwick, *History of the Popes 1830–1914*, 173.

7. See Duffy, "Age of Pio Nono," 54.

8. See Bokenkotter, *Concise History of the Catholic Church*, 218–308, and Duffy, *Saints and Sinners*, 247–86.

grumbled that the clock of Europe had stopped in Rome, which was seen to combine feudal pretensions with Renaissance extravagance and whose rigidity and isolation led to stagnation, lamenting that while the world had changed, the church and its leaders had not. The papacy, and their perspective, represented a relic of the past, finding its persistence to the present ironic and unacceptable."[9] When it comes to the social and economic circumstances of the citizens of the Papal States, it has been pointed out that they were certainly no worse off than the working classes of European democracies, and in some respects were better off. There was no parallel in the Papal States, for example, to the Great Famine in Ireland (1845–52), largely mismanaged by the "enlightened" British government. However, Anti-papal sentiment at the time would never have acknowledged anything but what they took to be egregious mismanagement in papal government. "The Papal State was a benevolent theocracy. There was no longer a place in the Europe of 1864 for benevolent theocracies, and it may have been in the nature of things that the rising tide of the *Risorgimento* [the movement to unite Italy] should sweep this State away. But that is not a reason for stigmatizing Pio Nono's [i.e., Pius IX's] government as oppressive, or corrupt, or economically backward...."[10] The overly negative opinions of the Papal States were, of course, well known to Pius IX. He could not have been unaware of them. However, there never was a time when Pius considered relinquishing the Papal States. He regarded their political independence as essential, indeed willed by God, to his spiritual leadership as pope. He was never to waver on this point.

At a personal level, no one disagreed with the universally acknowledged fact that Pio Nono was a most charming man. Eamon Duffy writes: "He was genial, unpretentious, wreathed in clouds of snuff, always laughing."[11] In a more popular book on the papacy Duffy goes somewhat further, but without acknowledging any detailed sources, in describing Pius's affability and charm: "He was devout, kindly, unstuffy and at ease in the company of women (there were vague rumors of romantic irregularities earlier in his life, which didn't necessarily do him any harm in Italian opinion)."[12] Even his critics have to admit that he was most likable. For example, John Henry Newman, no great admirer of the Pope, wrote of him: "His personal

---

9. Coppa, *Politics and Papacy*, 1–2.
10. Hales, *Pio Nono*, 170.
11. Duffy, *Saints and Sinners*, 293.
12. Duffy, *Ten Popes Who Shook the World*, 95.

presence was of a kind that no one could withstand.... The main cause of his popularity was the magic of his presence.... His uncompromising faith, his courage, the graceful mingling in the name of the human and the divine, the humor, the wit, the playfulness with which he tempered his severity, his naturalness, and then his true eloquence."[13] Newman was to take exception to what he saw as a growing narrowness of theological and ecclesiological vision, especially in regard to the issue of papal infallibility, and so that makes his generous description of Pius significant.

Apparently, Pius's sense of fun virtually knew no bounds. On one occasion, a number of Anglican clergymen were visiting Rome and asked for his blessing. Pius pronounced over them, with humor, the prayer for the blessing of incense: "May you be blessed by him in whose honor you are to be burned."[14] Pius moved with ease in the company of women. He was an admirer of Queen Victoria, and she sent him a personal letter of sympathy in 1848 at the time of the revolution that took him into exile. In some ways, he seems to have considered himself a progressive Victorian,[15] and may even have entertained the utterly unrealistic idea that Queen Victoria might one day become a Roman Catholic.[16]

As a thinker, Pius was no intellectual. Odo Russell, the British ambassador to the Holy See and a man who was genuinely fond of Pius, commented on his "amiable but weak mind."[17] In this regard, advisers became all-important, but here too Pius was not blessed with great success. "Inevitably, therefore," as Eamon Duffy writes, "he was surrounded by people who endorsed and exaggerated his opinions and prejudices: as in the cabinets of Margaret Thatcher, success at the court of Pio Nono depended on being and being seen to be 'one of us.'"[18] He placed too much faith and trust, for example, in Msgr. George Talbot, a converted Anglican priest. Talbot was unstable and reactionary. For example, he sowed suspicions in the Pope's mind about the orthodoxy and fidelity of Newman. Duffy describes the man in devastating terms: "He was certainly devious, feline, wreathed in

---

13. Vidler, *The Church in an Age of Revolution*, 147.
14. Duffy, *Saints and Sinners*, 293.
15. Hales, *Pio Nono*, 129.
16. Duffy, *Ten Popes Who Shook the World*, 95.
17. O'Malley, SJ, "Beatification of Pope Pius IX," 10.
18. Duffy, "Age of Pio Nono," 55. Church historian John W. O'Malley adds to this description of Pius: "Pius surrounded himself with mediocrities, adept principally at telling him what he wanted to hear, a fact commented on by many contemporaries otherwise favorably disposed toward him" (*Catholic History for Today's Church*, 55).

intrigue, his view of the world and the church a perpetual game of cowboys and Indians, heroes and villains."[19] Somewhat less devastating is Cardinal Manning's view of Talbot as "the most imprudent man that ever lived."[20] In 1868, Talbot was removed from the Roman Curia and placed in a mental institution near Paris, where he died in 1886.

CARDINAL GIACOMO ANTONELLI (1806–76)

While George Talbot was papal chamberlain, Cardinal Giacomo Antonelli was Secretary of State. Antonelli was born into a family that was wealthy in its own right, but his father, Domenico, realistically recognized that both securing and promoting his wealth in the Papal States would demand an ecclesiastic in his family. Giacomo was to be that ecclesiastic and so in 1823 he was enrolled in Rome's University of the Sapienza, gradually finding himself fully engaged in the faculty of jurisprudence. To make headway in a good civil-service position in the Papal States one had to take holy orders, and so in 1841 Giacomo was ordained a deacon. He was an ecclesiastical careerist who never moved beyond diaconate toward priesthood. "[Domenico] was most anxious for his son to become a priest—a step which Giacomo scrupulously avoided, despite parental encouragement."[21] He received promotion upon promotion in the service of the Papal States on two counts: first, his fairly consistent conservative political positions, and second, his established and growing competence in the area of economic management.

After the election of Mastai-Ferretti as Pope Pius IX, Antonelli found himself trusted with ever more and newer responsibilities by the Pope. "Antonelli analyzed and understood Pius better than the others around him, appreciating that his reformism was moderated by his obsessive concern that no measure be undertaken which might compromise his spiritual mission. . . . Pius found himself torn between the need to effect economies, and the desire to provide for the country's social ills. Confronted with this

---

19. Duffy, *Saints and Sinners*, 294.

20. As reported in Shane Leslie, *Henry Edward Manning: His Life and Labors* (London, 1921), xii, cited in Sheridan Gilley, "New Light on an Old Scandal," 178. Gilley's own description of Talbot is closer to that of Duffy: "A born tittle-tattler and intriguer, whose low cunning seems the more unattractive for its sanction, an unctuous piety. His lack of mental balance eventually consigned him to a lunatic asylum at Passy, where the Pope wrote to him, charitably humoring his delusions."

21. Coppa, *Cardinal Giacomo Antonelli*, 31.

difficult choice, he sought assistance, calling upon Antonelli, who knew the finances of state inside and out."[22] Small wonder, then, that this papal reliance on Antonelli resulted in his being made a Cardinal in 1847, just forty-one years of age. Reliance on Antonelli continued throughout all the troublesome years of attempts at Italian unification, even when Piedmont annexed most of the Papal States. The conservative policies of Antonelli were seen as particularly problematic by those intent upon Italian unification. He was both feared and vilified by his enemies, both privately and publicly. "[Antonelli] reportedly sought to resign but Pius would not let him do so, imploring, 'You have been with me during easy times, now that troublesome times are upon us, you must remain.' Pius appreciated that he rather than Antonelli inspired the intransigent policy, and that the removal of his minister would only expose his personal responsibility, rendering all the more difficult the course he had chartered."[23] Probably more than anyone else close to the Pope, Antonelli realized the inevitability of the unification of Italy. Yet he seems never to have wavered in his support of Pius's insistence that his temporal power, the Papal States, were necessary to the exercise of his spiritual responsibilities.

Detailed and lurid accounts of Antonelli's sex life abound, making it exceedingly difficult to know what to believe. His attacks of gout were often put down to venereal disease. Church historian and historian of the papacy Eamon Duffy says that the Cardinal "practiced celibacy only episodically."[24] One wonders, however, how fair this judgment is. Frank J. Coppa, whose area of expertise is nineteenth- and twentieth-century Italian politics and church history, and who has written the most substantive and well-researched account of Antonelli in English, writes as follows: "Those who discounted the Cardinal's contributions and were prepared to believe the worst of him, have never adequately explained why Pio Nono, acknowledged by almost all to lead a saintly life, kept a 'libertine' in his service. We know that the Pope was aware of the stories which circulated about his Minister. Indeed, a series of anonymous letters were sent to the pontiff recounting the Cardinal's alleged escapades, lurid sex life, and disloyalty, calling for Antonelli's removal. Pius, distressed by these letters, discounted

---

22. Coppa, *Cardinal Giacomo Antonelli*, 38–39.
23. Coppa, *Cardinal Giacomo Antonelli*, 111.
24. Duffy, "It Takes All Sorts to Make a Saint," 1180. See also J. Derek Holmes, *Triumph of the Holy See*, 130.

them."25 It seems most unlikely indeed, although it could never be completely falsified, that Pius would have been unaware of Antonelli's "episodic celibacy" and not have confronted him about it, or distanced himself from him.

What is not in doubt is that Antonelli used his powerful office to promote his family to such an extent that he was accused of replacing the nepotism of popes with the nepotism of the Secretary of State. Three of his brothers were given well-paying jobs in the papal civil service, and all were made papal counts. At the same time, Antonelli attended Mass daily, received communion once a week, and dispersed large amounts of money to various charities. One of the recipients of Antonelli's charity was Don Giovanni Bosco, now St. John Bosco, in his work for abandoned children. Owen Chadwick sums up Antonelli in these words: "He had not been ordained to be priestly, he was ordained because that opened a career."26 That is not an unfair judgment, but in this world of messy human affairs perhaps one ought not to expect heroic and ideal performance.

THE UNIFICATION OF ITALY

Italy was not the unified state that it is today with Rome as its capital. It was divided up into various kingdoms and principalities, including the Papal States. The Papal States were the constant focus of political intrigue and ambition on the part of the rulers of France and Austria as well as the various Italian monarchical parties. Mid-nineteenth-century Italian politics and history are like a chess game between these various groups. The endpoint of the game, agreed virtually but in various ways by everybody, was the unification of Italy.

A movement, ultimately to be successful, was underway in the mid-nineteenth century to unite Italy under one leader, and for a time it seemed possible that that leader might be Pius IX, a sort of president of a united Italy. The Italian philosopher-theologian Antonio Rosmini (1797–1855) dreamed and hoped of such a possibility. As has been noted, Pius was perceived by many to be something of a reformer and a liberal. Soon after his election he embarked on a series of measures designed to improve the conditions in the Papal States. As well as declaring an amnesty for former revolutionaries in his territories—something that a number of seasoned

---

25. Coppa, *Cardinal Giacomo Antonelli*, 185.
26. Chadwick, *History of the Popes 1830–1914*, 94.

European politicians took issue with—he went on to initiate more immediately practical decisions and measures. For example, he introduced railways and gas street lighting in Rome itself and he put into place an agricultural institute to improve productivity and to help farmers make the most of their farms. He had the chains removed from the gates of the Jewish ghetto in Rome and after some time the gates were burned down. Jews had been required to attend Christian sermons weekly, but Pius abolished this absurd requirement.

Things were changing and changing fast in papal Italy. Pius ordered that insults against the Jews, fairly typical in the annual comedies of the Roman Carnival, were to cease. Frederic Ozanam, founder of the St. Vincent De Paul Society, described Pius in glowing terms as "the envoy sent by God to conclude the great business of the nineteenth century, the alliance of religion and liberty."[27] Ozanam was also an eyewitness of the torchlight processions to the Pope's Quirinal Palace celebrating his popularity and his liberal policies. Putting all this in summary form, one Englishman writing to another in 1848 remarked: "A pretty state we are in altogether, with a radical pope teaching all Europe rebellion."[28]

The prospect of a more liberal papal regime with whatever actual reality it had came sharply to an end in the year 1848, the year of European revolutions, and the year in which the city of Rome itself fell to Italian revolutionaries. "In spite of inevitable differences, the revolutions in Europe during 1848 were simultaneous and often inspired by a common ideology. . . . For a time it seemed that the whole of Europe was attempting to reorganize itself according to the principles of democracy and nationalism."[29] In that year, Pius established an elected municipal government and agreed to a new constitution for the Papal States that included an elected chamber with the power to veto papal policy. As popular sentiment increasingly demanded the expulsion of Austria from Italy, however, Pius was called upon to give his leadership and endorsement to this move. His response was to affirm that he would not send troops against the Catholic nation of Austria, and to invite Italians to return to their established princes and abandon the notion of a united and federal Italy under his proposed leadership. To say the least, this was singularly naïve. Duffy describes what happened:

---

27. Aubert, "Pius IX, Pope, Blessed," 11:385; see also Hales, *Pio Nono*, 50–51.

28. Robert Wilberforce to J. B. Mozley, cited in Vidler, *The Church in an Age of Revolution*, 148.

29. Holmes, *Triumph of the Holy See*, 106.

"Overnight, from being the most popular man in Italy, he became the most hated."[30] Romans began to speak of *Pio Nono Secondo,* the second Pius IX. In November of 1848, his prime minister, Pellegrino Rossi, was murdered, and in the same month Pius had to escape from the city dressed as a simple priest, an escape orchestrated with considerable political wisdom by his loyal ally Cardinal Antonelli. Rome was in revolt. From the safe position of Gaeta, in Naples, the Pope called upon the Catholic powers of Europe to restore him to Rome and the Papal States. Consequently, in July 1849 French troops took Rome, and Pius returned in 1850. Duffy writes: "He never recovered from his exile of 1848, and for the rest of his life remained convinced that political concessions to democracy merely fueled the fires of revolution. The liberal honeymoon was over."[31] For the next two decades the Pope depended on the presence of French and Austrian troops to maintain his position in the Papal States, and on Cardinal Antonelli's counsel and policies to maintain and to safeguard the primacy of his spiritual position. As always "[Antonelli] pledged his diplomatic expertise to implement the conservative policy flowing from the Pope's religious convictions."[32]

REACTION TO EUROPEAN LIBERALISM

Liberalism is a notoriously slippery notion, but we may take our point of departure for its definition from church historian Alec Vidler: "Broadly speaking, in the nineteenth century liberals were those people who were in favor of the new kind of state and society that had issued from the [French] Revolution."[33] That is an excellent starting-point. "Freedom, equality, brotherhood" had been the cry of the French Revolution, and liberals were those who wanted to see that cry echoed in every aspect of society. Liberalism referred to those who espoused constitutional and representative governments, who favored religious toleration, and who advocated the separation of church and state. These ideas were commonplace in Europe and in the United States of America and were daily gaining ground also among many Catholics. Although it is dangerous to make grand and general descriptions, it is probably fair to say that political liberalism marked France and parts of Italy especially, while a more intellectual liberalism was characteristic of

30. Duffy, *Saints and Sinners,* 288.
31. Duffy, *Saints and Sinners,* 288.
32. Coppa, *Cardinal Giacomo Antonelli,* 71.
33. Vidler, *The Church in an Age of Revolution,* 148.

England and Germany. After his brief two-year flirtation with liberal ideas, Pius IX set his face firmly against liberalism in all its forms, and to further this project he encouraged the Jesuits to found the conservative newspaper *Civilta cattolica* in 1849 and he gave strong support to the establishment of another news organ, *L'Osservatore Romano*, in 1860. Negatively both organs countered liberalism and positively supported ultramontane ideas.[34]

Pius was deeply opposed to religious toleration. He came out against, for example, the modest degree of tolerance shown toward Protestant worship by the Spanish government. He took issue with the grand Duke of Tuscany, who permitted Jews to attend the university. In Italy the center of liberalism was undoubtedly the city of Turin in the Kingdom of Piedmont. Its king, Victor Emmanuel II, with his prime minister, Count Cavour, continued to promote the cause of Italian unification, especially against the hated Austrian presence. "Count Cavour . . . favored a separation of Church and State. The Count explained his preference for the ecclesiastical freedom which prevailed in the United States, convinced that it would eventually take root in Italy."[35] A "liberal" policy overtly hostile to the "conservative" church was pursued in Piedmont. For example, in 1854 almost all monasteries and convents were suppressed, except for some nursing and teaching congregations. They had practical value for modern and progressive society in a way that contemplative religious foundations did not. In 1860, the Legations and the Marches of Ancona, both within the Papal States, were taken by Piedmont. This meant that a small residual strip of land on the west coast of Italy was all that remained of the Papal States. Defense forces from devout Catholics came together from all over Europe to fight on behalf of the Pope. French, Spanish, Portuguese, Polish, Irish—all rallied to the papal side. The Irish Brigade was under the command of one Major O'Reilly. Eamon Duffy notes wittily that the Pope was initially doubtful about the Irish contingent in these defense forces "because he feared the effects on Irishmen of the ready availability of cheap Italian wine."[36] From the perspective of Pius, the entire situation in Italy had a rather apocalyptic feel to it. On the one hand, liberal Piedmont represented the forces of evil and, on the other, he was leading the legions of God. Roger Aubert comments: "To realists who tried to persuade him that sooner or later he must

---

34. Heft, SM, "From the Pope to the Bishops," 59. See also Holmes, *Triumph of the Holy See*, 135.

35. Coppa, *Cardinal Giacomo Antonelli*, 77, slightly adapted.

36. Duffy, *Saints and Sinners*, 289.

negotiate, Pius IX opposed a mystical confidence in divine providence, nourished by the conviction that the political convulsions in which he was implicated were only an episode in the great battle between God and Satan, in which Satan's defeat was inevitable."[37]

POPE PIUS IX AND JUDAISM

The new and liberal Pope who had dismantled the Jewish Roman ghetto reinstated this ghetto after his return from exile. It was part and parcel of his struggle with liberalism. To Pius's struggle with liberalism we must add the Mortara episode.[38] Edgardo Mortara (1851–1940) was a Jewish boy whose family lived in Bologna, a city at that time within the Papal States. When he was still only one, Edgardo became seriously ill and a Christian servant in the Mortara household baptized him secretly, fearing that the child would die without the benefit of the sacrament, and so would forfeit the blessing of heaven. The story of the secret baptism broke, and the Inquisition moved in. Since Edgardo was now technically a Christian, and since the law forbade Christians to be brought up as Jews, the now six-year-old was taken from his parents in 1858 and put under the direct protection of the Pope himself. There was, as one might expect, an uproar throughout the world, but Pius was deaf to all pleas to return the child to his parents. Owen Chadwick summarizes not only the reaction of contemporaries to the event, but what must be the sentiment of any ordinary person when he says, "Even today it is hard to read with equanimity the curial defenses of what was done: a State stealing a little boy from his mother, persecution of the Jews—the rights of the family and the rights of humanity."[39] Without intending to do so and undoubtedly from his own personal theological commitment to protecting the precious soul of the child as he saw it, the Pope's involvement drew the church into the widest possible disrepute at the popular level. It confirmed the popular judgment that Papal Italy was in need of moral,

---

37. Aubert, "Pius IX, Pope, Blessed," 385.

38. See Kertzer, *The Kidnapping of Edgardo Mortara*. This the fullest account of the Mortara affair, at least in English. Contrast Kertzer's detailed account with other studies of Pius IX. Curiously there appears to be no treatment of the Mortara incident in Hales's finely documented account of Pius's papacy, *Pio Nono*. Coppa mentions the Mortara affair very briefly in his *Pope Pius IX*, 129, and with careful attention to detail against the broader horizon of the papacy's relationship with Judaism in his *The Papacy, the Jews and the Holocaust*, 95–98.

39. Chadwick, *History of the Popes 1830–1914*, 131.

social, economic, and political redemption. Duffy writes of the Mortara affair as it played out at the everyday level: "[Pius] made a pet of Edgardo, escorting him into public audiences, playing hide and seek with him under his cloak." The child was never returned to his parents, eventually became a priest, and lived into the 1930s. As a Catholic priest, Edgardo was known as Fr. Pio Maria Mortara. His autobiography was edited by the Italian religious journalist Vittorio Messori and published in English in 2017, and nowhere in it is Fr. Pio critical of what took place.[40] Not only that, but he writes of his gratitude for his vocation as a Catholic priest. All of that is very fine and well, but the issue of the kidnapping is still very problematic.

Church historian Eamon Duffy continues: "His case was both a human tragedy and a demonstration of the gulf which had opened up between the thought world of the papacy, and the secular, liberal values which were now the moral currency of Europe, even for many Catholics."[41] Duffy goes on to say that Pius himself was not particularly anti-Semitic, "except in the tragically general sense in which most Christians were anti-Semitic."[42]

THE SYLLABUS OF ERRORS

Pius distanced himself from every aspect of liberalism in 1864 with the publication of two documents: the encyclical letter *Quanta Cura* and the *Syllabus of Errors*. The immediate catalyst for the encyclical was a Catholic congress held at Malines, Belgium, in 1863. At this Congress Montalembert, a French Catholic liberal politician and friend of Félicité de Lammenais whose constant dream was the reconciliation of Catholicism and the modern world, strongly encouraged a reconciliation between the church and democracy. His speech was later published under the title "A Free Church in a Free State." In his speech, Montalembert said that too many Catholics associated the church with the pre-French Revolution Ancien Régime and, while the Ancien Régime may have had its merits, it had one major demerit—it was dead. He advocated the church's universal

---

40. Messori, *Kidnapped by the Vatican?* The book was reviewed by the American Dominican theologian Romanus Cessario in the journal *First Things*, February 2018, 55–58. In his review Cessario sides with Pope Pius IX and his associates. The review stirred up something of a controversy in the English-language Catholic press.
41. Duffy, *Saints and Sinners*, 289–90.
42. Duffy, "It Takes All Sorts to Make a Saint," 1181.

acceptance of democracy.[43] Montalembert's democratic views were not welcomed in Rome. Pius's Secretary of State, Cardinal Antonelli, rebuked both Montalembert and the Archbishop of Malines in 1864, and in December of the same year, the encyclical *Quanta Cura* was published. *The Syllabus of Errors*, a list of eighty condemned propositions based on the Pope's previous statements and allocutions was a comprehensive condemnation of liberalism reflecting mainly the problems Pius perceived throughout Italy, and especially in Piedmont.

The idea of a comprehensive papal attack on modern liberal errors may have originated with one Vincenzo Pecci, Bishop of Perugia, ultimately to become Pius's successor as Pope Leo XIII. The Syllabus had ten headings that dealt with a range of propositions: I, pantheism, naturalism, and absolute rationalism (propositions 1–7); II, moderate rationalism (8–14); III, indifferentism and latitudinarianism (15–18); IV, socialism, communism, secret societies, Bible societies, and liberal-clerical societies (citing earlier texts); V, the church and its rights (19–38); VI, civil society and its relation to the church (39–55); VII, natural and Christian ethics (56–64); VIII, Christian marriage (65–74); IX, the temporal power of the pope (75–76); X, modern liberalism (77–80). Proposition 77 in *The Syllabus* denied that non-Catholics should be free to practice their religion. Proposition 80 condemned the idea that "the Roman Pontiff can and should reconcile himself with progress, liberalism, and recent civilization." To be fair, the attention of *The Syllabus of Errors* immediately stemmed from and was focused on the Italian liberals who were bent on the suppression of the temporal power of the papacy and the unification of Italy. It had in mind the policies of the Piedmontese government against the church. However, it did not sound like that publicly. Taken as a whole and without contextual nuance, "it seemed that the Pope had declared war on modern society in all its aspects."[44] Virtually there was nothing good about modernity and it had to be condemned as incompatible with the church.

Alec Vidler maintains, and rightly, that it is only fair to admit that Pius near the end of his life recognized his limitations in this regard and confessed: "I hope my successor will be as much attached to the church as I have been and will have as keen a desire to do good: my system and my

---

43. See Chadwick, *History of the Popes 1830–1914*, 170–72.
44. Vidler, *The Church in an Age of Revolution*, 151.

policies have had their day, but I am too old to change my course; that will be the task of my successor."[45]

ULTRAMONTANISM

In an excellent series of essays devoted to ultramontanism, church historian Jeffrey von Arx, SJ, provides us with a fine segue into the phenomenon in his "Introduction": "Ultramontanism is a blind spot . . . in our understanding of the religious history of the Roman Catholic Church in the nineteenth and well into our own century. Whether inside or outside the Roman Catholic community, it is difficult for many intelligent people today to understand the depth of commitment to the ultramontane cause of so many Roman Catholics in the century and a half before Vatican II; sometimes distressing to contemplate its victory in the church; puzzling to discover how much attention and concern the progress of ultramontanism within the church drew, not only from Roman Catholics and politicians in mainly Roman Catholic countries like France, who must deal with the papacy, but also from non-Catholics and even from freethinkers in a country like Great Britain, where, saving Ireland, the Roman Catholic Church did not count for much."[46] Literally the term *ultramontanism* means "beyond the mountains," the mountains being the Alps beyond which lay Italy and Rome, and refers to an interpretation of the Christian reality that is totally centered on the papacy. It is a point of view in which the bishops of the Catholic world "are relegated to a subordinate level while everything centers on the Pope."[47] In today's parlance, ultramontanism has probably become papal-centrism, an excessive theological and especially ecclesiological centering on the pope.

Pius IX's reign witnessed the rapid development and perhaps the climax of ultramontanism, leading Alec Vidler to comment, "The mystique about the Holy Father, and what often seems an unwholesome adulation of his person, dates from Pius IX."[48] In some quarters, the pope was spoken of as "the vice-God of humanity." One French ultramontane bishop maintained that the pope was the continuation of the Incarnate Word. The Jesuit review *Civilta Catolica* put it about that when the pope meditated, God was

---

45. Cited in Vidler, *The Church in an Age of Revolution*, 153.
46. Von Arx, SJ, "Introduction," in his *Varieties of Ultramontanism*, 1–2.
47. Heft, SM, "From the Pope to the Bishops," 59.
48. Vidler, *The Church in an Age of Revolution*, 153.

thinking in him. Extreme language, indeed. At the popular level and as a result of photography, Catholics all over the world had pictures of Pius in their homes, and steamships and railways enabled relatively easy frequent pilgrimage to Rome. Pilgrims streamed to Rome. Add to this the emergence of foreign correspondents for national newspapers throughout the world, and Pius became, in the words of Jesuit historian John W. O'Malley, "the first papal mega-star."[49] Needless to say, not all Catholics were ultramontane in outlook. John Henry Newman was certainly opposed to ultramontanism. Speaking of an excessive devotion to the person of the pope, the Archbishop of Rheims stated that it was "an idolatry of the papacy."[50]

From the perspective of ultramontanism, anything less than a complete identification with and endorsement of the pope was less than Catholic and was immediately suspect. This is how Eamon Duffy describes ultramontanism in the church of Pius IX: "These ultramontanists saw the church as a monolithic and solitary beacon in a dark and ever-darkening world. It was an institution in which obedience was prized above all virtues and which insisted that its children—a telling epithet for adult believers—must march in step to the beat of the Vatican drum. This was a vision of the church centered above all not merely on the office but on the person of the pope."[51] Let us admit, as indeed we must, that Duffy's ecclesial description does not and cannot take into careful consideration all the differences of nuance and position in Pius IX's church. Yet, Duffy has his finger quite firmly on the ecclesial pulse here. There was little favor in Pius's church for those who did not share this ultramontane mindset.

Though the ultramontane perspective at Vatican I will be examined in more detail later, suffice it to say that Pius encouraged this point of view. He threatened bishops who were inclined to disagree with the definition of papal infallibility, and he raised to the episcopate men who were strongly ultramontane, in alignment with his own sympathies. One historian captures the mood in these words: "[Pius] used the apostolic nuncios as watchdogs to keep the bishops in line; recalcitrants were sometimes invited to a personal audience, which could be stormy."[52] This was also the time when national seminaries in Rome were encouraged, where young and impres-

---

49. O'Malley, "Beatification of Pius IX," 8; see also Chadwick, *History of the Popes 1830–1914*, 113.

50. Vidler, *Church in an Age of Revolution*, 154.

51. Duffy, "Age of Pio Nono," 47.

52. Bokenkotter, *A Concise History of the Catholic Church*, 319.

sionable seminarians could drink in this Roman ultramontane spirit in the holy city itself and take it back to their home countries and dioceses.

In similar fashion, in April 1870 while the First Vatican Council was in session, Pius summoned the premier Vatican archivist, Augustin Theiner, an Oratorian priest and a well-respected scholar, and charged him with providing documents to the anti-infallibilists, specifically the English Catholic historian Lord Acton. Pius considered anti-infallibilists his personal enemies and enemies of the church. In August of the same year, Theiner was required to give up his keys to the Vatican archives. Although he was not actually dismissed and retained his title of prefect of the archives, he continued to work under the same difficult conditions as any ordinary scholar using the data of the archives for research.[53]

THE PAPACY AND THE EPISCOPATE

Pius introduced new hierarchies into England in 1850 and into the Netherlands in 1853. During his pontificate he created two hundred new bishoprics or apostolic vicariates. Duffy notes the consequence when he says that "All this represented a massive growth of papal involvement and papal control in the local churches."[54] Bishops in the expanding church in the United States were appointed in Rome and developed a strong Rome-centeredness. Under Pius, missionary work, which he first encountered in 1823–25 when he was in Chile and Peru, expanded throughout the world. The episcopate had been firmly integrated with the papacy theologically, but now that integration had a new, more intense and structured dimension. Bishops appointed by Pius naturally felt a personally close bond with the Pope, and it can certainly be argued that while this close bond was of great value to Catholics worldwide, there was also something of a downside. If not entirely forgotten, the importance of the episcopate in its own right, so to speak, tended to fall into abeyance.

---

53. Chadwick, *Catholicism and History*, 63–66. Chadwick's book offers many examples of Theiner's scholarly reputation. Eamon Duffy suggests mistakenly that Theiner was actually dismissed in his article, "It Takes All Sorts to Make a Saint," 1181.

54. Duffy, *Saints and Sinners*, 304.

POPE PIUS IX AND POPULAR DEVOTION

When one looks at the latter half of the nineteenth-century Catholic Church, one recognizes that popular devotions were taking off throughout Europe. "A passion for the Middle Ages spread among romantic Catholics, who indulged in processions and pilgrimages, the veneration of relics and new devotions to Our Lady and the saints. Canonizations became more frequent during the nineteenth century and they were often carried out with impressive ceremonial. Pius IX himself took a personal interest in the rapidly expanding devotion to St. Joseph who was proclaimed patron of the universal church in 1870."[55] Church historian Thomas Bokenkotter writes: "Pius IX's real success was with the interior renewal of the church, and he deserves credit for the magnificent leadership he gave in deepening a sense of piety and spirituality."[56] No account of Pius would be complete if it did not turn attention to his promotion of devotion to the Sacred Heart and to the Blessed Virgin Mary. In 1856, Pius extended the feast of the Sacred Heart to the universal church. "Through these devotions, through declaring Francis de Sales a doctor of the church and through other means, Pius helped turn piety in a more heartfelt direction."[57] Some find it all too easy to pour scorn on such devotions as the Sacred Heart of Christ. Although much of the popular and widespread artwork associated with this devotion may be judged to be of a very poor quality, the very notion of the heart as a symbol of human love and commitment becomes a very powerful focus for expressing the divine love, something given particular emphasis, for example, by the twentieth-century Catholic theologian Karl Rahner.[58]

Not only piety but also the religious institutions of the church flourished during Pius's reign. During this time, the Society of Jesus almost doubled its membership, as did many other religious orders, for example, the Sulpicians, the Passionists, the Redemptorists, the Franciscans, and the Dominicans. There were new foundations too: The Blessed Sacrament Fathers, the so-called White Fathers, and the Society of the Divine Word, the latter two foundations having an especially missionary commitment, something favored by the Pope.

55. Holmes, *Triumph of the Holy See*, 138–39.
56. Bokenkotter, *A Concise History of the Catholic Church*, 327.
57. O'Malley, "Beatification of Pius IX," 8.
58. Consider, for example, the retrieval of this devotion by Karl Rahner, SJ, "Devotion to the Sacred Heart Today," in his *Theological Investigations*, especially 127–28. See also Callahan, *Karl Rahner's Spirituality of the Pierced Heart*.

The demands for the definition of the dogma of the Immaculate Conception of our Lady were being received in Rome long before Pius IX. The demand had been heard increasingly in France since 1830, the year of the vision of our Lady to St. Catherine Labouré in the Rue du Bac, Paris. As a result of St. Catherine's experiences, the cult of the Miraculous Medal very quickly gained ground. The medal was first issued in 1832, and on one side of the medal there was an image of Mary with the inscription, "O Mary, conceived without sin, pray for us who have recourse to thee." In 1847, Giovanni Perrone, the leading theologian of the Roman schools and a Jesuit, published a thesis to show that the doctrine of the Immaculate Conception could be defined. Pius appointed a commission to study the question, including another Jesuit theologian Carlo Passaglia. From exile in Gaeta in 1849, Pius issued the encyclical *Ubi Primum*, asking the advice and prayers of the worldwide episcopate. Of some six hundred episcopal replies, nine-tenths were entirely supportive of the dogma. The definition was drawn up by Passaglia and Perrone, creating the popular but false impression that it was an invention of the Jesuits. To offset this criticism, Pius invited a number of bishops at the last moment to modify the text of the definition. "We must accept this humiliation," he is reported to have said, "so that it won't be said that everything depended upon the Jesuits."[59]

The dogma of the Immaculate Conception was proclaimed on December 8, 1854. The proclamation of this dogma was "an innovation of the first-order, something no pope had ever done before."[60] Although the doctrine was warmly received by most Catholics and reflected popular Marian sentiment that had been growing and developing for centuries, there were those who did not accept it. One French priest, arguably mentally disturbed, who preached against the doctrine after the formal definition was suspended by the Archbishop of Paris, Marie Dominique Auguste Sibour. The priest then stabbed the Archbishop to death during a procession in a Paris church. Although Pius was in many ways following the movement of popular devotion in the proclamation of the Immaculate Conception, Owen Chadwick accurately states, "No previous Pope in eighteen centuries had made a definition of doctrine quite like this."[61] Needless to say, this development, allied to the growing ultramontanism, the increasing personal loyalty of so many bishops to the person of the pope, and the general and

---

59. Hales, *Pio Nono*, 148.
60. O'Malley, SJ, *A History of the Popes*, 246.
61. Chadwick, *History of the Popes 1830–1914*, 121.

popular awareness of the pope among Catholics, contributed to a Catholic super-star view of the papacy that has not been entirely healthy.

CONCLUSION

Pope Pius IX died on February 7, 1878, the longest pontificate in the history of the church. With him from December 22 until his death was Henry Edward Manning, the ultramontane Archbishop of Westminster, who had stalwartly supported the Pope since he first met him and asked his blessing as an Anglican Dean visiting Rome so many years before. Just one month before Pius's death, King Victor Emmanuel II died in the Quirinal Palace, about a mile away from the Vatican. Strictly speaking, the King had been excommunicated for the role he had played in what was known as "the spoliation of the church." Once Pius knew that the King was dying, he "quietly allowed the King's chaplain to absolve him on his deathbed of the excommunication . . . and Victor Emmanuel II, 'the Father of his Country,' died as a Catholic reconciled to the church."[62] Three years later when Pius's body was transferred to the Basilica of St. Lawrence-outside-the-walls in 1881, it was done at night because of the anticlericalism raging in the city. Even so, it was unpleasant and the Roman mob threw mud from the Tiber at the coffin.

The entire strategy of Pius's pontificate left its impress on the church for a century, a point well made by Eamon Duffy: "Pius IX's papacy helped lock the Catholic Church into a confrontation with the modern world from which it did not recover until the Second Vatican Council, and not entirely then."[63] While Pope Leo XIII and others attempted a friendlier and somewhat more open attitude to the modern world, according to Alec Vidler, "there was no substantial change in the authoritarian pattern which [Pius] had canonized until the dramatic reign of John XXIII."[64] The papacy be-

---

62. O'Malley, SJ, *A History of the Popes*, 252.

63. Duffy, *Ten Popes Who Shook the World*, 101. Historian Marvin R. O'Connell, *Critics on Trial*, 24, writes: "Pius IX's inability to differentiate among the diverse currents of thought that swirled through the nineteenth century was his greatest weakness. He never grasped, for example, the import of the profound changes European society underwent during his lifetime, when the old agricultural economy gave way to an industrialized system dominated by an aggressive middle-class and a vast urban proletariat, and when monarchies had to surrender their immemorial powers to more or less liberal and representative regimes."

64. Vidler, *The Church in an Age of Revolution*, 156.

came authoritarian in style, and the church at large became defensive and generally hostile to the modern world.

A NOTE ON POPE LEO XIII

Although Pope Leo XIII was the one who made Newman a cardinal, it was Pope Pius IX who was really Newman's pope, that is to say, the pontificate during which most of his struggles and challenges were waged. Pope Leo XIII was born in 1810 and died in 1903, he was nine years younger than Newman and outlived him by thirteen years, and he was pope from 1878. Suspicion had hung over Newman's head for many years. His great English rival, as it were, Cardinal Manning, thought of Newman as at least a borderline heretic. All this came to an end when Leo named him a cardinal. "My Cardinal (exclaimed the Pope to a Catholic peer, Lord Selborne)! It was not easy, it was not easy. They said he was too liberal, but I had determined to honor the church in honoring Newman. I always had a cult for him. I am proud that I was able to honor such a man."[65] Pope Leo's encyclical of 1879, *Aeterni Patris*, provided the charter for the revival of Thomism in the Catholic Church. Newman had never much more than a gentleman's acquaintance with the thinking of St. Thomas Aquinas and so this encyclical letter promoting Thomism had no real effect on his thinking. In 1896, however, six years after Newman's death, Pope Leo promulgated his encyclical *Apostolicae Curae* condemning Anglican orders as null and void. It is difficult to know what Newman would have made of this had he lived. It is very difficult to see Newman impugning the sacred ministry of his friends Edward Pusey and John Keble.

---

65. Cited in Dessain, *John Henry Newman*, 165.

2

The Oxford Movement

The leaders of the Oxford Movement wanted to find a place for the poetic or the aesthetic judgment; their hymnody shared in the feelings and evocations of the romantic poets; they wished to find a place and value for historical tradition, against the irreverent or sacrilegious hands of critical revolutionaries for whom no antiquity was sacred; they suspected the reason of common sense as shallow; they wanted to justify order and authority in church as well as state.

Owen Chadwick[1]

The Oxford Movement dominated the scene until 1845. There was magic of one kind or another about its principal personalities—John Keble, John Henry Newman, Richard Hurrell Froude and others too. It may be that there is magic in anything new that comes out of Oxford.

Alec R. Vidler[2]

INTRODUCTION

IT IS IMPORTANT AT the outset when thinking about the Oxford Movement to recognize that the Church of England was not by any means a uniform and

---

1. Chadwick, *Spirit of the Oxford Movement*, 2.
2. Vidler, *Church in an Age of Revolution*, 49.

united body. There were different currents of thought and practice within the church often described as "high," "low," "broad," and finally "evangelical." The high church tended to be more Catholic in terms of liturgy and devotional practices. The low church looked to the legacy of Puritanism and held very closely to the Thirty-Nine Articles of the church, statements of belief and conviction that give emphasis to the more Protestant elements of the church. The broad church was much more flexible and tended to incorporate all Christian points of view. The evangelical church placed its emphasis on such things as individual feeling, the reading of Scripture, preaching, and tended to downplay the sacraments and a priestly understanding of pastoral ministry.

Our two opening quotations, both from established and well-respected church historians, form an interesting contrast. In his wide-ranging yet accurate description, Owen Chadwick indicates an important connection between the leaders of the Oxford Movement and the English romantic poets such as William Wordsworth. In that sense, they were reacting against what they all would have regarded as rationalism, the apotheosis of human reason objectively understood as the touchstone of all truth, not unlike their continental European counterparts—Friedrich Schleiermacher of the University of Berlin, Johan Sebastian Drey, Johan Adam Möhler of the Catholic faculty of the University of Tübingen, and so forth. Truth, and most especially theological truth, may be experienced and discovered in the poetic, the symbolic, and the liturgical, most of which they deemed to have been lost since at least the time of the Caroline Divines of the seventeenth-century Church of England. Alec Vidler, on the other hand, and not without a touch of irony, points to a certain "magic" about the leaders of the movement. He is certainly right about this. If we think about the names he provides—Keble, Newman, Froude—and add Pusey, they all had each in his own way a vibrant and attractive sparkle. They were all Oxford men in every sense of the word. "In a peculiarly English sense, Oxford was a sacred city, and the loyalty to Oxford was a religious one. Oxford and Cambridge were the seminaries and intellectual powerhouses of the Church of England as by law established, the national church; the Fellows of the Colleges were for the most part celibate clergymen."[3] The Oxford magic, then, is a sacred Oxford magic.

Perhaps we need to say something further about Oxford before going on to the Oxford Movement itself. In his very fine book *The Anglican*

---

3. Gilley, "Keble, Froude, Newman and Pusey," 97.

Revival: Studies in the Oxford Movement, the Swedish theologian Yngve Brilioth points out that Oxford was the source for three movements of religious reformation in England.[4] The first of these movements had to do with the Oxford theologian John Wyclif (ca. 1330–84). "Wyclif was not only acknowledged at Oxford as the outstanding teacher of his time, but was also the leader of a reform movement of 'poor priests,' inspired by Franciscan ideals of apostolic poverty, for whom the obtaining of high office was not a prime consideration."[5] It is true that Wyclif denied certain aspects of traditional Catholic eucharistic doctrine but, however important that issue is, the wider aspects of his reform movement should not be forgotten.[6] Brilioth's second Oxford reform movement flows from John Wesley (1703–91), one generation before Newman. Wesley underscored the universal call to holiness of all Christians, and centered much of this universal call on a more regular celebration of the Eucharist. Then, finally, comes the Oxford Movement. Brilioth is not insinuating some inner causal connection between these three reforming movements, but rather recognizing their common source in Oxford as a center of theological learning.

THE OXFORD MOVEMENT

In the mid-nineteenth century, from 1833 to 1845, there took place a renewal movement within the Church of England centered on Oxford and its University, and hence the term "the Oxford Movement." The purpose of the movement was to restore those catholic elements of theology and liturgy exemplified especially by the Caroline Divines of the seventeenth century. The "Caroline Divines" is a term given to a group of theologians writing mainly during the reigns of Kings Charles I (1625–49) and Charles II (1660–85), but including also the great Lancelot Andrewes (1555–1626). The question may be asked, "Why *this* movement, and why *then*?" The answer is complex. Some would argue with plenty of supporting evidence that there was a decline of church life in England and moreover a decline that was exacerbated by the spread of "liberal" movements in theology. Alec Vidler in his celebrated book *The Church in an Age of Revolution* puts it like this: "No institution was more obviously in need of reform than the Established Church. There were glaring abuses and inequalities in its system that had

---

4. Brilioth, *Anglican Revival*, 29–32.
5. Wilks, *Wyclif: Political Ideas and Practice*, 2.
6. See Cummings, *Eucharistic Doctors*, 145–50.

continued uncorrected since the time of feudalism, and would no longer be tolerated now that the middle classes were winning power."[7] One historian, with accuracy and not a little wit, takes Vidler's perception further when he writes: "[The Church of England in the eighteenth century] concentrated on the temporal plums and forgot about the spiritual pie. The Establishment slept: it was the sleep of the snug rather than of the just."[8] At the same time, it needs to be asserted that the "high" liturgical and sacramental theology, spirituality, and devotion of the Oxford Movement had plenty of antecedents in the Anglican tradition before them, and was never lost from the tradition.[9] "If we look at the three main themes or facets of Tractarianism—the doctrine of the church, its apostolicity, unity, independence and relation to the State; the rule of faith, the role of tradition and the Fathers; and finally, spirituality and its different elements, along with sacramentalism and the symbolic significance of rite and ceremony—we can find ample evidence of renewal and resurgence in each, within the high church tradition in the forty or fifty years preceding the dawn of the Movement."[10] This fine summary by Peter Nockles is amply verified in the literature referred to in his essay. The difference between these high church emphases and the re-Catholicizing elements of the nineteenth-century Oxford Movement and its tracts is twofold: first, the latter had a carefully structured system for the widespread dissemination of their ideas; second, the degree and length to which some of the Tractarians went was far beyond the horizon of their forebears, with some of their prominent leaders going over to Rome and many others giving institutional expression to Catholic elements of ritual and devotion in their local Church of England parishes.

At another level, the passing of the Catholic Emancipation Act of 1829 was feared by some to occasion a flood of movement from the Anglican Communion to the Roman Catholic Church. Added to this was the British government's insistence on suppressing ten Anglican Irish bishoprics, known as the Temporalities' Bill of 1833. This decision by the British government made so much sense since the majority of the Irish population

---

7. Cummings, *Eucharistic Doctors*, 45–46.

8. Brendon, *Hurrell Froude and the Oxford Movement*, xiv.

9. This is well demonstrated in the essays edited by Geoffrey Rowell, *Tradition Renewed: The Oxford Movement Conference Papers*, the original publication. Two essays are particularly helpful: Richard Sharp, "New Perspectives on the High Church Tradition: Historical Background, 1730–1780," 4–23 and Peter Nockles, "The Oxford Movement: Historical Background 1780–1833," 24–50.

10. Nockles, "Oxford Movement," 26.

were Roman Catholic and yet they were tithed by the established Church of Ireland and, of course, they resented and resisted this tithing. From the English point of view, however, it looked as if the government was interfering in the church. This led the priest-theologian-poet John Keble to deliver his famous sermon in the university church of St. Mary the Virgin in Oxford entitled "National Apostasy," on July 14, 1833. This sermon is generally regarded, and particularly by Newman, as the beginning of the Oxford Movement.[11] The occasion was the summer Assize Court, the local law courts, when the judges, lawyers, and functionaries of that circuit court of England were assembled. It was really nothing more than a formality. It took John Keble about thirty-five minutes to deliver the sermon, and it was his way of taking a firm stand against the "liberalism" of the British government having its way with the established Church of England. The church was not to be understood as a department of state, but as of divine foundation, and clergy, especially bishops, should be appointed and should function out of that conviction rather than in accordance with secular and political criteria. "The political background to Keble's sermon was the perception that [the established Church of England] was increasingly in the grip of Dissenters, agnostics, atheists, and even Roman Catholics."[12] If the British Parliament was open to people who were not members of the Church of England and so might possibly become government ministers, then they could very well be engaged in making decisions about the church, and clearly this was unacceptable, not least from a theological point of view.

When Keble returned home he made arrangements to have the sermon printed and circulated. If this liberal British government was going to interfere in the church as if the church were another organ or department of state, then it was high time for the church to reassert and reemphasize its divine institution, and to look to its leaders as the successors of the apostles. Owen Chadwick puts the point well. "It was necessary, politically necessary, that the clergy of the Church of England should look to leaders who would declare that the authority of the church does not rest upon the authority of the state; that the church possesses a divine authority whatever the state may do, even if the state should be represented by an indifferent or a persecuting government; that the authority of the bishop or the vicar

---

11. Frank Leslie Cross believes that the idea that the start of the Oxford Movement is to be found in Keble's sermon is a myth. In my judgment, he overstates his case, but he most valuably points out the wider and deeper roots of the movement. See Cross, *Oxford Movement and Seventeenth Century*.

12. Cornwell, *Newman's Unquiet Grave*, 57.

rests not upon his national or his social position, but upon his apostolic commission."[13] Thus was born the Oxford Movement and its leaders, apart from Keble himself, were John Henry Newman and his close friend Edward Bouverie Pusey, and various others affiliated with Oxford.

TRACTS FOR THE TIMES

In direct and clear opposition to what was seen as the government's meddling in the church in suppressing bishoprics in Ireland, the movement emphasized the Church of England as a divine institution. Furthermore, it underscored the episcopal doctrine of "apostolic succession," thus recognizing the descent of the bishops from the twelve apostles and so distancing them from any degree of government interference. These aims began to take shape through what became known as the "Tracts for the Times," a series of theological pamphlets begun by John Henry Newman later that year in 1833. Ecclesiology was a key issue, and central to ecclesiology was a high theology of the episcopate, and this was already in place, at least partly, prior to the Oxford Movement. "Pre-Tractarian High Churchmen, following the lead of the Caroline Divines, believed that 'the Church of England's claim to be a true branch of the church universal stood or fell by its preservation of apostolic order through the succession.'"[14] What the tracts did was to take this note to a higher key, and it caught on. The first tract, just three pages in length, appeared anonymously (but Newman was the author), in September 1833 and began with these words: "I am but one of yourselves, a presbyter; and therefore I conceal my name, lest I should take too much on myself by speaking in my own person. Yet speak I must; for the times are very evil, yet no one speaks against them."[15]

The tracts exercised a very definite influence among the clergy, an influence well described by Owen Chadwick in these words: "The Movement reached out so forcefully from Oxford because it understood the needs of the country parish, because its teaching passed into the shelves of the vicarage library and the ideas of its sermons (or the sermons themselves) into the village pulpit."[16] Shortage of funding for the publication and dissemina-

13. Chadwick, *Spirit of the Oxford Movement*, 3.

14. Thus, Peter Nockles, cited in Rowell, "The Ecclesiology of the Oxford Movement," 217.

15. Cited in Graef, *God and Myself*, 48.

16. Chadwick, *Spirit of the Oxford Movement*, 25.

tion of the tracts was a significant challenge, and at least in the beginning the authors paid for the printing costs themselves. They began as relatively short pamphlets, then the pamphlets were bound together in various volumes. As the tracts developed they went on from being short pamphlets to much longer theological treatises on all the issues that seemed important to the leaders of the movement.

As the tracts continued to be developed, published, and spread throughout the country there gradually arose within the movement two distinct paths—one that grew more and more sympathetic to Rome, and the other that looked to theological, liturgical, and devotional renewal within the Church of England. Some members of the movement "swam the Tiber," that is to say went over to Rome, but the majority remained in the Church of England, attempting to renew their church from within.

In 1841, Newman published the famous *Tract 90*, "Remarks on Certain Passages in the Thirty-Nine Articles," in which he tried to establish consonance between the Anglican Thirty-Nine Articles—the set of doctrinal formulas regarded as definitive by the Church of England—and Roman Catholic theology. Newman may have taken this consonance much too far for the taste of most Anglican clergy, but it was not simply a Newman emphasis, a line of interpretation that he himself was pushing on his own. It would have had a definite appeal to other members of the movement.[17] *Tract 90* sold ten thousand copies in a few weeks. The sheer sales indicate something of its widespread influence. The tract was condemned by many Anglican bishops and in 1842 Newman retired to Littlemore.

SCRIPTURE, SACRAMENTAL THEOLOGY, SPIRITUALITY

Scripture, sacramental theology, and spirituality may be distinguished in the theological writings of the Tractarians, but they can never be separated. They are interwoven one into the others. Consider what the Swedish theologian Alf Härdelin has to say about the Tractarian appreciation of Scripture: "I think it is legitimate to say that, with regard to the re-evaluation of classical Christian exegesis, de Lubac was anticipated in no small degree during the nineteenth century; by Newman in his book on the *Arians*, but even more by Pusey in his unfortunately still unpublished 'Lectures on Types

---

17. See Chadwick, *Spirit of the Oxford Movement*, 43, who writes: "The Idea behind Tract 90 was integral to the theology of the Movement. It was defended and applauded by Pusey and by Keble."

and Prophecies of the Old Testament,' and above all by Keble in Tract 89."[18] This laudatory evaluation of the Tractarian appreciation of Scripture is best understood, in accord with patristic theology and exegesis, as a sacramental understanding of Scripture. Thus, John Keble in *Tract 89* writes: "[Christ is] the end of the ancient types and the beginning of a new series. In him all that happened before was, as it were, brought to a point; and all again that should come after, was but so many developments of what he said, did, and suffered among us."[19] This leads Härdelin to pull together Keble's (and one can equally say the Tractarian) theological understanding as follows: "As many patristic and medieval writers have spoken of Christ and the church as forming *una mystica persona,* so in people's language Christ, 'in union and communion with his members,' may be said to constitute 'in a certain sense, one great and manifold Person, into which, by degrees, all souls of men, who do not cast themselves away, are to be absorbed.'"[20] The mysteries of Christ, found in Scripture and celebrated in sacrament, pass over into the ecclesial Body of Christ, so that Christ and his members form one organic communion, and this communion moreover is to be the ultimate destiny of all, unless definitively and eschatologically it is rejected.

In subsequent chapters there will be a treatment of some of the Oxford Movement leaders—John Henry Newman, John Keble, Hurrell Froude, and Edward Pusey. Here we shall continue briefly to sketch some of the general themes of the movement's ecclesiology, spirituality, and sacramental theology. For members of the Oxford Movement the church was not to be understood in the first place as a human institution. "However lethargic and even corrupt the church may appear it is divine in origin and is the theater for the drama of God's special acts of grace."[21] Thus, great emphasis was placed on ecclesiology and on the sacraments as the premier instruments of God's grace. In Newman's preface to the publication of the first collection of the tracts, he set forth what he regarded as unacceptable: "The neglect of the daily service, the desecration of festivals, the Eucharist scantily

---

18. Härdelin, "Sacraments in the Tractarian Spiritual Universe," in Rowell, *Tradition Renewed,* 78. Härdelin (1927–2014) was a Swedish Lutheran theologian who developed an interest in the Oxford Movement and wrote an excellent book, *The Tractarian Understanding of the Eucharist.* A medievalist and a hymn writer, he was received into the Catholic Church in 1963.

19. Keble, "Tract 89," cited in Härdelin, "Sacraments," 83.

20. Keble, "Tract 89," cited in Härdelin, "Sacraments," 83.

21. Borsch, "Ye Shall Be Holy," in Rowell, "Sacraments," 72.

administered, insubordination permitted in all ranks of the Church."[22] The divine establishment of the church went hand-in-hand with their very high theology of liturgy and the sacraments. This high ecclesiology and high sacramental theology led to a high theology of those who celebrated the liturgy. "Yet while in their priestly offices and personal lives the Oxford leaders remained distrustful of display, the almost magnetic energy produced by so much passionate intensity held under control by a restraining simplicity of life was a source of powerful attraction. To many who gathered about them it made them appear to glow with an inner light. They seemed to make the unseen world real. They stood close to the holy God."[23] This is certainly the case with Keble, Newman, and Pusey.

Owen Chadwick makes the following comment about these three major leaders of the movement: "It would be too sharp a dissection but not therefore without its truth to say that Newman represented the moral and intellectual force of the Movement, Keble the moral and pastoral, Pusey the moral and devotional."[24] Notice that in Chadwick's description of each of these leaders "moral" features are the common factor. They wanted to see authentic Christian discipleship, founded in sacramental incorporation into Christ, made manifest in a serious and at times ascetical moral life. The emphasis on moral conscience probably came to all three of them from the work of Bishop Joseph Butler, *The Analogy of Religion*, as well as his sermons and other writings, which would have been textbooks for Newman and Keble. For all three of them conscience was from God and obedience to conscience was what led to an awareness of God's presence. Isaac Williams (1802–65), another leader of the Oxford Movement and drawn into it through John Keble, puts this notion of the role of obedience for the Christian life into very strong words in *Tract 80*: "If people were now asked what was the most powerful means of advancing the course of religion in the world, we should be told that it was eloquence of speech or preaching . . . whereas, if we were to judge from Holy Scripture of what were the best means of promoting Christianity in the world, we should say obedience, and if we were asked about the second, we should say obedience; and if we were to be asked about the third, we should say obedience."[25] Williams,

---

22. In "Tracts for the Times I," iv, cited in Borsch, "Ye Shall Be Holy," 72.

23. "Tracts for the Times I," iv, cited in Borsch, "Ye Shall Be Holy," 73.

24. Chadwick, *Spirit of the Oxford Movement*, 38.

25. Isaac Williams, "On Reserve in Communicating Religious Knowledge," 82, cited in Frederick H. Borsch, "Ye Shall Be Holy," 69–70.

understood here as standing also for Keble, Newman, and Pusey, was not advocating some kind of extrinsic or external obedience to a distant God, as it were. The obedience described by him is an obedience that emanates from ecclesiological awareness, an awareness that one is "in Christ," and an awareness that finds grace-filled focus and energy in Scripture and sacrament. There is no question here of a moral imitation of Christ from the outside but rather of Christ "mystically reiterating in us" the paschal mystery of his life, death, and resurrection so that we ourselves as members of his body become corporately and individually sacraments of his presence.[26]

Arguably, this understanding of Christian obedience spilled over into a more developed personal spirituality for members of the movement. They advocated such spiritual exercises as regular examination of conscience, meditation and prayer, and the use of devotional books. Newman, for example, was fond of *The Imitation of Christ*, which he had been reading since about 1822. Now, however, with the momentum of the movement he found himself drawn to Lancelot Andrewes (1555–1626) and his book of prayers and meditations. Andrewes's book had been published in Latin. Newman translated it into English and it was published as a tract, and Newman regularly used it in his own personal prayer.[27]

CONCLUSION

To get some sense of the power of the Oxford Movement to make a singular impact on the life of an individual, let us take the example of William George Ward—admittedly an extreme example. William George Ward (1812–82), fellow of Balliol College Oxford and a devoted follower of Newman, published in 1844 *The Ideal of a Christian Church*. Ward's "ideal" was the Roman Catholic Church. Oxford was the very center of the Anglican establishment. Consequently, his book was censured by the convocation of the University of Oxford on February 13, 1845. Ward was deprived by the University of his degrees—and from now on he signed himself William G. Ward, undergraduate—and he entered the Catholic Church in 1845.[28] Alec Vidler comments fairly, although it was not so obvious to Ward him-

---

26. Härdelin, "Sacraments," 89.

27. For a brief introduction to Lancelot Andrews, Cummings, *Eucharist and Ecumenism*, 77–91.

28. Ward subsequently became a lecturer in moral philosophy at St. Edmund's College, Ware, and was an ardent and even extreme ultramontane and controversialist.

self perhaps, that "Ward and those whom he influenced soon came to feel that the Church of Rome—which they may have seen through rose tinted spectacles—possessed means of fostering the fruits of the Spirit which the Church of England had discarded and perhaps irretrievably lost."[29] Something similar, albeit with qualification, could be said of the others who went over to the Roman Catholic Church.

Apart from the effect on individual persons like Ward, either in the Oxford Movement itself or in some way or another attracted by the movement, the question arises, "What influence did the Movement have in the Church of England as a whole?" Owen Chadwick, without a doubt one of the most careful and influential interpreters of the Oxford Movement, puts it like this: "[It] succeeded, far beyond the expectations of many, in transforming the atmosphere of English worship, in deepening the content of English prayer, in lifting English eyes, not only to their own insular tradition, but to the treasures of the Catholic centuries, whether ancient or modern."[30] He believed that its influence on theological thought in England came somewhat later, and was less effective in influencing doctrine, for example, in the area of ecclesiastical authority. Other major and pressing issues were claiming the attention of English theologians—Charles Darwin's *Origin of the Species* (1859), the impact of science on the general public and in the academy, and the consequences of developments in biblical criticism. Arguably, an appreciation of patristic theology, liturgy, and ecclesiology continued to hold its own in the theological schools, but these other issues demanded immediate attention.

---

29. Vidler, *Church in an Age of Revolution*, 53.
30. Chadwick, *Spirit of the Oxford Movement*, 49.

3

John Henry Newman (1801–90)

Newman is far less dead to me, than many of my contemporaries; and less dead, even, than Socrates for whom, in the day-dreams of my young youth, I thought it would be lovely to lay down my life. . . . It was by way of Newman that I turned Roman Catholic. Not all the beheaded martyrs of Christendom, the ecstatic nuns of Europe, the five proofs of Aquinas, or the pamphlets of my Catholic acquaintance, provided anything like the answers that Newman did.

Muriel Spark[1]

Conversion changed [Newman's] explicit allegiance and had immense consequences for the course of his life, but it did not overturn the pattern of his thinking. The continuities in his thought before and after conversion are in many ways more striking than the discontinuities.

Patrick Allitt[2]

No account of the church or theology in the nineteenth century would be complete without attention to John Henry Newman, Anglican and Catholic, and Anglican and Catholic in such a way that the continuities

---

1. Muriel Spark, Foreword, in Vincent F. Blehl, SJ, *Realizations*, v–ix, cited in Gilley, "Newman and the Convert Mind," 6.
2. Allitt, *Catholic Converts*, 3.

between the one and the other are, in Patrick Allitt's words, "more striking than the discontinuities." The life and commitment of John Henry Cardinal Newman demonstrate the best of what it means to be a catholic Christian in both ecclesial traditions. The immediate difficulty is how to deal with the enormous amount of data and interpretations. There is an entire Newman industry with detailed studies on every part of his life and thought. Few theological authors have provided us with such rich autobiographical data as Newman—his *Apologia pro Vita Sua*, his diaries, and his letters are all now available in print. When it comes to a basic introduction to Newman, selection of material becomes, therefore, all-important. Thus, there are three parts to this chapter under the headings "Newman, Man of the University," "Newman, Man of the Church," and "Newman the Man." These admittedly artificial divisions will enable us to see the continuities and discontinuities to some extent, but more importantly, will make Newman more manageable. One might wonder, however, why attention is given to "Newman the Man." Why not be content with an elucidation of Newman's contribution to and understanding of the university and the church? Why probe into his humanity, his character traits, his person? One might be the greatest scholar in the world, the most devout Christian in the church, but somehow one's real and substantive contribution seems to shine through simply and with conviction in one's person, in how one talks, relates, deals with problems, flourishes in friendships and commitments. Newman was a very fine man—distinguished, yes; famous, undoubtedly. But he was also a very good man, a very ordinary man in so many ways, a man with whom one can easily identify as this description from Newman biographer John Cornwell will demonstrate: "He was quick to tears; but he would laugh out loud, especially at puns and malapropisms. He had the gentlest apologetic smile. He worried about his health to the point of hypochondria; he was plagued by bad teeth. He was anxiously curious about the ailments of others. He could be catty . . . self-disciplined, ascetic, he beat himself weekly with a discipline until age forbade; the discipline was always in his luggage. He was prone to fasting, yet he enjoyed his food and wine. On a holiday . . . we find him whining over the small size of a single lamb cutlet served up to him in a hotel dining room: a 'portion of cutlets' in the plural, he pointed out, had been listed on the menu."[3]

---

3. Cornwell, *Newman's Unquiet Grave*, 18.

John Henry Newman (1801–90)

BRIEF BIOGRAPHICAL SKETCH

Newman's life spans the whole of the nineteenth century, but it was a difficult life in so many ways. Louis Bouyer, the French Oratorian, says of Newman: "It is not an exaggeration to say that Newman was a little or not at all understood by his contemporaries."[4] This is one of the continuities in Newman. Bouyer is referring to the fact that when Newman left the Church of England, his leaving was little understood by many of his fellows in the Oxford Movement, and his leaving took many with him to Rome. Equally, however, he was not entirely accepted by many Catholics, who found his way of doing theology and some of his ideas curiously suspect, at least until the time of Pope Leo XIII, who undid much of this suspicion by making Newman a cardinal.

John Henry Newman, the eldest of six children—John, Charles, Harriet, Francis, Jemima, and Mary—was born in London on February 21, 1801, and he died in Birmingham on August 11, 1890. Here are noted the main essentials of his life as a prelude to a closer examination of his person and meaning. He attended a private boarding school at Ealing and was a star pupil, excelling in the Greek and Latin classics, but demonstrating considerable skill in music—the violin being his instrument. He set up a newspaper in the school, in which he did most of the writing. One contribution interestingly comes from a certain John Quincy Adams, later president of the United States, whose son was also at the school. Newman was not much of a sportsman, but he liked to swim—his schoolboy diary is full of entries of bathing in the river. He was also very religious, and at the age of sixteen Newman tells us that he underwent a conversion, from "an unbelieving boy" to a "Christian." During his earlier teenage years he read a number of authors, including David Hume, that made him somewhat skeptical about traditional religion. "He no longer wanted to be religious, but he did want to be 'virtuous'; there was something in the idea of being religious that he did not like, nor did he understand what it meant to love God."[5] Newman's emergence from this adolescent skepticism to a more vibrant Christian faith was partly due to an evangelical master at school, Walter Mayers.[6]

The England into which Newman was born was changing rapidly. Newman remembered as a small boy the candles that people sat in their

---

4. Bouyer, *Newman's Vision of Faith*, 9.
5. Graef, *God and Myself*, 12.
6. Dessain, "Newman's Spirituality," 139.

windows to mark the triumph of the battle of Trafalgar on October 21, 1805. It would be another ten years before Napoleon Bonaparte was finally overthrown at the battle of Waterloo. In that interim decade, Newman was growing up and England was transforming. Historian Marvin O'Connell has captured something of these changes in this most descriptive paragraph: "The spoils of war have a way of turning to dust in the victors' hands, but the hard times after Waterloo reflected something deeper than an ordinary postwar deflation. There was a dramatic shift going on in the economic life of the nation and, indeed, of the whole Western world. Steam-driven machinery was about to alter the habits of a thousand years. The painful process took a long time to accomplish; it began long before 1820 and would continue for generations after. It brought with it dislocation and insecurity and unconscionable greed. It threw up ugly cities and ghastly sweatshops in which women and children were systematically maimed in the name of an abstract economic theory. It scarred the countryside with slag heaps and blinded the eye with industrial haze. And it provided ordinary people with comforts and leisure beyond the wildest dream of their ancestors."[7] This was the fast-changing world of Newman's entire life and, especially after he became a Catholic and moved to the great industrial metropolis of Birmingham, a world in which he and his Oratorian brothers had to face pastorally.

After going up to Oxford and later Newman contributed as best he could to the family financially, a role that would continue until his mother died and his sisters married in 1836.[8] For the most part, he got on well with his sisters—Jemima, Harriet, and especially the youngest, Mary—not so with his brothers, Francis and Charles. He put Francis through Oxford University, so that in 1826 Francis achieved a "double first," and was soon elected to a fellowship at Balliol College. He wrote in his journal at times of being "ill tempered with Francis," and then in 1827, "Frank is off my hands, but the rest are now heavier."[9] Francis Newman traveled a very different path from his better-known brother, going on an ill-thought-out Christian missionary expedition to the Middle East, and moving later in life into various educational institutions as a teacher. It would be impossible to say that Francis and John Henry were close.

---

7. O'Connell, *The Oxford Conspirators*, 6.
8. Turner, *John Henry Newman*, 122.
9. Tristram, *John Henry Newman: Autobiographical Writings*, 110.

John Henry Newman (1801–90)

Starting in 1823, John began a long-running debate with Charles, who had become involved in a socialist movement devoted to the political and religious thought of Robert Owen. The Irish Newman biographer Seán O'Faoláin describes Charles's situation accurately but with a degree of wry humor: "To his heart-riven family [Charles] might just as well have declared himself an atheist, an anarchist, an abortionist, or a Roman Catholic."[10] Faced with such odds, one can understand that this fraternal debate, if that is the right word, between Charles and John continued throughout Charles's life.

The youngest sister, Mary, born in 1809, died in early January 1828, a devastating blow for Newman. Though Newman seldom commented in his letters on his father's death, he frequently spoke of Mary's. In February 1829, just over a year after Mary's death, he was still dreaming vividly of her.

The evangelical milieu of the school in Ealing also had its influence on John Henry's younger brother, Francis Newman (1805–97). They were very different. Indeed, Basil Willey describes the differences in this way: "In the history of nineteenth-century English thought there is no story more striking, or more full of moral significance, than that of the divergent courses of the brothers Newman. It is as if two rivers, taking their rise in the same dividing range, should yet be deflected by some minute irregularity of level, so that one pours its waters into the Mediterranean, the other into the German Ocean."[11] The analogy is particularly apt. Newman became a Mediterranean Catholic, and Francis, after a spell of evangelical fervor that took him as a missionary to Baghdad, became something of a northern European rationalist. Willey does not speak of the third Newman brother, Charles, who especially in the context of Seán O'Faoláin's description adds to the complexity of this family. But more about Charles Newman later.

After boarding school, Newman went up to Trinity College, Oxford, in 1817. While he clearly enjoyed his studies, he found his first two years in university difficult. The late Meriol Trevor, in her splendid biography of Newman, expresses Newman's difficulties in her own inimitable way: "He was two years younger than most men of his year and came from a very different background. Trinity was certainly gentlemanlike—nobody did much work and everybody drank a lot of wine."[12] Francis followed him to

---

10. O'Faoláin, *Newman's Way*, 85.
11. Basil Willey, *More Nineteenth Century Studies*, 11.
12. Trevor, *Newman's Journey*, 18.

Oxford, to Worcester College, and John considered him a superior Greek scholar.

After his studies, John was ordained a deacon of the Church of England in 1824 and a priest the following year. Stephen Dessain, the premier Newman scholar of his generation, tells us that after ordination "[Newman] wrote a sentence which gives the key to all his subsequent history: 'I have the responsibility of souls on me to the day of my death.'"[13] He remained in Oxford from 1817 to 1846 in various capacities: as a fellow of Oriel College, as a college tutor, as vicar of the University Church of St. Mary the Virgin, and its community of Littlemore, but the care of souls remained central to everything he did.

In 1832, Newman went on a Mediterranean trip with his friend Richard Hurrell Froude, the high Anglican who had introduced him to the full doctrine of the sacraments, the eucharistic presence of Christ, and devotion to Mary, Mother of God. Froude had tuberculosis and his archdeacon-father hoped that this trip would be beneficial for his health. Newman joined them. "The whole of this journey was to be for Newman a voyage into his own soul, ending with a death and resurrection in Sicily."[14] When the Froudes were ready to return to England, Newman decided to stay, against their advice, and to explore Sicily for himself. He became seriously ill, the illness compounded by the initial doubts he had begun to feel about various aspects of his own Anglican church. "As I lay in bed the first day, many thoughts came over me. I felt God was fighting against me—and felt at last I knew why—it was for self-will. . . . Yet I felt and kept saying to myself 'I have not sinned against the light.'"[15] Though he felt he had not sinned against the light, he sensed a keen opposition between his own self-will and what God wanted from him, and perhaps ambition and pride. It was on his delayed return to England that Newman composed perhaps his most famous piece of verse, "Lead, kindly Light." This poem will be examined in a later chapter.

On the very same day that John arrived back in England from Sicily, Francis arrived back from his ill-starred mission to Baghdad. Coincident with John's return to England was the birth of the Oxford Movement in the Church of England, when John Keble preached his famous sermon on "National Apostasy." The Oxford Movement was a complex phenomenon,

13. Dessain, "John Henry Newman," 22.
14. Trevor, *Newman's Journey*, 48.
15. Trevor, *Newman's Journey*, 51.

but "essentially, the movement was the rediscovery of the church as an autonomous community, organically one with the first disciples of Christ."[16] To so many outsiders, however, the movement was seen as a Romanizing of the Church of England, as a selling out of the Reformation. Through his preaching and teaching and writing Newman was thought of as a crypto-Romanist by many of his peers in the church. Though he professed obedience to his own Anglican bishop, the Bishop of Oxford, it did not look like that to his critics. Newman's theological views were becoming more and more Roman Catholic, despite his allegiance to his bishop. Meriol Trevor rightly comments that Newman's influence, both as an Anglican and as a Catholic, tended to intimidate bishops of either church. She writes: "Newman's personal influence was to make him, all his life, far more important than any bishop, Anglican or Catholic, under whom he acted as a simple clergyman. It was like having an unexploded bomb in your diocese."[17] This emerges especially from some of the *Tracts for the Times* that Newman authored. For example, in *Tract 1* he wrote: "Black event as it would be for the country, yet . . . we could not wish [the bishops] a more blessed termination of their course than the spoiling of their goods and martyrdom."[18] Not too many bishops would have found this sentiment an ideal termination of their episcopal course. Or again, in the final *Tract 90* on the Anglican Thirty-Nine Articles, in which Newman suggested that there were no barriers in the Articles to the acceptance of Roman Catholic doctrine. The spoiling of one's goods and the prospect of martyrdom may be seen as a sort of rhetorical flourish, but the acceptance of Roman Catholic doctrine? Now the bomb was ready to explode! The reactions to *Tract 90* ranged "from thinking it was an attempt to join England with Rome, to hold it to be a dastardly example of sophistry."[19] It was the end of the Tracts, and although still 1841, it was the end for Newman as an Anglican.

After a long and difficult personal struggle, Newman entered the Catholic Church on October 8, 1845, being conditionally baptized and received by the Italian Passionist priest Blessed Dominic Barberi. Before he left his Oxford, a number of his friends came to see him, to make their farewells: "Pusey last of all, late at night. Newman left Oxford next morning at half-past eight and did not see it again, except from the train, for thirty-two

---

16. Trevor, *Newman's Journey*, 55.
17. Trevor, *Newman's Journey*, 76.
18. O'Connell, *The Oxford Conspirators*, 147.
19. Lease, *Witness to the Faith*, 69.

years."[20] All considered, he had spent twenty-five years in his beloved Oxford, and he would not see Edward Bouverie Pusey, the Regius Professor of Hebrew and one of his closest friends again until they were both old men. That same year, 1846, saw Francis Newman appointed Professor of Latin at University College London, a post he was to hold until 1863.

In 1847, Newman was ordained a Catholic priest in Rome and joined the Oratory of St. Philip Neri with some companions. At the end of that year he returned to England, and in 1848 established in England the Oratory in Maryvale, at that time just outside the city of Birmingham in the English Midlands. The year 1849 saw the Oratory moved to a former gin distillery in downtown Birmingham, and finally in 1852 to its present site in Edgbaston, Birmingham.

Throughout his life Newman was a writer. He wrote theological works mainly, but in 1852 a series of lectures in Dublin, Ireland, on university education that saw life in print as *The Idea of a University*. This conceptual blueprint was to take living flesh as the Catholic University of Ireland to which Newman was appointed as rector in 1854. Superficially, it may seem strange to appoint an Englishman as rector of a Catholic university in Ireland in the politically turbulent mid-nineteenth century, a time when Irish nationalism was growing rapidly. But who would have seemed more suitable than this distinguished Oxford convert? Newman remained in that position until 1857 when, for both personal and ecclesiastical reasons, he resigned. During this period he was constantly crossing St. George's Channel between England and Ireland, dividing his time between the Birmingham Oratory, of which he was the founding father, and the Catholic University of Ireland as rector.

During the 1860s Newman found himself in a difficult position. Many, especially Anglican converts like Henry Edward Manning, Archbishop of Westminster, were pushing for a definition of papal infallibility, but a very wide-ranging definition. One Newman expert describes the situation accurately: "A violent campaign seemed to turn the Pope into an oracle independent of the church."[21] Newman disagreed. Though he accepted the notion of papal infallibility, he felt it would be widely misunderstood and that it was not really necessary. This rendered him even further suspect in an English Catholic church whose leadership was very ultramontane at the

---

20. Trevor, *Newman's Journey*, 118.
21. Dessain, "John Henry Newman," 24.

time. Papal infallibility was defined at the First Vatican Council in 1870, the year in which Newman published *An Essay in Aid of a Grammar of Assent*.

The cloud of suspicion under which Newman lived was lifted when he was made a cardinal by Pope Leo XIII in 1879. "'My cardinal,' declared Leo promptly, 'It was not easy . . . they said he was too liberal.'"[22] This act vindicated him against those extremist critics who, especially in respect of papal infallibility, had regarded him as unsound or less than fully Catholic.

When Newman died in 1890, the end was very simple. "There were no last words. Newman went out of this world as quickly and quietly as he went in and out of the rooms in it, surprising people who had expected a more formal presence."[23] After his death, however, hundreds filed past his coffin in the Oratory in Birmingham, and thousands lined the route to his final resting place at Rednal, just south of the city. The *Daily News* at his death said that "thousands know that they have lost one in whom their faith rested, one who was a living incarnation of the defensibility of faith, one on whose authority they could quote an argument to sustain them in their acceptance of the unseen."[24]

NEWMAN, MAN OF THE UNIVERSITY

In a memorandum written in 1863, Newman wrote, "From first to last . . . education has been my line."[25] Newman always believed in the central importance of thinking for oneself, trying out ideas, being open to the critical and corrective judgments of others. "He devoted much of his day to writing—hence the vast collection of private letters. He thought on paper."[26] In his *Idea of a University*, Newman wrote: "Great minds need elbow-room, not indeed in the domain of faith, but of thought. And so indeed do lesser minds, and all minds. . . . Every human system, every human writer, is open to just criticism. Make him shut up his portfolio; good! And then perhaps you lose what, on the whole and in spite of incidental mistakes, would have been one of the ablest defenses of Revealed Truth (directly or indirectly

---

22. Cited in Adrian Hastings, "John Henry Newman," in Hastings et al., eds., *Key Thinkers in Christianity*, 123.

23. Trevor, *Newman's Journey*, 265.

24. Quoted in H. Francis Davis, "Cardinal Newman," in Charles Davis, *English Spiritual Writers*, 123.

25. Tristram, *John Henry Newman: Autobiographical Writings*, 259.

26. Chadwick, *Newman, A Short Introduction*, 10.

according to his subject) ever given to the world."[27] Thinking for yourself, however, did not mean for him thinking by yourself or thinking that all thinking was equally valuable. He was opposed to both solipsism—that the discrete individual somehow is the criterion of all truth—and to what he called liberalism. Newman was consistently opposed to liberalism, but he meant by liberalism something quite precise. For Newman liberalism is the notion that one opinion is as good as another. He was open to new ideas, for example, to the advancement of science as he understood it at the time. When Charles Darwin's *Origin of the Species* came out in 1859, shocking many devout Christians with its ideas of human evolution, the theory did not shock Newman. He wrote to a correspondent at the time that he was willing "to go the whole hog with Darwin."[28] In fact, Newman had a dynamic view of the universe long before many of his contemporaries. This dynamic perspective emerged especially from his studies of Christian antiquity.

Newman became immersed in the fathers of the church and in all aspects of patristic theology.

> The appeal to the Fathers was an older part of the Anglican tradition, but no Anglican had read them before with the intensity of Newman, in his efforts to show the resemblances between ancient and modern heresy, ancient and modern faith. . . . It was from the Fathers, and in particular from his hero, St. Athanasius, the combative fourth-century Bishop of Alexandria, that Newman believed that he had given intellectual substance to the principle that the Catholic faith of Christian antiquity had stood *contra mundum*, against the world, and that the modern Church should do the same.[29]

Newman was aware of German theology in the nineteenth century up to a point. His very good friend Edward Pusey studied Oriental languages and Protestant theology in Germany and was in constant contact with Newman. "Pusey set himself to learn German with a tutor, and in June 1825 he left England for Germany. During the next two years Pusey spent about fifteen months visiting various German universities. He met Friedrich Schleiermacher and Joachim Neander and formed friendships with several young, rising theologians. Pusey was alternately appalled and

---

27. Newman, *The Idea of a University*, 383–84.
28. Cited in Trevor, *Newman's Journey*, 111. See Wilson, *The Victorians*, 100–101.
29. Gilley, "Keble, Froude, Newman, and Pusey," 101.

John Henry Newman (1801–90)

fascinated by what he found in Germany."[30] Newman was also aware of German Catholic theology in at least a very limited fashion. For example, on May 11, 1834, Thomas D. Acland, a friend of Newman, wrote to him: "[Nicholas] Wiseman has desired me to draw your attention to a German work by Möhler, on Athanasius and his times. Very Roman Catholic, I believe."[31] It is not clear how much German theology Newman knew in detail, and it is especially unclear if he was aware of more than the names of Johann Adam Möhler and Matthias Scheeben. If the theological work of Möhler and Scheeben was to lead to theological renewal not only in Germany but throughout continental Europe, the contribution of John Henry Newman would do the same primarily, though not only, for the English-speaking theological world. Pusey picked up for him folios of the fathers at a shilling each. From his patristic studies Newman learned that change was essential to human flourishing, essential to the church. "The church was not a changeless idea; it was a living community. Christ was one and the same, but the understanding of him must grow as the collective mind of the human race grows in the search for truth; the guidance of the Spirit was promised to, and mediated through, the united body. And St. Peter's successor was the divinely appointed center of unity."[32]

When eventually Newman found himself in Rome studying for the priesthood in the Catholic Church, the standard of university theology did not match the standard he had known in Oxford. According to his friend Ambrose St. John, he often fell asleep during lectures on moral and dogmatic theology. He was disappointed to find that theology was taught from second-rate manuals, and seldom from original sources. Few read St. Augustine or St. Thomas Aquinas. He referred to St. Thomas as "the champion of revealed truth," and when Pope Leo XIII later published an encyclical on Aquinas, Newman wrote to the Pope to thank him for it. Nonetheless, Newman had nothing more than a layman's acquaintance with Aquinas. "He left Rome without having any introduction to Thomistic philosophy or theology. His natural disinclination for metaphysics, added to this lack of

---

30. O'Connell, *The Oxford Conspirators*, 98.

31. Mozley, *Letters and Correspondence of John Henry Newman*, 2:40. The Wiseman referred to is Nicholas Wiseman (1802–65), later to be Cardinal-Archbishop of Westminster. From 1828 to 1840 Wiseman was in Rome as rector of the English College. He had a solid acquaintance with Oriental languages and patristic theology, and hence the reference to him in this letter.

32. Trevor, *Newman's Journey*, 112.

any encouragement, left him all his life with no deep knowledge of Thomist metaphysics."[33]

When Newman was appointed rector of the Catholic University in Dublin, his ideal and his practice in the university shocked the then Archbishop of Dublin, Cardinal Paul Cullen, who was himself responsible for Newman's appointment. Newman was all too aware of the many difficulties the new university faced, both from church authorities and from external forces. But he did not give up. Newman wanted the best available scholars appointed to teach in the university and in that respect, for example, in 1853 he invited the German historian and theologian Ignaz von Döllinger to become a professor. "In gaining you, we should gain the presence and countenance of a world wide reputation."[34] While it did not come to pass, it illustrates Newman's desire to make his university a center of real excellence. "Newman had no patience with the notion that the essence of a university is an assembly of learned men, busy in acquiring knowledge, and allowing the young the privilege of watching.... The ideal activity is to engender a habit of mind ... which lasts through life, of which the attributes are freedom, equitableness of mind, calmness, moderation, and wisdom."[35] Therefore, Newman gave the students very considerable freedom, both moral and intellectual—far too much, according to the Archbishop of Dublin. Newman established a science faculty and a school of medicine. Although the British government of the day refused to grant accreditation to the new university, which was seen as in opposition to the Queen's Colleges established in Belfast, Galway, and Cork, the Royal College of Surgeons in Dublin gave recognition to this new school of medicine, and it flourished from the beginning. Newman also appointed lay professors. Cardinal Cullen was opposed to this, not least because the political views—that is the republican views—of many of the Irish laity conflicted with his own. When Newman suggested to the bishops of Ireland who formed the board of governors of the university that it was necessary to appoint a vice-rector, they invited him to suggest one. When he suggested a layman and named him, silence ensued, and by the time Newman left, no one had been appointed. With both insight and wit Meriol Trevor describes Newman's attitudes towards the student body: "Newman expected the young men to keep horses

---

33. Davis, "Newman and Thomism," 158.

34. Dessain and Blehl, *The Letters and Diaries of John Henry Newman*, vol. 15, 506.

35. Chadwick, "The University on Mount Zion," in his *Spirit of the Oxford Movement*, 101.

and went riding with them himself. He encouraged music and debating societies and even, horror of horrors, supplied them with a club room and a billiard table, so that they could enjoy the favorite game of the day without resort to the places of entertainment in the town."[36]

Successive historians have emphasized the role of Newman in the university at the expense of Cardinal Cullen. The latter is most often seen as an obstacle to the flourishing of Newman's project. It is true that there were real differences between the two men. The fact remains, however, that it was Cullen who had recruited Newman and who had tried to keep him in Dublin. Cullen, of course, ever-cautious, moved much more slowly on issues facing the university than Newman would have wished. Newman's advocacy of lay professors and lay involvement was all fine and well, but Cullen was only too aware of the nationalistic and anti-British young Irelanders, and of the volatile political climate.[37]

Newman has some fine things to say about the role of the teacher. He views the teacher, regardless of discipline, as a necessary intermediary in presenting the world of knowledge to the student. It is not simply the case that the teacher supplements what the student can learn from books and self-education. There is also what may best be described as "the personal presence of the teacher."[38] The text person that is the teacher is every bit as important as the textbook. And so it comes as no surprise that teachers in Newman's judgment should exercise a certain personal-pastoral care for their students, especially in terms of their intellectual development. Contrary to many of his peers in Oxford at the time, Newman believed that tutors—in our terminology, professors—should directly supervise students' work, and should take a real interest in the young men in their care. "This, in fact, was what tutorship became in Oxford," partly influenced by Newman's example.[39] Newman wanted scholars of distinction to be appointed. To name but one of the professors appointed to Newman's University, Sir Peter le Page Renouf (1822–97) was a most distinguished Egyptologist. Renouf was Professor of Ancient History and Oriental Languages at the University from 1855 through 1864.[40]

36. Trevor, *Newman's Journey*, 162.
37. See Barr, *Paul Cullen, John Henry Newman and the Catholic University of Ireland*.
38. Mulcahy, "Personal Influence, Discipline and Liberal Education," 152.
39. Trevor, *Newman's Journey*, 41.
40. Newman's University eventually morphed into University College Dublin. Renouf's legacy developed into the Department of Oriental/Semitic Languages. For a brief

Newman was intellectually curious and thought that the university should likewise be a place of genuine intellectual curiosity. He loved visiting zoos until he was well over eighty. One companion of his to the Dublin zoo wrote in his diary: "To see Fr. Newman and [go] with him to the Zoological. His wonder at and speculation on the design and end of beasts; their ferocity; their odd ways; birds especially."[41] Wide-ranging intellectual curiosity and religious devotion were not at odds for Newman. Here is his mission statement, as we would call it today, for the university: "I wish the intellect to range with the utmost freedom and religion to enjoy an equal freedom; but what I am stipulating for is, that they should be found in one and the same place, and exemplified in the same persons. . . . I want the same roof to contain both the intellectual and the moral discipline. Devotion is not a sort of finish given to the sciences; nor is science a sort of feather in the cap . . . an ornament and set-off to devotion. I want the intellectual layman to be religious and the devout ecclesiastic to be intellectual."[42]

Nor was Newman upset at intellectual differences between friends, among students, and even within the church. Writing to a critic who was also a friend from Oxford days, W. G. Ward, he said:

> I do not feel our differences to be such a trouble as you do; for such differences have always been, always will be in the church; and Christians would have ceased to have spiritual and intellectual life if such differences did not exist. No human power can hinder it; nor, if it attempted it, could do more than make a solitude and call it peace. . . . Man cannot and God will not. He means such differences to be an exercise of charity. Of course, I wish as much as possible to agree with all my friends; but if, in spite of my utmost efforts, they go beyond me, I can't help it, and take it easy.[43]

Friends need not be clones one of another, even in the most important areas of religious belief and expression.

Ultimately Newman's idea of what a university education should produce is a gentleman. He had very strong and, it seems to me, entirely valid convictions about what a gentleman should be, and were he alive today, when access to university education is open to everyone, he would say the same of a lady. Here is his description from *The Idea of the University*: "It is

---

history see Owen F. Cummings, "A Century of Near Eastern Languages," 30–36.

41. Cited in Trevor, *Newman's Journey*, 164.

42. Cited in Trevor, *Newman's Journey*, 184.

43. Cited in Trevor, *Newman's Journey*, 225.

well to be a gentleman, it is well to have a cultivated intellect, a delicate taste, a candid, equitable, dispassionate mind, a noble and courteous bearing in the conduct of life; these are the connatural qualities of large knowledge; they are the objects of a university; I am advocating, I shall illustrate and insist upon them."[44] Two aspects of Newman's gentlemanly bearing ring out very clearly in this famous passage: a gentleman is to be intellectually cultivated, by which Newman means alive, aware, open to insight, pursuant of truth; he is to be courteous in his conduct. Every generation interested in higher education would benefit from seeing these high ideals bound indissolubly together.

NEWMAN, MAN OF THE CHURCH

Probably most people think of Newman as Cardinal Newman, an eminent prince of the church. Newman was always a man of the church, church understood in the broadest possible sense. He was thoroughly an Anglican churchman before becoming a Roman Catholic churchman. When he became a Roman Catholic, he was forty-four. In this regard, the late Bishop Geoffrey Rowell, one of the premier contemporary historians of the Oxford Movement, points out: "This simple fact is one we are apt to forget. His spirituality, his theological outlook, were already largely settled: men do not change drastically at such an age. In leaving the Church of England and joining the Church of Rome, he looked only for the more perfect realization of that faith by which he had tried to live as an Anglican."[45]

As a deacon in the Church of England, for example, this young intellectual threw himself into pastoral work. Mariel Trevor describes him in these words:

> He started visiting, especially the sick, and keeping notes. Often he was taken in by pious talk and afterwards discovered that the person was a drunkard or had deserted his wife and children. From the dying he tried to elicit penitence and induce them to take the Sacrament which, as he was only a deacon, he could not administer himself. The case of a sick girl was very painful—"It is like a sword going through my heart." And there was a young married woman with consumption. "Her eyes looked at me with such meaning. I felt a thrill I cannot describe—it was like the gate

44. Newman, *The Idea of a University*, 110.
45. Rowell, "The Roots of Newman's 'Scriptural Holiness,'" 13.

of heaven." She died half an hour after he left, much comforted by his reading from St. John, though very ignorant of religion, as most of these poor people were.[46]

Pastoral care was never far from Newman's mind, either in the Church of England or in the Catholic Church. He was constantly concerned with the care of souls. In the 1860s, the pompous Msgr. George Talbot wrote to Newman inviting him to preach in Rome to an audience ostensibly superior to anything he could find in the industrial maze that was Birmingham. Newman refused the invitation, writing the famous words "Birmingham people have souls."

Newman was a great advocate of the laity in the church. The same Msgr. George Talbot in a famous article—which was also a caricature of Newman's views—written in a periodical called *The Rambler* described the role of the laity in the church as follows: "They wish to govern the church in England by public opinion.... What is the province of the laity? To hunt, to shoot, to entertain."[47] The laity should have nothing to do with ecclesiastical affairs. In a memorandum of some correspondence he had with the editor of *The Tablet*, a British Catholic weekly, Newman wrote in reply, "The church would look foolish without them."[48]

Newman avoided any sense of the church as sectarian, as exclusive, as isolated, as insular. He accepted the role of the papacy in the church as the final adjudicator in matters of doctrinal and moral teaching, but he objected to a sweeping application of infallibility to all the pronouncements of the pope and to the way in which the proponents of such sweeping infallibility accused those who disagreed of being unorthodox. During the time leading up to the declaration of papal infallibility, and in the light of the positions that emphasize the role of the pope out of all proportion to his real role in the church, Newman wrote: "Instead of aiming at being a worldwide power, we are shrinking into ourselves, narrowing the lines of communion, trembling at freedom of thought, and using the language of dismay and despair at the prospect before us, instead of, with the high spirits of the warrior, going out conquering and to conquer."[49] In point of fact, Newman had been invited to go to Rome for the First Vatican Council as an expert

---

46. Trevor, *Newman's Journey*, 29.
47. Cited in Trevor, *Newman's Journey*, 230.
48. Cited in Trevor, *Newman's Journey*, 194.
49. Cited in Trevor, *Newman's Journey*, 227.

theologian, but he turned down the invitation on the grounds of age and health, and commitment to his writing.

In terms of his own spiritual life, Newman had a constant and profound sense of God, a sense of the immediate presence of God. He wrote in his *Apologia Pro Vita Sua* "From a boy I had been led to consider that my Maker and I, His creature, were the two beings, luminously such, *in rerum natura*."[50] Before God, the soul was, in his words, *sola cum Solo*.

> Common men see God at a distance ... but the long practiced Christian, who, through God's mercy, has brought God's presence near to him, the elect of God, in whom the Blessed Spirit dwells, he does not look out of doors for the traces of God; he is moved by God dwelling in him, and needs not but act on instinct. I do not say there is any man altogether such, for this is the angelic life; but it is the state of mind to which vigorous prayer and watching tend.[51]

This permeative sense that Newman had of God's presence, of the loving union of the soul with God, perhaps best understood as a mystical presence, as an "ontological mysticism,"[52] is finely described by Owen Chadwick in these words: "God ... was too instant for debate.... God is simply there."[53]

The human person before God, *sola cum Solo*, is, however, not unconnected, not a discrete, atomistic individual, as it were. Newman has a relational view of the Christian person, embodied with others in Christ. Newman's understanding of the church is as communion, communion with the Triune God and communion with one another.

> This then is the special glory of the Christian church, that its members do not depend merely on that which is visible, they are not mere stones of a building, piled one upon another, and bound together from without, but they are one and all the births and manifestations of one and the same unseen spiritual principle or power, "living stones," internally connected, as branches from a tree, not as the parts of a heap. They are members of the Body of Christ.[54]

---

50. Newman, *Apologia Pro Vita Sua*, quoted in Davis, "Cardinal Newman," 127.
51. Newman, *Apologia Pro Vita Sua*, quoted in Davis, "Cardinal Newman," 128.
52. The phrase comes from Dessain, "Newman's Spirituality," 153.
53. Chadwick, "John Henry Newman," 152.
54. Newman, *Parochial and Plain Sermons*, 4:169–71.

At least in some respects his ecclesiology would resonate with the communion ecclesiology emergent from Vatican II.

Reading through the *Apologia Pro Vita Sua* leads one to a further appreciation of Newman's communion ecclesiology. Charting his spiritual and theological development, he makes constant mention, with gratitude, of so many of his Anglican professors, priests, and peers—Walter Mayers of Pembroke College Oxford; Daniel Wilson, later to become Bishop of Calcutta; Richard Whately, principal of Alban Hall Oxford and later Archbishop of Dublin; William James and Edward Hawkins of Oriel College; John William Bowden, Richard Hurrell Froude, John Keble, Hugh Rose; William Palmer of Dublin and of Worcester College, and Edward Pusey of Christ Church. Their names and so many more unfold throughout the *Apologia*. Newman, now a Roman Catholic, recalls them graciously and with great kindness. This leaves the historian Owen Chadwick to comment as follows: "[Newman] taught [Catholics of the nineteenth century] to be more generous to other denominations, for no Roman Catholic priest had ever said thank you to the Anglicans with such heartfelt eloquence."[55]

Like Möhler and Scheeben, the great scholars of the Catholic Faculty of Theology in the University of Tübingen, Newman was captivated by the theology of the patristic era. This theology along with a broader awareness of the early history of Christianity helped to move him from an earlier evangelical sense of the church to a more Catholic sense of the church.[56] Newman had been asked by Hugh James Rose, a high Anglican clergyman, to write a history of the early councils of the church. This threw him into the complexities of doctrinal exchange and debate and conciliar resolution during this crucial period of Christian development. He never quite finished the project that Rose had asked for, but his researches reach their conclusion in his first major theological publication, *The Arians of the Fourth Century* (1833). In ways that would not be accepted without nuance and qualification by the scholarly community today, Newman set out to contrast the Antiochene school of theology and the Alexandrian school of theology. He associates Arius and his faulty Christology and soteriology with the traditions of exegesis and reflection of Antioch, and St. Athanasius and his orthodox Nicene Christology and soteriology with

---

55. Chadwick, "John Henry Newman," 152.

56. On Newman's historical sensibility, see the still very useful Louvain doctoral dissertation of Thomas S. Bokenkotter, supervised by the great church historian Roger Aubert, *Cardinal Newman as an Historian* (1959).

the traditions of exegesis and reflection of Alexandria, with the latter being clearly superior to the former. Rowan D. Williams, former Archbishop of Canterbury, writes in his introduction to a contemporary edition of the book: "Newman's 'Antioch' is an ideal type not an historical reality. It is the type of a theology dictated by human wisdom, human desire, the reluctance to be humble before revelation. Alexandria, the home of true theology, is characterized by reverence, by the expectation that the Bible will always be deeply mysterious, working through elusive symbolism over a lifetime of contemplation; this is a theology giving priority to God. Newman's purpose in terms of the 1820s was evidently to challenge any English assimilation of German critical scholarship and doctrinal revisionism."[57] In terms of a close study of patristic texts themselves, Newman began in 1836 along with his friend Edward Pusey both to translate and to put together a team of translators for the *Library of the Fathers*. One result of this patristic saturation was to push him closer to Catholicism, as he himself remarks in *An Essay on the Development of Christian Doctrine*, "Of all existing systems, the present communion of Rome is the nearest approximation in fact to the Church of the Fathers. . . . Did St. Athanasius or St. Ambrose come suddenly to life, it cannot be doubted what communion he would take to be his own."[58] We shall return to this important quotation shortly. The Jesuit patristic theologian Brian E. Daley has captured very nicely what might be called the contemporaneity of the fathers of the church for Newman in doing theology. Daley writes: "Newman offers a gentle and attractive portrait of the patristic style of theological argument that seems also to be a portrait of the kind of theologian . . . he wants to be. . . . For Newman, who always strove to listen and to speak with the heart, the Fathers always remained in touch, always were ideal partners in conversation."[59]

Newman's *An Essay on the Development of Christian Doctrine* was written between March 1844 and September 1845, just before Newman was received into the Catholic Church by Blessed Dominic Barberi, the Passionist priest. The book was published later that year. The English patristic scholar Anthony Meredith, SJ, helps us to understand the trajectory of Newman's 1845 *An Essay on the Development of Christian Doctrine* when he says: "[According to Newman] development in the church is a particular

---

57. Williams, "Introduction," xxxix. I owe the reference to Brian E. Daley, "The Church Fathers," 31–32.

58. Newman, Lecture 12, "Ecclesiastical History," 367.

59. Daley, "The Church Fathers," 43.

example of the more general problem and phenomenon of change. The Church is a living historical organism; therefore it is only natural that she should also change."[60]

Newman himself was changing in 1845. W. G. Ward, his friend in the Oxford Movement, had been stripped of his Oxford degrees in February of that year, and in the midst of the controversy surrounding this event it was inevitable that Newman's name and reputation would be involved. In March, he wrote to his sister Jemima:

> I have a good name with many; I am deliberately sacrificing it. I have a bad name with more; I am fulfilling all their worst wishes, and giving them their most coveted triumph. I am distressing all I love, unsettling all I have instructed or aided. . . . Pity me, my dear Jemima. What have I done thus to be deserted, thus to be left to take a wrong course, if it is wrong?[61]

The pain, including the pain of contemplated ecclesial change of allegiance, is self-evident in this letter to his sister. In the *Essay on the Development of Christian Doctrine*, Newman was inquiring into the possible criteria for acknowledging appropriate change/development in doctrine, an inquiry that was both the fruit of his studies in early church history and patristic theology, and also his "transition from the static to the dynamic view of the world which his contemporaries found it so hard to make."[62]

Newman-specialist Nicholas Lash cautions us in this vein, "To summarize Newman's thought is, notoriously, to distort it. . . . There is simply no substitute for a close, patient, critical and sympathetic attention to his own text." However, for the sake of brevity in the context of this book we must attempt a summary.[63]

Newman wrote the book standing at the desk he had been given by Henry Wilberforce.[64] In his "Introduction," Newman makes eminently

---

60. Meredith, *The Theology of Tradition*, 65. The edition I am using of the *Essay* is John Henry Newman, *An Essay on the Development of Christian Doctrine*, the edition of 1845, edited with an introduction by J. M. Cameron.

61. Cited in Turner, *John Henry Newman*, 533.

62. Trevor, *Newman's Journey*, 11.

63. Lash, *Newman on Development*, 153. Similarly, Avery Dulles warns us that "The *Essay* is not a brief for a kind of dogmatic Darwinism" in his *John Henry Newman*, 74.

64. Trevor, *Newman's Journey*, 109. Wilberforce (1807–73) had been a student of John Henry Newman's at Oxford and followed Newman into the Catholic Church in 1850.

John Henry Newman (1801–90)

clear that from his historical investigations the Protestantism of his day is far from the obvious heir to the early church.

> Whatever be historical Christianity, it is not Protestantism. If ever there were a safe truth, it is this.... It is shown by the long neglect of ecclesiastical history in England, which prevails even in the English Church.... It is melancholy to say it, but the chief, perhaps the only English writer who has any claim to be considered an ecclesiastical historian, is the infidel Gibbon.[65]

Newman's judgment here is not entirely persuasive. He seldom takes into consideration the Eastern Orthodox Church. Be that as it may, while it is true that no modern church or Christian tradition exactly replicates the face of the ancient church, nonetheless he recognizes that ancient face in the Catholic Church. "There is one modern face ... wherein one can see the wrinkles and the lines, the slant of the head and the angle of the shoulders and the glance of eyes, which remind the observer of the face in the portrait."[66] The Catholic Church has a strong family resemblance and likeness to the antique patristic church. And so Newman illustrates this point in the passage noted above that has come to be very well known:

> Did St. Athanasius or St. Ambrose come suddenly to life, it cannot be doubted what communion they would mistake for their own. All surely will agree that these Fathers, with whatever differences of opinion, whatever protests, if we will, would find themselves more at home with such men as St. Bernard or St. Ignatius Loyola, or with the lonely priest in his lodgings, or the holy sisterhood of mercy, or the unlettered crowd before the altar, then with the rulers or the members of any other religious community.[67]

Newman provides seven criteria for distinguishing true from false developments in Christian doctrine, although he insists that "development does not take place by a mere 'mechanism of reasoning.'"[68] The process is far more complicated. First, preservation of type. He uses a biological analogy. A doctrinal development is genuine if we can discern an underlying type in various manifestations. A butterfly preserves type when it morphs from egg to caterpillar, from caterpillar to chrysalis, from chrysalis to but-

---

65. Newman, *An Essay*, 72.
66. Chadwick, *From Bossuet to Newman*, 141.
67. Newman, *An Essay*, 185.
68. Chadwick, *From Bossuet to Newman*, 156.

terfly. Or using a metaphor from human development, "Just as an adult keeps the same members and organs as the newborn child, so the church and its teaching must always remain recognizably the same."[69] In Newman's judgment, the ecclesial communities of the Reformation tradition had not preserved the distinctive and characteristic features of the early Christian church, and the Roman Catholic Church had done so.

Second, continuity of principles. These are the basic and fundamental principles of Christian doctrine such that, were they to be negated, the entire infrastructure of doctrine would collapse or at least be left in a very reduced state. Newman uses the helpful analogy of language.

> The science of grammar affords another instance of the existence of special laws in the formation of systems. Some languages have more elasticity than others, and greater capabilities. . . . We feel the presence of a certain character or genius in each, which determines its path and its range; and to discover and enter into it is one part of refined scholarship. And when particular writers, in consequence perhaps of some theory, tax a language beyond its powers, the failure is conspicuous.[70]

Newman appears to be saying that there is a difference between literacy in a language and fluency, and furthermore that individual creative fluency may reach a point of distortion in terms of the basic intelligibility of the language. Some of the basic principles which, if abandoned, would result in the severest reduction of Christianity would be: dogma, the sacramental principle, the priority of faith over reason, the propriety of intellectual inquiry into the meaning of revelation, and the principle of development itself. These are such foundational principles that, if denied, would result in the collapse of traditional Christian faith.

Third, power of assimilation. This is the ability of the Christian doctrinal tradition to assimilate new knowledge, for example, the assimilation of the biological theory of evolution into the doctrine of creation. Evolution adds new significance and wonder to that doctrine. "As a healthy organism builds itself up by ingesting food, so the church takes in what is assimilable in the cultures it meets, and transforms what it appropriates."[71]

The fourth, logical sequence. This needs particular care because it is not so much straightforward deduction of new truths from others as it is,

---

69. Dulles, *John Henry Newman*, 74.
70. Newman, *An Essay*, 124–25.
71. Dulles, *John Henry Newman*, 75.

in the words of John Macquarrie, "a slow growth of knowledge based on meditation on a few basic ideas that seem to possess a certain dynamic which, once it has been glimpsed, impresses itself more and more upon the believer."[72] Macquarrie offers the example of the doctrine of the Trinity over the first three or four centuries. "It was a deepening rather than an extension of knowledge."[73]

Fifth, anticipation of the future. Some doctrines emerged and were received later on in the Christian tradition, but in fact, had their roots within an earlier time. Although Newman does not use this example himself since the *Essay* was written between 1841 and 1845, it affords a good example, namely, the doctrine of the Immaculate Conception of the Virgin Mary. Promulgated in 1854, it finds its roots in earlier patristic descriptions of the utter holiness of Mary as Theotokos.

Sixth, conservative action on its past. What this means is put very succinctly as Avery Dulles comments on it: "Does the new doctrine confirm or weaken adherence to the ancient faith?"[74] Does what is proposed as a new development, in other words, preserve and conserve the best of the traditional faith?

Seventh, chronic vigor. This is a very pragmatic way of commenting on doctrinal development. "False developments . . . had a transitory character, whereas the genuine development shows vigorous and continued growth."[75] Or, in Newman's own words, "While a corruption is distinguished from decay by its energetic action, it is distinguished from a development by its transitory character."[76]

It has been pointed out, and rightly so, by Aidan Nichols, OP, that these seven criteria do not stand on their own for Newman. Nichols considers that the center of gravity of the *Essay* lies elsewhere:

> The center of gravity of the *Essay* lies in the three great church-historical tableaux which Newman paints: the church of the first three centuries; the church of the fourth-century Arian crisis; the church of the patristic golden age in the fifth and sixth centuries.

---

72. Macquarrie, *Stubborn Theological Questions*, 163. Macquarrie's essay in this volume, "Development of Doctrine," is a very helpful and eminently clear approach to the question of doctrinal development.

73. Macquarrie, *Stubborn Theological Questions*, 163.

74. Dulles, *John Henry Newman*, 75.

75. Macquarrie, *Stubborn Theological Questions*, 163.

76. Newman, *An Essay*, 147.

> Each tableau culminates with Newman drawing a parallel with the nineteenth-century Roman communion, showing that the changes brought about by the Tridentine reformation of the church are insubstantial compared with the overwhelming sameness between the earlier Christians and the modern Roman Catholics.[77]

There can be little doubt that that is Newman's ultimate goal. However, in a century in which development was very publicly in the air—recall that Newman once said that he could go the whole hog with Darwin—it was and it remains immensely useful to surface criteria for determining authentic development of doctrine, even if these may not be applied in a woodenheaded fashion.[78] In the 1845 edition of the *Essay*, Newman referred to the criteria as "tests," but in the 1878 edition as "notes." The difference in nomenclature between the two editions is not insignificant, though it continues to be debated in some measure.[79]

In chapter 1 in *An Essay on the Development of Christian Doctrine*, Newman famously wrote that "In a higher world it is otherwise but here below to live is to change and to be perfect is to have changed often."[80] The idea of evolution, of change and development was very much in the air at this time, stimulated, of course, as it would ultimately be by the publication in 1859 of Charles Darwin's book, *The Origin of the Species*.

NEWMAN THE MAN

Man of the church, man of the university, in many ways an ideal man and an ideal priest, but also an ordinary man. Newman's very ordinariness is one of his most attractive features. A female admirer so showed her disappointment at Newman's ordinariness when she first met him that he wrote to her, "As for myself, you are not the first person who has been disappointed in me. Romantic people always will be. I am, in all my ways of going on, a very ordinary person."[81] There seems to have been little pretense in the man. He evinced so many ordinary characteristics of what it is to be human.

---

77. Nichols, *From Newman to Congar*, 51.

78. Trevor, *Newman's Journey*, 111. In an introduction to the *Essay*, Newman scholar Ian Ker thinks of it as "comparable to Darwin's *On the Origin of Species*." See Newman, *An Essay on the Development of Christian Doctrine*, xxv.

79. McCarren, "Development of Doctrine," 125–30.

80. Newman, *An Essay*, 100.

81. Cited in Trevor, *Newman's Journey*, 100.

John Henry Newman (1801–90)

One of these was the common, perhaps universal experience of shame. Newman's father was not a great businessman. His business enterprises seldom were marked by success. There seems little doubt that this not only pained Newman but gave rise to shame. In later years, when his sister Harriet told her husband, Tom Mozley, that her father had been a chief clerk in a London firm, this greatly annoyed Newman. Speaking to Mozley, he insisted that his father had been a partner, not just a clerk. In point of fact, Newman was accurate, but one gets a sense that his desire for accuracy was in part fueled by a sense of shame at his father's commercial failures.[82]

Newman was extraordinarily introspective. In a manuscript he entitled *Memoranda*, which he marked as "personal and most private," covering the years 1804–26, we are given glimpse after glimpse of Newman's introspection. The very production of the manuscript demonstrates this, as described by Seán O'Faoláin: "He first wrote it in 1820–21; transcribed it in 1823, with additions; in 1840, with omissions; in 1872 he marked it 'to be partially and finally transcribed with great omissions and put aside for good'; but in 1874 he went at it again and cut out fifteen precious pages at the beginning."[83] Newman was constantly writing. "[The work of John Cornwell] has stressed the compulsive character of Newman's writing: he was seldom without a pen in his hand."[84] We see Newman's introspection-in-writing at work with finesse in the *Apologia*. Indeed, so much of Newman would be utterly opaque, unknown to us without his introspection. Such introversion and self-scrutiny, however, are not always blessings. Partly because of this introspection, Newman was able to cope with loss in this world. If the world and everything in it is only penultimately real—and Newman says things like this with different meanings at different times—then loss can never finally be loss. Whether it is the loss of a childhood home, or of status, or the death of friends, the conviction that there is no finality to it enables one better to deal with it. This is not to say that such loss is not keenly felt in its own way, but it is also fitted into a metaphysical scheme of things, for Newman a religious scheme of things, so that while it has its place, one is not overwhelmed by loss. Perhaps O'Faoláin comes close to the truth when he remarks, "[Newman's] weakness was that he

---

82. O'Faoláin, *Newman's Way*, 6–7.
83. O'Faoláin, *Newman's Way*, 42.
84. Gilley, "Keble, Froude, Newman, and Pusey," 98.

would always love most passionately when all was gone, always speak his love too late."[85] Many could identify with Newman in this regard.

Newman was a great reader of novels, and especially enjoyed the work of George Eliot and Anthony Trollope. He also loved music, a love that was born when he was at boarding school. In a letter to a friend, he wrote: "I never wrote more than when I played the fiddle. I always sleep better after music. There must be some electric current passing from the strings through the fingers into the brain and down the spinal marrow. Perhaps thought is music."[86]

As an adolescent, Newman often clashed with his father who thought he was becoming too religious for his own good. He recorded in his journal his father's words: "Have a guard. You are encouraging a nervous and morbid sensibility, and irritability, which may be very serious. I know what it is myself perfectly well. I know it is a disease of the mind. Religion, when carried too far, induces softness of the mind."[87] His father's bias was wide of the mark. No one could accuse Newman of softness of the mind. His journal shows something of the man. He judges himself to be vain of his attainments, too conscious of social differences and class, and prone to bad temper and bad thoughts. When he became a Catholic in 1845, Newman wrote to his brother Francis to ask for his forgiveness for his bad temper and cruelty when they were both young. In his much edited *Memoranda*, he wrote: "While with Frank at Oxford I have felt a spirit of desperate ill-temper, and sullen anger rush on me. . . . So violent has this sometimes proved that I have quite trembled from head to foot and thought that I should fall down under excess of agitation." Seán O'Faoláin's description has the ring of accuracy: "[Newman] had a devilish temper, passions so ungovernable as to unman him, and a tongue that could clip a hedge."[88] While that may be so, it takes a big man to seek out forgiveness and effect reconciliation, and that was Newman's way. Frank visited John frequently, even into his eighties, in the Oratory in Birmingham. His older brother, Charles, born one year after John in 1802, was a trying and constant challenge to the Newman family throughout his life, and an atheist. He was financially supported by both Frank and John. Charles lived in the Welsh town of Tenby for the last thirty to forty years of his life. John went to visit

85. Gilley, "Keble, Froude, Newman, and Pusey," 55.
86. Cited in Trevor, *Newman's Journey*, 223.
87. Cited in Trevor, *Newman's Journey*, 22.
88. O'Faoláin, *Newman's Way*, 64.

him in September 1882, sensing probably that the end could not be far off, but Charles would not see him. We can only imagine how Newman felt. But, when Charles died in 1884, it was John who paid for the funeral and the gravestone with the inscription, "O Lord, of your eternal mercy, do not despise the work of your hands."

It has been pointed out by A. N. Wilson that despite all his fine qualities as a priest, an intellectual, and a man, Newman did not have an obvious concern for the mass of ordinary people, or for the difficulties of their lives. Wilson contrasts Newman rather negatively with the Anglican theologian and social prophet Frederick Denison Maurice.

> While the Irish starved [during the famine years], Newman worried his mind about Augustine's controversy in the fourth century with the Donatists. . . . Newman wrote from the middle of the slums of Birmingham as if he were an Oxford don . . . whereas Maurice was always engaged with realities external to himself. To this degree Maurice—the Anglican professor hounded out of his theological chair for "heresy"—was in many ways more "Catholic" than Newman, the Roman convert who was to die a cardinal.[89]

Even acknowledging a degree of *animus* on Wilson's part toward Newman, there is something in what he says. Theology is always done somewhere, and if that place in no way affects the doer of theology, that is problematic, to say the least. Wilson goes on to point out that, when it was to his taste, Newman was very aware of contemporary events. He followed, for example, the Crimean War, cutting out from *The Times* the maps showing how the campaign was developing.[90] Undoubtedly, Newman must have felt compassion toward the famine-suffering Irish and toward the poor of Birmingham. It remains a legitimate question, however, why such factors did not seem to enter more explicitly into his theological reflection.

Newman made and kept friends and was devoted to them. Msgr. Francis Davis of Oscott College drew an interesting and in some ways humorous contrast between Newman and St. Thomas Aquinas:

> "St. Thomas," wrote Chesterton, "was a huge heavy bull of a man, fat and slow and quiet; very mild and magnanimous but not very sociable, even apart from the humility of holiness; and abstracted, even apart from his occasional and carefully concealed experiences of trance and ecstasy." Newman, on the other hand, was

---

89. Wilson, *The Victorians*, 149.
90. Wilson, *The Victorians*, 180.

thin and pale and slightly bent. He walked and talked rapidly, and spoke incessantly as he walked. He had large, lustrous eyes, seeming to pierce through both men and things. Though naturally shy on first acquaintance, he always found, and needed, friendship.[91]

Later chapters will consider some of Newman's friendships. Here we present just a few words on Hurrell Froude and Ambrose St. John anticipating something of that later chapter. After his friend Hurrell Froude died, Newman collected various essays of his for publication. While he was readying these essays, he wrote at the back of his diary for 1839 these words about Froude: "Farewell, most loved, so much missed, until that Day which shall make you, known to so few, manifest to all as you were."[92]

Newman never forgot his dead. "Nobody was forgotten; when they died, their names were stitched into the little anniversary book with his cross-stitched cover. . . . Every week, nearly every day had its memorials and Littlemore parishioners jostled with Fellows of Oriel, Anglicans with Catholics, nuns, children, duchesses, theologians, doorkeepers—a long human litany."[93] He prayed for his sainted dead on the occasion of their anniversary. Friends were friends for life and into eternity.

---

91. Davis, "Newman and Thomism," 157.
92. Cited in Trevor, *Newman's Journey*, 70.
93. Trevor, *Newman's Journey*, 263.

4

In Newman's Circle from Oxford
John Keble, Hurrell Froude, Edward Bouverie Pusey

No one has ever had such friends as I have had.

John Henry Newman[1]

John Henry Newman valued loyal friendship. Ever since his Oxford days as leader of the Tractarian Movement, he set an enormous store on the value of spiritual "amicitia."

Peter Nockles[2]

JOHN HENRY NEWMAN LIVED and ministered as both an Anglican and, from 1845, as a Catholic. Some of his close Anglican friends followed him to Rome, but certainly not all of them. Yet he did not see his conversion to Catholicism as a reason to sever relationships with longtime Anglican friends with whom he had walked in fellowship over the years. Close friends in the Oxford Movement who remained committed Anglicans were John Keble, Edward Pusey, and Richard Hurrell Froude, the latter dying prematurely. Other friends who became Catholics included Ambrose St.

---

1. Cited in Gilley, *Newman and His Age*, 394.
2. Nockles, "Foreword."

John and Edward Caswall, both of whom joined Newman's Oratory. All of these men were closely associated with Newman in one way or another, and in this chapter we shall briefly take a look at each of them.

Before doing so, it may be helpful to address something of a discordant note about Newman's friendships, especially his male friendships. Since at least the publication of Geoffrey Faber's *Oxford Apostles* in 1933, some commentators consider that there was a homoerotic element in the Oxford Movement, and perhaps in Newman himself. While the consensus of scholarship seems to be against this—think, for example of the outstanding biographical account of Newman by Ian Ker—there are some things to consider. While he himself espoused celibacy from an early age, he seems at times to have thought or felt that the marriage of his close male friends was something of a betrayal. This was true, for example, of Tom Mozley who married Newman's sister Harriet, and of his very close Oxford friend Henry Wilberforce. Newman wrote in 1840: "All my habits for years, my tendencies, are towards celibacy. I could not take that interest in this world which marriage requires. I am too disgusted with this world—and, above all, call it what one will, I have a repugnance to a clergyman's marrying. I do not say it is not lawful—I cannot deny the right—but, whether prejudiced or not, it shocks me."[3] However scholars comment on this perplexing aspect of Newman's friendships, it seems to me that in this respect Newman fails to appreciate fully the sacramentality of marriage.

FROM OXFORD: JOHN KEBLE (1792–1866)

> *The re-birth of eucharistic piety is the most active of all the forms of fermentation which the Oxford Movement set working in the spiritual life of England.*
>
> Yngve Brilioth[4]

John Henry Newman regarded the 1833 sermon, "National Apostasy," by John Keble as the beginning of the Oxford Movement, the catholicizing movement in the nineteenth-century Church of England. In that sermon, Keble denounced the British Parliament for suppressing, for various economic and political reasons, a number of arguably redundant Irish bishoprics. With a very high theology of church and episcopacy, he saw this

---

3. Cited in Tristram, *John Henry Newman, Autobiographical Writings*, 137.
4. Brilioth, *Eucharistic Faith and Practice*, 215.

state interference with the church as nothing less than apostasy, and it was this sermon that roused Newman to reforming action after his return to England from his Mediterranean trip. While many have heard of Newman, fewer will have come across John Keble.

John Keble was born in 1792 at Fairford in Gloucestershire, England, to John Keble, the Vicar of Coln St. Aldwyn. The younger John Keble breathed in a high church atmosphere from the beginning. His father stood in a line of tradition that went back to the strongly liturgical Caroline Divines of the seventeenth century, the high church Anglican theologians who wrote mainly during the reigns of Kings Charles I (1624–49) and Charles II (1660–85). When his friends John Henry Newman and Hurrell Froude began to discover various forgotten strands of catholic theology, Keble in a sense had the upper hand. Thus, Georgina Battiscombe, Keble's biographer, writes: "When Newman and Froude were all enthusiasm for some item of Catholic faith or practice, which had burst upon them with the force of a new revelation, Keble would nod approval and remark in tones of highest commendation, 'Yes, that is exactly what my father taught me.'"[5] Keble saw himself as standing theologically, liturgically, and spiritually in the great tradition of such divines as Richard Hooker, George Herbert, William Laud, Lancelot Andrewes, and Jeremy Taylor. Indeed, one historian of the Oxford Movement goes so far as to say that "Keble was the last of the Caroline Divines and the Non-jurors; and the best of them."[6]

Having been a brilliant student at Corpus Christi College, Oxford, Keble was elected in 1811, aged nineteen, to one of the coveted fellowships at Oriel College, Oxford. Oriel was regarded as the most intellectual of the Oxford colleges at the time, and boasted a group of liberal thinkers known as the "Noetics," a group that was doctrinally liberal and highly critical of religious orthodoxy and far from congenial to the young Keble. Nonetheless, and this seems typical of Keble's personality, he seems to have got on well with the Noetics.[7]

He was ordained deacon in 1815 and priest the following year. Although he became a tutor at Oriel College in 1817, he left to assist his father in his country parish, and that was to be his life's work. Being a parish priest

5. Battiscombe, *John Keble: A Study in Limitations*, 11. See Gilley, "Keble, Froude, Newman, and Pusey," 102, where Gilley says apropos of Battiscombe's biography, "[it] underestimated his considerable intellectual and spiritual abilities and his influence on others."

6. O'Connell, *The Oxford Conspirators*, 91.

7. O'Connell, *The Oxford Conspirators*, 91.

was his vocation. He moved on to a living at Hursley, near Winchester, in 1825 at the invitation of a former pupil, Sir William Heathcote, and, apart from some years when again he assisted his priest-father, he was there until his death in 1866. A very long and committed tenure as a parish priest! This is how Louis Bouyer puts it: "Though Keble was an accomplished scholar, he was first and foremost a man of prayer and the devoted parish priest of a small rural community."[8] The devoted parish priest was always his vocation. "[He embodied] his teaching in a rural ministry which became a model for other High Churchmen, reflecting his own belief that were the Church of England as a national institution to fail, the true Church would still be found in his parish."[9] He ministered obviously to his patron, Sir William Heathcote, but most of his parishioners were ordinary working-class people, not known for their devotion to the liturgy and practice of the Church of England. The great Edward Bouverie Pusey, Hebraist and leader in the Oxford Movement, thought Keble's ministry a waste of his gifts and talents: "Through human mismanagement . . . the writer of *The Christian Year* should, for the chief part of his life, preach to a peasant flock, of average mental capacity."[10] Contrast Pusey's perception with that of a close friend and follower of Keble and later his biographer, Charlotte Yonge, who offers this fine description of his pastoral care: "The vicar was the personal minister to each individual of his flock—teaching in the school, catechizing in the church, most carefully preparing for Confirmation, watching over the homes, and, however otherwise busied, always at the beck and call of everyone in the parish."[11] Even allowing for some degree of hero worship in Yonge's description, is pastoral ministry to be counted a waste over against academic achievement in theology? Surely not, and perhaps that is not quite what Pusey intended. Keble must be judged an intellectual, but being an intellectual was subordinate to life in Christ. "To be clever was the gift of some, holiness was God's calling to all."[12] Keble was not to sever entirely his academic connection with Oxford, being elected Professor of Poetry in 1831 and holding this position until 1841. The professorship of poetry did not require residence, and demanded only four lectures a year. In Keble's time, they were delivered in Latin.

8. Bouyer, *Orthodox Spirituality and Protestant and Anglican Spirituality*, 208.
9. Gilley, "Keble, Froude, Newman, and Pusey," 103.
10. Cited in Johnson, *John Keble: Sermons for the Christian Year*, 5.
11. Johnson, *John Keble: Sermons for the Christian Year*, 6.
12. Rowell, "John Keble: A Bi-Centenary Sermon," 244.

Despite Newman's judgment about Keble's 1833 sermon and the beginning of the Oxford Movement, this is a controversial issue. Certainly, the sermon "National Apostasy" created a stir, but would it, or would Keble alone, have been able to "create" the Oxford Movement? Certainly not, according to Owen Chadwick. Chadwick believes that Newman "charitably rendered Keble a disservice by hailing him as the true and primary author of the Oxford Movement. . . . Keble was the author of no movement."[13] Chadwick's judgment is surely correct, given all that is known of Keble. He was not the towering figure whose personal charisma and suasive rhetoric was capable of launching such a turbulent renewal movement in the Church of England. Yet, it must be said that Keble played his part, and a significant part. Not only Newman's words about the sermon "National Apostasy," but the testimony of virtually all who were caught up in the movement bear witness to Keble's influence.

Historically, three men are commonly regarded as intimately associated with the inception of the Oxford Movement: Keble, Hurrell Froude, the passionate and somewhat radical thinker, and Newman. Each had his own contribution to make to the catholicizing of the Church of England, but they were quite different. Perhaps the historian Christopher Dawson gets it right when he writes of the trio: "Each of them played an essential part, but no one of them could have realized himself without the cooperation of the rest. Froude alone would have gone up like a rocket and left nothing behind him but a shower of sparks. Keble alone would have been a conservative county clergyman who wrote pleasing religious verse. . . . Newman alone would certainly have done something, but who can say what?"[14] It was Froude who brought Keble and Newman together—the one good thing he said he had done in his life—and Keble took a key role in the movement's publications. He contributed to the *Tracts for the Times*, the theological pamphlets promoting and defending the views of the Oxford Movement. After the *Tracts* had come to an end, Keble remained on good terms with Newman until the latter went over to Rome in 1845, and even then he felt a strong connection with Newman. After that, Keble remained in close touch with E. B. Pusey, trying to maintain the high church emphasis in the Church of England.

---

13. Chadwick, "The Limitations of Keble," *Theology* 67 (1964), 47. This essay has been reproduced in Chadwick's *The Spirit of the Oxford Movement*, 54–62.

14. Dawson, *The Spirit of the Oxford Movement*, 12.

In 1836, Keble put out an edition of the *Works* of Richard Hooker, one of the founders of the Anglican theological tradition. That year also saw Keble as Vicar of Hursley, near Winchester. There he remained as parish priest for the rest of his life. Ten years after his death, in 1876, Keble College, Oxford, was established in his memory, giving a sense of his very considerable impact on English ecclesiastical society.

Bishop Geoffrey Rowell has it right when he says of Keble: "He had a natural sense of awe and wonder at the mystery of God, and a consciousness of the limitation of human language in speaking of God. He shunned ecclesiastical gossip and theological slogans."[15] A fine accolade for any Christian minister! Writing elsewhere of Keble's spirit, the bishop says:

> No blustering, no bragging, no knocking people over the head with dogmas, no thumping of Bibles, no multiplication of schemes and organizations—but an awareness that to worship is to adore, and that the prayer of adoration is the prayer of love, and that this inner core of our lives, our responsiveness to God, is a living out of a mystery, which always eludes our ability to express it in words.[16]

Rowell's description leads one to suggest that John Keble was a mystic, even if in theologian John Macquarrie's words "a moderate mystic, a sacramental mystic."[17]

Even the most ordinary, daily, trivial experiences may have this mystical-sacramental quality to them, like sleeping and waking: "Every evening we do in a certain way, in the way of type and parable, represent and enact the mystery of Good Friday, and no less plainly, every morning we enact the mystery of Easter."[18] Nothing could be more ordinary, even trivial, than our sleeping and rising. But for the mystic Keble this is an existential participation in the Paschal Mystery. His moderate mysticism enables him to read all reality as charged with God's presence, but sinfulness clouds this vision:

> *Two worlds are ours: 'tis only sin*
> *Forbids us to descry*
> *The mystic heaven and earth within,*
> *Plain as the sea and sky.*[19]

15. Rowell, "John Keble and the High Church Tradition," in his *The Vision Glorious*, 22.

16. Rowell, "John Keble: A Bi-Centenary Sermon," 244.

17. Macquarrie, *Two Worlds Are Ours*, 218–22, slightly adapted.

18. Cited in Rowell, "John Keble: A Bi-Centenary Sermon," 246.

19. Keble, *The Christian Year*, 42–43.

In 1827, Keble published *The Christian Year*, a volume of religious poetry built around the liturgical year as found in the Book of Common Prayer. One historian comments accurately, "What Keble set out to do was to provide a thoughtful commentary in verse to the Prayer Book."[20] It proved immensely popular, going through multiple editions from the date of publication until the year of Keble's death. Newman remarked of the volume: "Keble's hymns are just out . . . they seem quite excellent." Keble was as suspicious of popular evangelicalism as he was of theological rationalism, but poetry mediated a sacramental sense for Keble—he dedicated *The Christian Year* to William Wordsworth—and his own poetry very deliberately so. Indeed, poetry and sacramental/mystical awareness are very close.[21]

There is no doubt of Keble's influence on Newman. As Geoffrey Rowell puts it: "If Newman came to hold so strongly that faith was communicated by personal influence, that 'heart spoke to heart' (the motto he chose when he was made a cardinal), then it was surely Keble who taught him so much of the priest who bears his people in his heart."[22] When it comes to preaching, there is a difference. While Keble's sermons are not in the same literary genre as Newman's, nevertheless his preaching was intended to provide the best of what the Oxford Movement had to offer to his working-class parishioners, a vision that is "profoundly sacramental, the visible world permeated through and through by the invisible world."[23]

"The liturgy is the divine script for a moral and spiritual drama, both the reenactment of salvation history and the actual enactment of personal sanctification."[24] Frequent celebration of the Eucharist was rare in the nineteenth-century Church of England, but Keble saw to a monthly celebration, moving later to a weekly celebration of the sacrament. He was up against

---

20. O'Connell, *The Oxford Conspirators*, 93.

21. Macquarrie, *Two Worlds Are Ours*, 220. Not everyone holds Keble's poetry in such high regard. Consider these words from historian Owen Chadwick in *Spirit of the Oxford Movement*, 52: "It is necessary, perhaps, to be capable of pleasure in Wordsworth, or parts of Wordsworth. I will confess that I can only understand, with a bare assent of the intellect, the influence exerted by *The Christian Year*. Keble has moments of grandeur, moments of deep sincerity and simplicity; but the moments of bathos, or of superficiality, bring you down again to the dust too soon after you have soared above it. . . . I give this only as a reflection of personal taste."

22. Geoffrey Rowell, *The Vision Glorious*, 24.

23. Johnson, *John Keble: Sermons for the Christian Year*, 10.

24. Johnson, *John Keble: Sermons for the Christian Year*, 15.

the ways of the parish here. Despite his more frequent celebration of the Eucharist, and his equally frequent encouragement of his congregation to receive the eucharistic Christ, it seems that they were reluctant to do so. They were just as reluctant to heed his call for the sacramental confession of sin as a preparation to receive Holy Communion: "We go on working in the dark ... until the rule of systematic Confession is revived in our Church."[25]

Two quite different scholars who have made a special study of John Keble's theology have reached identical judgments about his understanding of the Eucharist: Maria Poggi Johnson, a Roman Catholic historian of theology, and the late Geoffrey Rowell, an Anglican bishop and former professor of theology at Oxford University. Johnson writes: "Keble's views on the Eucharist are at the heart of his vision. . . . In fact, in his teaching on the Eucharist all of Keble's theological and pastoral thought comes together."[26] Rowell writes: "Keble's theology was particularly concerned with sanctification and it became increasingly a eucharistically centered theology."[27]

The celebration of the Eucharist involved for Keble a strong and passionate belief in the real presence of Christ. Maria Johnson puts it like this: "He takes every occasion that text or topic or season offers to press home both the reality of Christ's immediate presence where the sacrament is being celebrated and the immense importance of that presence for Christians."[28] No less was his belief in the eucharistic sacrifice. In the poem from *The Christian Year* entitled "Holy Communion," we find this stanza:

> *Fresh from th' atoning sacrifice*
> *The world's Creator bleeding lies,*
> *That man, His foe, by whom He bled,*
> *May take Him for his daily bread.*[29]

It is very clear in this verse that the Eucharist re-presents the unique sacrifice of Christ in such a way that this sacrificed Christ is taken in Holy Communion—"may take *Him*" for "daily bread." Both elements of doctrine, eucharistic presence and sacrifice, come together in this fine passage:

---

25. Keble, *Letters of Spiritual Counsel*, 1870, 39, cited in Rowell, *The Vision Glorious*, 37.

26. Johnson, *John Keble: Sermons for the Christian Year*, 29–31.

27. Rowell, *The Vision Glorious*, 35.

28. Johnson, *John Keble: Sermons for the Christian Year*, 29.

29. Keble, *The Christian Year*, 187.

> "For their sakes I am sanctifying myself, that they also may be sanctified through the Truth." ... This one saying of Christ conveys apparently in itself the two chief points of the evangelical doctrine concerning the holy and blessed Eucharist: first, that it is His memorial Sacrifice, a means of obtaining God's favour and pardon for all such as truly repent: next that it is a most high Sacrament, a means whereby we are united to Christ, and so made more and more partakers of His righteousness here, and His glory hereafter. "I sanctify myself": there is the Sacrifice; "that they also may be sanctified through the Truth": there is the Sacrament.[30]

Like so many Anglican churchmen, Keble was opposed to transubstantiation. Not to the belief in and acceptance of the real presence of Christ, but to what he took to be a too rationalist approach to the mystery of the Lord's presence. He was just as keenly opposed to those who would deny the real presence, as he says, "Wherever Christ is, there he is to be adored."[31] In fact, he sees both parties as being quite similar:

> Transubstantiation on the one hand, ... the denial of Christ's real presence on the other. ... The two errors in the original are perhaps but rationalism in two different forms; endeavours to explain away, and bring nearer to the human intellect, that which had been left thoroughly mysterious both by Scripture and tradition. They would turn the attention of man from the real, life-giving miracle to mere metaphysical or grammatical subtleties, such as our fathers never knew.[32]

He was a supporter of eucharistic adoration in the Church of England, and published a book *On Eucharistical Adoration* in 1857, the work in which Owen Chadwick considers that Keble, who often declared himself incompetent theologically, "came nearest to being a theologian."[33] His basic position is that if the Incarnate Christ is the subject of our adoration, the eucharistic Christ cannot be less:

> That, therefore, of which we eat, the same we are most humbly to worship; not the less, but the more, because in so giving Himself to us He is stooping so very low for our sakes. ... If we really believe

---

30. Keble, *Sermons Academic and Occasional*, 259, cited in Rowell, *The Vision Glorious*, 36.

31. Cited in Rowell, "John Keble: A Bi-Centenary Sermon," 245.

32. Keble, "Primitive Tradition," in his *Sermons Academical and Occasional*, 213, cited in Rowell, *The Vision Glorious*, 34.

33. Chadwick, "The Limitations of Keble," 50.

that which He declares to be His own Flesh and Blood is Jesus Christ giving Himself to us under the form of Bread and Wine, how can we help thanking, and therefore adoring, (for to thank is to adore), the unspeakable Gift, as well as the most bountiful Giver? seeing that in this case both are one.[34]

Owen Chadwick, the *doyen* of church historians of nineteenth-century England, is our best lead into a somewhat controversial poem of Keble's to do with the Eucharist: "Froude believed the doctrine of the Real Presence and brought Newman to value it; a poem in Keble's *Christian Year* seemed to deny it. Even the closest of associates may sometimes contradict each other, and on matters which are not unimportant."[35] Chadwick is wisely saying that we ought not to look for exact uniformity even on important matters among the closest of friends, and, it may be argued, even within oneself. The poem to which he makes reference is as follows:

> *O come to our Communion Feast:*
> *There present in the heart,*
> *Not in the hands, th' eternal Priest*
> *Will His true self impart.*[36]

In the version first published in 1866 after Keble's death, the clause "Not in the hands" was changed to "As in the hands," thus making it consonant with Catholic theology. Taken at surface value, the original words suggest a very reduced version of the real presence, so that Chadwick describes this as "a near receptionist doctrine of the Eucharist."[37] John R. Griffin, in an unsatisfactory book that is far from the scholarly consensus on Keble, reaches the rather tendentious conclusion, based on these lines, that Keble did not actually believe in the real presence.[38] Griffin takes Keble's words with great seriousness, albeit in isolation from the total context of his life's *oeuvre*. Aligning myself with Chadwick—"[Keble] *seemed* to deny it"—it is necessary to say that there *seems* to be a contradictory element here in Keble's eucharistic theology. But the poem occurs in the early 1827 *The Christian Year*, some six years prior to his sermon "National Apostasy." If this poem is laid alongside his later views, especially in *Eucharistical*

---

34. Keble, *On Eucharistic Adoration*, 75–76, cited in Rowell, *The Vision Glorious*, 37.
35. Chadwick, *Spirit of the Oxford Movement*, 21.
36. Towards the end of the poem "Gunpowder Treason."
37. Chadwick, *The Mind of the Oxford Movement*, 31.
38. Griffin, *John Keble, Saint of Anglicanism*, 71–74.

Adoration, it cannot be interpreted as his mature or final position, but must be seen as an intemperate expression of a eucharistic theology in progress. His eucharistic theology, along with so many other of his points of view, continued to develop.[39] That is what it means to grow and mature religiously. To arrest such theological development with one stanza from *The Christian Year* seems flawed.

The French Catholic spiritual writer Léon Bloy has wisely said that "There is only one sadness, the sadness of not being a saint."[40] By all accounts of those who knew him well, John Keble was a saint. As Bishop Geoffrey Rowell puts it, "If we would look for the secret of Keble's influence it is surely in that combination of magnetism and reserve, the hidden qualities of humility and holiness, that led his contemporaries to venerate him as something close to a saint."[41] However, he was saint in his own tradition, the Church of England. This was something of a challenge to his friend John Henry Newman.

On September 12, 1865, when Keble had less than a year to live, the three old Oxford Movement friends—John Keble, Edward Pusey, and John Henry Newman—met for the last time at Keble's Hursley Vicarage. Newman wrote of the occasion: "There were three old men, who had worked together vigorously in their prime. This is what they have come to—poor human nature—after twenty years they meet together round a table, but without a common cause . . . and all of them with broken prospects."[42] They never lost their affection for one another. Writing from the Birmingham Oratory to Edward Pusey some seven years after Keble's death, Newman recalled words spoken in his hearing by Keble: "I think I have heard Keble say, 'Well, all I can say is, that, if the Roman Communion is the One True Church, I do not know it, I do not know it.'"[43] These sentiments were difficult for Newman, but it seems to me he regarded Keble as a saint. Newman viewed these words as demonstrating invincible ignorance on Keble's part, and thus, from his theological perspective, opening heaven to this self-evidently saintly man.

---

39. See Chadwick, "The Limitations of Keble," 49.
40. Nicholl, *Holiness*, 28.
41. Rowell, *The Vision Glorious*, 40.
42. Cited in Gilley, *Newman and His Age*, 339.
43. Dessain and Gornall SJ, *The Letters and Diaries of John Henry Newman*, vol. 26, 299.

FROM OXFORD: RICHARD HURRELL FROUDE (1803-36)

Richard Hurrell Froude was the son of Robert Hurrell Froude, the Rector of Dartington and Archdeacon of Totnes, a country gentleman and a landowner in his own right, and was the first of eight children. His mother Margaret died in 1821, when he was but eighteen years old, and yet she exercised a profound influence on her oldest son. Reading her journal years after her death brought tears to his eyes. She recommended to her son the keeping of a journal and this he did, and it became the first part of his posthumously published *Remains*. In his journal we find Hurrell very introspective and very judgmental of himself, examining in great detail especially his faults and failings, such that Piers Brendon writes of him, "Hurrell Froude was more responsible than anyone for introducing the practice of close analysis of motives and action, both of self and others, into the Oxford Movement."[44] Educated at Eton and Oriel College Oxford, Froude became a Fellow of Oriel in 1826, and impressed his peers with his brilliance. Oriel College was generally regarded as the most intellectually outstanding of the Oxford colleges and the senior common room was a regular locus for the cut and thrust of intellectual analysis and debate. At Oriel Froude got to know Newman: "Newman is a very nice fellow indeed, but very shy."[45]

Hurrell developed a close friendship with John Keble of Oriel, a friendship founded on Keble's holiness of life and personality rather than simply intellectual prowess. He spent vacations with Keble, who guided his reading and offered challenges to the younger man in conversational exchange. One historian of the Oxford Movement speculates that there were two Hurrell Froudes:

> The hard-riding, tough-talking, hater of sham and pretense; and a small boy, unsure and afraid, calling out wordlessly to his mother through a perpetual dark night of the soul. One wonders what bluff old Archdeacon Froude made of it all when he read this curious line from his son, written in 1823: "I think the more I see of Keble the more I get to like and admire him; in everything but person and manner he seems so very like mother."[46]

---

44. Brendon, *Hurrell Froude and the Oxford Movement*, 13.

45. In a letter to his father Archdeacon Froude, cited in Brendon, *Hurrell Froude and the Oxford Movement*, 59.

46. Cited in O'Connell, *The Oxford Conspirators*, 102.

As the section on Keble has shown, Keble had a very strong sacramental sensibility and his and Hurrell's mutual influence on one another is amply verified in their correspondence. Hurrell had a great love for the Middle Ages, not least for the integrated way that he believed the church operated throughout the fabric of society at that time. From the medieval worldview and from the Romantics generally he absorbed an understanding of creation as sacramental, "the visible order of nature as an index of the invisible one."[47] Part of his interest in the Middle Ages was Gothic architecture, architecture in England that had been destroyed during the reign of Henry VIII, architecture that Froude saw as inter-linked with liturgy, theology, and spirituality. Owen Chadwick comments as a result of Froude's love for all things medieval and especially architecture that a "sentiment for monastic ruins generates no sympathy for a Reformation which ruined monasteries."[48] Chadwick's comment sums up Froude's position on the Reformation—it was a false, iconoclastic turning away from the authentic Christian tradition, doctrinally, liturgically, and spiritually. His Catholic orientation was already well underway.

Froude experienced a serious spiritual crisis in 1826–27, a crisis described as "not a momentary psychological convulsion but a prolonged period of religious turmoil."[49] He was over-examining himself in a scrupulous way about his spiritual life, and especially his moral failures as he saw them. Sexuality was an area of moral failure for him—some authors have over-psychoanalyzed Froude in the direction of homosexuality but the evidence is very thin indeed—and other failures include, from his journal, greed, insincerity, laziness, vanity, and bad temper, the kind of moral failures from which no one is exempt. Keble was of great assistance to him during this crisis, warning him constantly about the dangers of excessive introspection. Along with Newman but not with Keble, Froude began to espouse celibacy, not only as his own existential choice, but as a Catholic-Christian ideal. At the same time, his appreciation of the sacraments was developing rapidly and especially his appreciation of the Eucharist as the center of the sacramental system. Celibacy and the high valuation of the sacraments were to feed into the Oxford Movement.

Although Froude's health had never been great, by about 1831 he was presenting incipient symptoms of tuberculosis. In the summer of

47. Brendon, *Hurrell Froude and the Oxford Movement*, 31.
48. Chadwick, *The Victorian Church*, vol. 1, 174.
49. Brendon, *Hurrell Froude and the Oxford Movement*, 61.

1831, he and Newman took a ship from the city of Southampton to the Devonshire resort of Torquay and Froude caught a cold on the deck of the ship, which seemed further to hasten the onset of his illness. Journeying to a warmer climate was the prescription of the day. Thus, Hurrell and his archdeacon father along with John Henry Newman boarded the steamship *Hermes* heading for the Mediterranean. The journey did not improve Froude's health very much. Newman parted company from the Froudes so that he could return to Sicily for further personal exploration. They had warned him against this but he paid no heed. *En route* home to England the Froudes traveled through France and this provided Hurrell with knowledge of Félicité de Lammenais and his ideas. Lammenais's desire to have a church entirely free of state control resonated very powerfully with Froude's developing ecclesiology. He wanted something very similar for the Church of England. He really wanted nothing short of disestablishment. "Lammenais confirmed the ideas of radicalism and disestablishment which Froude had already developed."[50] When Froude arrived back in England he was ready for the crisis fomented by Keble's Assize Sermon and, indeed, he may have been partially responsible encouraging Keble to preach it. And so the Oxford Movement began. Piers Brendon does not exaggerate when he comments "During the summer and autumn of 1833 the course of the Movement was determined by a triumvirate consisting of Newman, who held the reins, Keble, who provided the motive power, and Froude, who wielded the whip and yelled directions."[51]

Froude's yelling directions had as their major purpose guiding the Oxford Movement towards more Catholic points of view. Whenever he came across anything in the Tracts for the Times that smacked of Protestantism as he understood it, he never hesitated to protest and condemn. "In spite of the paucity of evidence it cannot be doubted that Froude's constant epistolary expectation to Keble and Newman pushed them and the Tracts in a more decisively Catholic direction. Froude acted as a kind of censor: nothing Protestant escaped his eye."[52] He kept up his scrutiny of the Tracts even from abroad.

All this time Hurrell's health was failing. He left for Barbados in November 1833 in the hope that the warmer climate of the Caribbean would help. He threw himself into various kinds of work, especially teaching, for

50. Brendon, *Hurrell Froude and the Oxford Movement*, 120.
51. Brendon, *Hurrell Froude and the Oxford Movement*, 128.
52. Brendon, *Hurrell Froude and the Oxford Movement*, 147.

the Anglican diocese in Barbados and the West Indies generally. Brendon thinks that Froude's "most important single composition" was something that he put together in Barbados in 1834, the "Essay on Rationalism." The essay is wide-ranging but, as one might expect, it comes very close to Catholic theology and understanding. He had been developing his Catholic orientation for a long time along with his consequent anti-Protestant direction, and in this essay he puts forth a most Roman Catholic understanding of the Eucharist. He defends the doctrine of the real presence of Christ in the eucharistic gifts against what he takes to be Protestant reductionism and at the same time he distances his position from the rationalist Catholic understanding of transubstantiation. "Froude's high conception of the Eucharist and his recognition of its vital function in the life of the church must be regarded as his most significant contribution to the tenets of the Oxford Movement."[53]

Froude returned to England in the spring of 1835. He was not getting better. He paid a brief visit to Oxford, visiting his friends and encouraging the movement as best he could, and then left for home. He continued to push the Catholic line, corresponding especially with Newman. Newman's final visit to his friend in Dartington ended on October 11, 1835. He said of that final visit: "[Froude's] face lighted up and almost shone in the darkness, as if to say that in this world we were parting forever."[54] Newman wrote these words in his last letter to his friend: "My dear Hurrell, I will only say that you are ever in my thoughts and prayers and (by God's blessing) ever shall be—may I ever be in yours. Though you are at a distance, I feel you are now with me in Oxford. Ever yours most affectionately, John H. Newman."[55]

Hurrell died early in 1836. Four volumes of his writings were published posthumously by Keble and Newman, known as the *Remains*. The first volume consists largely of Froude's letters to various friends and extracts from his private journal. The other three volumes contain sermons and essays, many of which exemplify his Catholic orientation. They were well received by some but regarded with considerable hostility by many, not least because taken together they seemed to set out to "unprotestantize" the Church of England.

---

53. Brendon, *Hurrell Froude and the Oxford Movement*, 161.
54. Cited in Brendon, Brendon, *Hurrell Froude and the Oxford Movement*, 175.
55. Cited in Brendon, Brendon, *Hurrell Froude and the Oxford Movement*, 177.

FROM OXFORD: EDWARD BOUVERIE PUSEY (1800-1882)[56]

> *Of the three unquestioned leaders of the Oxford Movement (Keble, Newman, Pusey) Pusey is perhaps the least known. Neither he nor John Keble have received ... the attention which they deserve.*
>
> A. M. Allchin[57]

> *Since the flurry of post-mortem recognition, Pusey has largely dropped from public memory, and from prominence among scholars of nineteenth-century British Christianity.*
>
> Rowan Strong and Carol Englehardt Herringer[58]

Edward Bouverie Pusey was educated at Eton College, and then from 1819 at Christ Church Oxford, going on to become a Fellow of Oriel College, placing him in the company of John Keble and John Henry Newman, also Fellows of Oriel College Oxford in 1823. Newman describes his first meeting with Pusey in these words: "His light curly head of hair was damp with the cold water which his headaches made necessary for comfort; he walked fast with a young manner of carrying himself, and stood rather bowed, looking up from under his eyebrows, his shoulders rounded, and his bachelor's gown not buttoned at the elbow, but hanging loose over his wrists. His countenance was very sweet, and he spoke little."[59]

In 1825, Pusey spent some time studying theology and Oriental languages at the German universities of Göttingen and Berlin, something he was encouraged to do by his tutor, the Regius Professor of Divinity (and later Bishop of Oxford), Charles Lloyd. At Göttingen he attended the lectures of the Orientalist and Old Testament scholar Johann Gottfried Eichhorn (1750-1827) and at Berlin he got to know systematic theologian Friedrich Schleiermacher (1768-1834) and the patristic scholar Johann Neander (1789-1850). Schleiermacher seems to have had some particular influence on Pusey. His *The Christian Faith* had been published in 1821-22, just a few years before Pusey's arrival in Germany. Schleiermacher's emphasis on

---

56. All subsequent scholarship on E. B. Pusey is indebted to the four large volumes of H. P. Liddon, *Life of Edward Bouverie Pusey*, published between 1893-97. More recent scholarship has made greater use of the unpublished letters and papers of Pusey deposited in Pusey House, Oxford, especially by David Forrester.

57. Allchin, "Pusey, The Servant of God," 366.

58. Strong and Herringer, *Edward Bouverie Pusey and the Oxford Movement*, xi.

59. Tristram, *John Henry Newman, Autobiographical Writings*, 74.

"feeling" in theology undoubtedly helped Pusey come to terms with what he considered the two theological extremes: religious rationalism—although he still considered Schleiermacher something of a rationalist—and religious enthusiasm.[60] This made him "one of the few English theologians to have first-hand acquaintance with German theological thought."[61] The year 1826 saw Pusey yet again visiting Germany mastering other Semitic languages. In 1828, he was ordained priest in the Church of England and was also appointed (with the support once more of Charles Lloyd) Regius Professor of Hebrew and Canon of Christ Church. Although he was appreciative of German theology, Pusey criticized German scholars for treating Scripture less as the living Word of God and more as "a dead repository of barren technicalities."[62] So was Pusey theologically a rationalist, a liberal, a conservative, or an enthusiast? A letter of 1828 to his future wife Maria Barker shows that he was aware that he could be misunderstood perhaps "as one third mystic, one third skeptic, and one third (which will be thought the worst imputation of all) a Methodist, though I am none of the three."[63]

Once the Oxford Movement got going Pusey found himself as a strong supporter, but not immediately. In 1828-30, he published in two parts *An Historical Enquiry into the Probable Causes of the Rationalist Character lately Predominant in the Theology of Germany*. The book was critical of what Pusey took to be German theological rationalism—though some charged him with being a theological liberal—and eventually in 1848 he withdrew it from sale and bought up the remaining copies. What is clear is that by the mid-1830s he was certainly on board with the movement's theology and so he wrote *Tract 18*, "Thoughts on the Benefits of the System of Fasting, Enjoined by Our Church," published in 1834. In 1836, he published three more Tracts, 67-69, on "Scriptural Use of Holy Baptism," really three parts of one volume running to some 400 pages. In this volume, he argued against a very widespread and popular point of view that communion with God took place through many and varied individual practices

---

60. Frappell, "'Science' in the Service of Orthodoxy: The Early Intellectual Development of E. B. Pusey," in Butler, *Pusey Rediscovered*, 9–11.

61. Rowell, *The Vision Glorious*, 72. Allchin writes: "Pusey brought with him a weight of biblical and oriental erudition and the knowledge of current philosophical and theological thought in Germany which no one in Oxford at that time could rival." See his essay, "The Theological Vision of the Oxford Movement," in Coulson and Allchin, *The Rediscovery of Newman*, 51.

62. Cited in Rowell, *The Vision Glorious*, 77.

63. Cited in Frappell, "'Science' in the Service of Orthodoxy," 16.

such as faith, prayer, and contemplation. Pusey argued that the church and the sacraments are "the ordained and direct visible means of conveying to the soul what is in itself supernatural and unseen."[64] His argument rested on his acquaintance with early Christian liturgies as well as patristic theology. These powerful sources deepened his understanding of salvation as a participation in the divine nature. His very substantial contributions moved the Tracts on from being relatively short theological pamphlets to more academic volumes. Pusey's interest in patristic theology inspired his support for the *Library of the Fathers*. Newman's very close friend Hurrell Froude said of Pusey that he was "so uncommonly learned that it is impossible to keep pace with him."[65] Pusey was not just a learned academic but took a keen interest in the poor and the marginalized of his society. "It is not customary for Regius Professors to spend their Long Vacations tending cholera victims in Bethnal Green, London," wrote A. M. Allchin in 1983, "I suppose an equivalent today would be working with the dying in the streets of Calcutta or Beirut."[66]

After leaving school at Eton College and before going to Oxford University, the young aristocratic Pusey fell in love with a girl, Maria Catherine Barker (1801–39), who was a year younger than he was. Some nine years later, in 1828, Pusey married Maria, a marriage to which Pusey's father, Philip, was initially very opposed. A keen student of Pusey's life and work, David Forrester, provides us with a description of Pusey's parents in these words:

> Both his mother and father were firm upholders of the traditions, privileges, and responsibilities associated with the landed ruling classes of the eighteenth century, and both of them were noted for the narrowness and rigidity of their outlook which occasionally bordered on the eccentric. Pusey's mother, a practical and unsentimental woman, reinforced or silently adopted the precision required in everything by her husband. . . . As late as 1850 and whenever resident in London, Lady Lucy Pusey had herself carried by sedan chair to church twice on Sundays and in winter she was invariably preceded by footmen bearing lighted flambeaux. Throughout her life she was never known to lean back in a chair, always considering such a practice a sign of laxity. Pusey's father, who was fifty-two by the time he married, utterly set in his ways,

---

64. Cited in Rowell, *The Vision Glorious*, 75.
65. Cited in Rowell, *The Vision Glorious*, 74.
66. Allchin, "Pusey, The Servant of God," 366–67.

... can only be described as an autocratic though benevolent martinet.[67]

There can be no doubting the fact that Pusey brought to his relationship and ultimately to his marriage with Maria very considerable baggage. Commentators uniformly suggest that from the time that his father vetoed the relationship with Maria Pusey he suffered from serious depression.

Edward Pusey and Maria Barker, very different in both backgrounds and temperament, were clearly immensely devoted and committed to each other. One historian of the Oxford Movement has captured well what Maria meant to Pusey: "For nine years he had struggled for her, for eleven years he was destined to keep and cherish her; and when he lost her, it was for him a catastrophe beyond all reckoning."[68] The Puseys had a son and three daughters. It seems to have been the case that Maria dominated Edward in most things, except religion. Religion was an area in which she experienced real difficulty. In a letter she wrote to Pusey before their marriage, Maria describes something of her difficulties.

> Religion has never been to me the source of comfort and serenity which it has to others. I could not but admire the beauty of its precepts and the sublimity of its views, and as far as a trust in a Supreme Being in temporal concerns goes, so far I have felt its use in calming my mind; but there does appear to me so much uncertainty, if not of contradiction in Scripture itself, so much more of that contradiction in the opinions of men . . . that I could frequently only find peace of mind in banishing the subject from my thoughts.[69]

Maria was also aware of the damage done to some of her friends from an excessively narrow interpretation of Christianity, for example, eating only the poorest kind of food, self-condemnation as a great sinner, and spending hours praying on one's knees. In his eighties, John Henry Newman, now Cardinal Newman, offers us a description of Mrs. Pusey, albeit a description reflected upon over some decades. Newman writes as follows:

> She was a tall, handsome person. Before her marriage she had no interest in religion, but she must always have had qualities of goodness . . . which only required to be drawn out by Grace. She was

67. Forrester, "Dr. Pusey's Marriage," 123.
68. O'Connell, *The Oxford Conspirators*, 99.
69. This excerpt from the unpublished letter comes from Forrester, "Dr. Pusey's Marriage," 131–32.

however at first, after their marriage, very odd, and I did not like to go to the house. Her oddities were the talk of Oxford: Whately (former Fellow of Oriel and later Archbishop of Dublin), who was a rough, noisy talker, was open-mouthed about it. She underwent a great change: and I loved her exceedingly in later life.[70]

The Puseys' daughter Katherine died in 1832, and Pusey saw this as chastisement for his sins, for his not being rigorous and sufficiently self-disciplined in his Christian practice. Maria died in 1839 and this left him utterly devastated. Some years later Pusey asked John Keble to hear his confession and in that regard wrote to him as follows:

> My dear wife's illness first brought to me the review of my past life, how, amid special mercies and guardianship of God I am scarred all over and seamed with sin, so that I am a monster to myself; I loathe myself; I can feel myself only like one covered with leprosy from head to foot.... I am so shocked at myself that I dare not lay my wounds bare to anyone.[71]

By all accounts Pusey was a very saintly churchman, albeit with a certain severe puritanical streak. What we hear in these excessively expressed sentiments is his awful grief at his wife's death, allied to a powerful sense of God's presence in which utmost unworthiness becomes the natural sense of the soul, and also a preoccupation with self-mortifying disciplines and austerities. Keble was very kind and gentle with Pusey and advised him not to be too hard on himself and to modify some of his asceticism.

Pusey's high theology of the sacraments was matched by an equally high theology of Scripture. The Old and New Testaments were not to be understood as a set of texts waiting to be analyzed and taken apart by Semitic and Greek philologists—the "dead repository of barren technicalities." From the church fathers and their understanding of allegory and typology he understood Scripture as the living Word of God to humankind. In many ways he anticipated the contemporary interest in revisiting patristic commentaries on Holy Scripture. Pusey's position is well summarized by Geoffrey Rowell in these words: "Pusey was a prime mover in making the works of the Fathers more widely known, emphasizing the patristic interpretation

---

70. From the record of a conversation between Pusey's biographer H. P. Liddon and Newman in 1883 and cited from Forrester, "Dr. Pusey's Marriage," 121–22.

71. Cited in Rowell, *The Vision Glorious*, 79–80.

of Scripture as setting out 'ancient Catholic truth' in contrast to 'modern private opinions.'"[72]

In the summer of 1836, while Pusey was developing his interest in the *Library of the Fathers*, he also produced a manuscript with the title "Lectures on Types and Prophecies of the Old Testament," an important manuscript for understanding Pusey's theology and exegesis, and as yet unpublished. This manuscript provides a substantive account of his approach to exegesis. Patristic study, combined also perhaps with some influence from Romanticism, led the Tractarians in general to develop a symbolic or a sacramental view of nature, and equally a symbolic or sacramental view of Scripture.[73] This is Pusey's understanding. Prophecy for him should not be understood in the first place as predictions of future events in the New Testament. Rather, types and prophecies should be seen as a complex, organic system whose purpose for the believer is best understood as mystagogic, that is, leading the believer to closer communion with God. This is what Pusey writes:

> When moderns then attempt to translate into plain terms the figurative language of Holy Scripture, and to substitute abstract, and as they would fain have it, clearer terms for the types and typical language of the Old Testament, they uniformly by this transmutation evaporate much of their meaning. We have not, it is true, visible propitiatory sacrifices, a visible theocracy, a visible temple; but it is still through the medium of these figures that we understand, (as far as we do understand) the reality: we have no better way of understanding the main truths of the Gospel than through these very figures, "the sacrifice of Christ," "the kingdom of God," "the temple of the Holy Ghost"; and he who would lay aside these types and typical language, and understand the mysteries of God without them, will be acting contrary to the teaching of Scripture and so very wrongly and foolishly. Men think that they gain in clearness, but they lose in depth; they will employ definite terms, in order to comprehend that which is infinite![74]

Now, of course, an exegete has to give attention to the historical-critical dimension of Scripture, to understand the particular historical circumstances of Scripture. That is entirely legitimate for Pusey up to a point, but

---

72. Rowell, *The Vision Glorious*, 78

73. Härdelin, "Sacraments in the Tractarian Spiritual Universe," 81–82.

74. Cited in Jasper, "Pusey's Lectures on Types and Prophecies of the Old Testament," 58.

it is not enough. There is so much more than that particular level of critical interpretation. The more consists in the sacramental or the mystagogic. Scripture leads to Christ, the Old Testament leads to Christ, everything in the Old Testament foreshadows Christ, and so "[Pusey's] Old Testament exegesis is consistently christocentric."[75]

Pusey's approach to Scripture harmonizes well with the more rounded approaches to biblical study that are being rediscovered or retrieved today. One thinks, for example, about the contemporary rediscovery of patristic exegesis, with its understanding of typology and allegory. At the same time, Pusey's conservatism, perhaps reinforced by his negative reaction to liberal German approaches to exegesis, hindered his appreciation of the historical-critical approaches. One author writes as follows: "When the *Origin of the Species* was published, E. B. Pusey, a theologian of staggering erudition, could be found asking scientific friends whether Noah could possibly have squeezed all the animals existing 5,000 years before, into an ark of the Biblical dimensions."[76] Even if this is true, arguably, Pusey was afraid of where historical-critical approaches to the Bible would go, ending up as "Biblical Studies" rather than as "Holy Scripture." Take God and his revelation out of Scripture and we are left with a series of interesting ancient texts.

"Pusey's sacramental mysticism sometimes drew near to ecstasy as he used biblical imagery to tell of dying and rising with Christ in baptism and continuing in relationship with that body of Christ through the Eucharist."[77] These words of Frederick Houk Borsch (1935–2017), New Testament scholar, theologian, and former Episcopalian Bishop of Los Angeles, are a fitting introduction to Pusey's understanding of the sacraments and especially of the Eucharist. The biblical imagery to which Borsch alludes is especially that of St. Paul whose mystical-sacramental language bonds the Christian with Christ in such intensity that for the Christian "to live is Christ." This emphasis is pervasive for the Tractarians, and Pusey begins to articulate it most powerfully in his 1836 Tract on Baptism. Pusey's christocentrism leads naturally to his theocentrism, so that A. M. Allchin can claim, with justification, that "he is very clearly a panentheist. God is in all things, all things are in God, God comes to us in all things. . . . [Pusey's

---

75. Jasper, "Pusey's Lectures on Types and Prophecies of the Old Testament," 64.

76. Tuckwell, *Reminiscences of Oxford*, 145, cited in Brendon, *Hurrell Froude and the Oxford Movement*, xi.

77. Borsch, "Ye Shall Be Holy: Reflections on the Spirituality of the Oxford Movement," 70.

theology] sees the doctrine of deification as a necessary corollary to the doctrine of incarnation, and as the fitting way to express our entry into the life and love of the Triune God."[78]

After Newman withdrew from the Oxford Movement, the leadership passed to Pusey. In 1843, he preached a sermon at the University Church in Oxford, "The Holy Eucharist, a Comfort to the Penitent," a sermon that was very supportive of the real presence of Christ in the Eucharist. Later in life Pusey acknowledged that his belief in the eucharistic presence of Christ was a legacy to him from his mother, a legacy confirmed by his subsequent reading of patristic theology and the Caroline Divines.[79] The sermon was not received as something central to and characteristic of the Anglican tradition and it was condemned by the vice-chancellor of Oxford and various theologians and consequently Pusey was barred from preaching in the University Church for two years. Nevertheless, the sermon sold eighteen thousand copies. There was a genuine receptivity in the Church of England to his strongly traditional and Catholic eucharistic theology.

This eucharistic theology flows from the profoundly incarnational Christology of the patristic era. For Pusey, reflecting patristic Christology, "Christ took our nature into himself so that in Him it is In-Godded, Deitate."[80] The language—"In Godded, Deitate"—is a little cumbersome and may sound strange to modern ears. But it is exactly accurate. The mystery of Christ's incarnation flows into the mystery of Christ's eucharistic presence. If we may describe this as a vertical theology of eucharistic presence, it must also be insisted that Pusey had a horizontal theology of eucharistic presence also. The vertical and the horizontal may be distinguished but never separated for him. In a magnificent passage that sounds very like St. John Chrysostom, we find his vertical and horizontal eucharistic theology laid out with great clarity.

> If we would see him in his sacraments, we must see him also, wherever he has declared himself to be, and especially in his poor. . . . Real love to Christ must issue in love to all who are Christ's, and real love to Christ's poor must issue in self-denying acts of

---

78. Allchin, "Pusey, The Servant of God," 373–86. See also Allchin's "The Theological Vision of the Oxford Movement," 54–71.

79. The influence of Lady Pusey on her son in this regard has been seriously questioned by Greenfield, "'Such a Friend to the Pope,'" 162–84. Greenfield certainly points to tensions in the developing theology of Pusey, especially as he moved towards the Tractarians, but it seem unnecessary to be so skeptical of Pusey's own understanding.

80. Cited in Rowell, *The Vision Glorious*, 82.

> love towards them. Casual alms-giving is not Christian charity;
> ... the poor, rich in faith, have been the converters of the world;
> and we ..., if we are wise, must seek to be like them, to empty
> ourselves, at least, of our abundance; to empty ourselves, rather of
> our self-conceit, our notions of station, our costliness of dress, our
> jewelry, our luxuries, our self-love, even as he ... emptied himself
> of the glory which he had with the Father, the Brightness of his
> Majesty, the worship of the Hosts of Heaven, and made himself
> poor, to make us rich.[81]

In another sermon, we see his vertical eucharistic theology most beautifully expressed:

> We could not be united to [God] save by his communicating himself to us. This he willed to do by indwelling in us through his Spirit; by making us, through the Sacrament of Baptism, members of his Son; by giving us, through the holy Eucharist, not in any carnal way, but really and spiritually, the Flesh and Blood of the Incarnate Son, whereby "he dwelleth in us, and we in him; he is one with us, and we with him."[82]

It comes as no surprise, then, that Pusey was an ardent promoter of more frequent celebrations of the Eucharist. In Christ Church Cathedral, Oxford, where he was a canon, there was but a monthly pattern for the celebration of the Eucharist. At the same time, Pusey rejected transubstantiation. His primary reason for this rejection is that he considered it a too "physical" and too "rational" approach to the mystery of the sacrament. From a historical point of view, it may be the case that the term transubstantiation carried too much baggage and perhaps too little understanding with it in the post-Reformation era. However, it is clearly not the case that the rejection of the term for Pusey meant the rejection of the reality of eucharistic presence. He referred to the eucharistic presence of Christ as "sacramental, supernatural, mystical, ineffable, deifical."[83] With his strong sacramental awareness Pusey was also a stout defender of the private confession of sin and of priestly absolution.

Newman's going over to Rome was a severe blow to Pusey. He was never thus tempted. However, he began to develop a sense of Providence

---

81. Pusey, *Sermons During the Season from Advent to Whitsuntide*, 58–59. The original date of publication was 1848.

82. Pusey, *Presence of Christ in the Holy Eucharist*, 9–10. Original publication was 1853.

83. These terms may be found in Rowell, *The Vision Glorious*, 88–89.

at work. "Because of his conviction that Newman was being called to play a unique role in the Roman Catholic Church, Pusey gradually came to look upon the reunion of the two churches as part of this special dispensation and saw it as his responsibility to help prepare the Church of England for the reunion to come."[84] This is certainly part of his three *Eirenica*. An "Eirenicon" is an attempt to bring seemingly contradictory doctrines into concord and harmony. In his first *Eirenicon* of 1865, Pusey was responding as an Anglican to the former Anglican now Roman Catholic Henry Edward Manning. Manning had written a book in 1864 with the title *The Workings of the Holy Spirit in the Church of England*, a book that was very critical of the Church of England. In his somewhat polemical response to Manning, Pusey made the important distinction between the official teaching of the Catholic Church and the many variations of popular piety and devotion. The text seems very dated from a post-Vatican II perspective, but it may be understood on Pusey's part as a serious attempt to arrive at what Vatican II called "the hierarchy of truths": "When comparing doctrines with one another, they [theologians] should remember that in Catholic doctrine there exists a 'hierarchy' of truths, since they vary in their relation to the fundamental Christian faith."[85] Reading the text from today's point of view, and perhaps even then, suggests that Pusey may have been too severe and unfair in his analysis. Nonetheless, Pusey's condemnation of certain Roman Catholic devotional practices was so harsh that Newman said to him in a letter, "You discharge your olive branch as if from a catapult."[86] The second *Eirenicon* came out in 1869, and in his third *Eirenicon* he returned to the notion of differentiating between official church teaching and what he took to be the excesses of public devotion and piety, and also the extreme ultramontane positions that were developing fast in the run-up to the First Vatican Council of 1869–70, in which papal infallibility was defined.

The three leaders of the Oxford Movement—John Keble, John Henry Newman, and Edward Pusey—traveled different paths after Newman was received into the Catholic Church in 1845. Keble continued in parish ministry, Pusey in Oxford University, and Newman as a Catholic priest. In 1865, news of Charlotte Keble's illness brought the three friends together.

---

84. Greenfield, "'Such a Friend to the Pope,'" 171.

85. Vatican II, "Decree on Ecumenism," par. 11.

86. Cited in Strong and Herringer, *Edward Bouverie Pusey and the Oxford Movement*, 5.

After two decades of separation, Pusey and Newman arrived at Keble's Hursley vicarage and they dined together, in Newman's words "simply by themselves for the first and last time."[87] The meeting was reported in the press as a *reconciliation* between friends after many years. Pusey took great exception to this and wrote to the newspaper:

> I much regret having to intrude upon the public my own private feelings, but the statement which you copied from some local paper (inaccurate in every particular, except that I spent some happy hours with my friend Dr. Newman) is so intensely painful that I cannot help myself. The statement is, so that Dr. N. and myself were "*reconciled* after twenty years." The deep love between us, which now dates back for above forty years, has never been in the least overshadowed. His leaving us was one of the deep sorrows of my life; but it involved separation of place, not diminution of affection.[88]

After the definition of papal infallibility at Vatican I, Pusey did not try to pursue the cause of reunion with Rome. Although he was deeply disappointed in the definition of infallibility, he never lost his affection for Newman. About ten years after the Council, Pusey wrote to Newman, "You may assure your friends that nothing has or can come between [sic] my deep love for John Henry Newman."[89]

In the last few weeks of his life, Pusey wrote to a friend:

> You, I hope, are ripening continually. God ripen you more and more. Each day is a day of growth. God says to you, "Open thy mouth and I will fill it." Only long. He does not want our words. The parched soil, by its cracks, opens itself for the rain from heaven and invites it. The parched soil cries out for the living God. Oh! then long and long and long, and God will fill thee. More love, more love, more love![90]

After a long life devoted to teaching and preaching, building up his beloved Church of England biblically and sacramentally and through the

---

87. Dessain and Gornall, *The Letters and Diaries of John Henry Newman*, vol. 24, 142.

88. Cited in Strange, "Reflections on a Controversy: Newman and Pusey's 'Eirenicon,'" 332–33.

89. Dessain and Gornall, *The Letters and Diaries of John Henry Cardinal Newman*, vol. 29, 144.

90. Cited in Allchin, "Pusey, The Servant of God," 388.

restoration of the religious life, reaching out towards reunion with Rome, Pusey died on September 16, 1882 and is buried in the nave of Christ Church Cathedral in Oxford where he had served for decades.

5

In Newman's Circle from the Oratory
Ambrose St. John, Frederick William Faber, Edward Caswall

> *There is one subject on which Newman is very "human," and that is friendship. His view of it is also very different from that of certain Catholic saints and spiritual writers, who warned against what is technically called "special friendships." Newman himself had an exceptional gift for friendship and was throughout his life surrounded by men who were deeply devoted to him.*
>
> Hilda Graef[1]

FROM THE ORATORY: AMBROSE ST. JOHN (1815–75)

A NUMBER OF NEWMAN'S friends preceded him into the Roman Catholic Church, including Ambrose St. John, who was probably Newman's closest friend. Educated at Westminster School and Christ Church College Oxford, St. John had studied Hebrew and Syriac under Edward Pusey. Ordained priest in the Church of England, he was the assistant priest to Newman's friend Henry Wilberforce and it was through Wilberforce that St. John met Newman in 1843. After this first meeting, Newman wrote to Wilberforce

---

1. Graef, *God and Myself*, 70.

about St. John: "St. John goes tomorrow and I ought to thank you for letting me have the great pleasure of making his acquaintance. He wishes to pay me a longer visit—and I assure you I do." Meriol Trevor comments, "St. John's longer visit lasted the rest of his life."[2]

St. John was received into the Catholic Church on October 2, 1845, at the Catholic College Prior Park near the city of Bath. St. John eventually found his way to Newman's community at Littlemore, and for the rest of his life Newman thought of him as his "Guardian Angel"; indeed, some think that the "Guardian Angel" in Newman's *The Dream of Gerontius* reflects St. John.[3] He was very close to Newman. There is speculation that they were both gay men. That is possible, of course, but there is no way finally to know. One Newman biographer has written of him, "though Newman's intellectual inferior, he came to fill the void in his heart left by Froude."[4] He accompanied Newman in 1846 to Rome where they would both be students at the Propaganda College.

In Rome, Newman and St. John were given very short notice to have an audience with Pope Pius IX. It had been raining very hard and their outer garments were pretty dirty as they met the Pope. In a letter to a friend, Newman described the audience: "When I knelt down to kiss [the Pope's] foot on entrance, I knocked my head against his knee—a friend of mine, Miss Giberne, on being presented took up his foot in her hands; it is a wonder she did not throw him over."[5] The friends were ordained together as deacons on May 29, 1847, and as priests the following day in the chapel of the Propaganda.

St. John remained with Newman at his side through thick and thin for the rest of his life, working both in the parish and in the Oratory school, supporting and supported by Newman in almost everything except his smoking, which Newman disliked intensely. He was a skilled translator, an almost natural philologist, not a systematic theological thinker. He translated into English the *Raccolta*, the Roman collection of indulgenced prayers. Bishop Joseph Fessler, who had been Secretary-General at the First Vatican Council, published a book whose title in English was *The True and False Infallibility of the Popes*. Newman was engaged in writing his famous letter to the Duke of Norfolk on papal infallibility and he wanted to have access

---

2. Trevor, *Newman's Journey*, 99.
3. Adams, "Elgar's Later Oratorios," 90–91.
4. Gilley, *Newman and His Age*, 224.
5. Gilley, *Newman and His Age*, 257.

to Fessler's book. Unable to read German, he turned to Ambrose St. John and asked him to translate the text for him. Given all his pastoral duties at the Oratory and his work in the Oratory school, it is an understatement to say that St. John was severely overworking.

Fatigued by excessive work and responsibilities, complicated by his anxiety and concern for Newman, St. John became quite ill and died in the spring of 1875. On the last afternoon of St. John's life, Newman describes his final visit with his lifelong friend. Newman writes: "[He] hugged me close to him, so close that I laughed and said 'he will give me a stiff neck.' I did not understand that he was taking leave of me."[6]

When Ambrose died quite suddenly at the age of sixty in 1875, Newman was almost paralyzed by grief. He was remembered as conducting the absolutions at the funeral Mass in the Oratory Chapel with great difficulty. Meriol Trevor describes the scene, recorded by a boy in the congregation who was later to become an Oratorian: "As Newman was giving the absolutions to the dead, after the Mass, he broke down and wept; the boy heard a strange noise all over the church and for a moment thought the people were laughing. But they were crying."[7] When Newman died, he was buried, according to his own wishes, in the same grave as Ambrose St. John at Rednal near Birmingham.

In the weeks and months after St. John's death, Newman revealed his feelings to a number of correspondents who had written to him offering their condolences. "As far as this world was concerned I was his first and last. He has not intermitted this love for an hour up to his last"; "From the very first he loved me with an intensity of love, which was unaccountable"; "He has been Raphael to my Tobit. . . . Ruth to my Naomi."[8] John Cornwell, a biographer of Newman, makes the following comment in a chapter of his biography describing the death of St. John: "What comes across is that Newman had taken St. John's love for granted; that he had not understood his emotional dependence on him until after he had died. In the depths of his grief he wrote to a correspondent: 'I have ever thought no bereavement was equal to that of a husband's or a wife's, but I feel it difficult to believe that any can be greater, or anyone's sorrow greater than mine.'"[9]

---

6. Gilley, *Newman and His Age*, 392.
7. Gilley, *Newman and His Age*, 252.
8. These citations are taken from Cornwell, *Newman's Unquiet Grave*, 206.
9. Cornwell, *Newman's Unquiet Grave*, 206.

FROM THE ORATORY: FREDERICK WILLIAM FABER (1814–63)

What Newman was to the Oratory in Birmingham, Faber was to the Oratory in London, though not easily, with much worry and concern, and with much misunderstanding. Frederick William Faber was born on June 28, 1814, in the vicarage of his grandfather at Calverley, Yorkshire. Frederick was baptized some six weeks later—"a delay of which the future Tractarian would certainly have disapproved"—in the parish church which was dedicated to St. Wilfrid, "a saint whom Frederick was greatly to admire."[10] In December of that year, his father Thomas Faber was appointed secretary to the Bishop of Durham and so the family moved to Bishop Auckland, the out-of-town residence of the Bishop. The young Faber grew up in a very religious family, a clerical family, but a family living in the north of England especially as it reached towards the Lake District, a most beautiful part of the country and the haunt of the poet William Wordsworth. He loved the Lake District and the poetry of Wordsworth. All of this made Faber intensely aware of God's presence, so much so that his biographer writes, "If Faber had not found God in Christianity and the church he would have found him in nature and pantheism."[11] At Harrow School Faber did well, fell in love with literature and poetry, and fell under the influence of an evangelical clergyman, so that in his teenage years his Christianity was marked by an evangelical moral earnestness and a certain anti-Catholic attitude. He went up to Oxford in 1833, the year of John Keble's famous Assize Sermon. Not surprisingly, he fell under the influence of Newman and attended his Sunday services at the University Church of St. Mary's, and began his association with the Tractarian movement, very gradually moving away from his evangelicalism. He was ordained a priest of the Church of England in 1839.

At Oxford Faber was unhappy theologically, as it were. "An Evangelical by temperament and a Tractarian by principle he upheld both sides of his religion with poetic exaggeration. He disconcerted Tractarians, puzzled Evangelicals, and disgusted High Churchmen. . . . He lay in that unhappy limbo between Canterbury and Rome—intellectually distrusting the one, emotionally distrusting the other."[12] He seems to have found much solace in

---

10. Chapman, *Father Faber*, 3.
11. Chapman, *Father Faber*, 9.
12. Chapman, *Father Faber*, 40–41.

writing poetry, something that he did all his life. Several trips to continental Europe gave him greater exposure to the practicalities of Catholicism, and his awareness of Rome developed in him a devotion to St. Philip Neri, the founder of the Oratory.

1843 was a difficult year for Faber. In his Anglican parish at Elton, he introduced a number of Catholic customs and even brought together a small quasi-monastic community, and published his strongly Roman Catholic *Life of St. Wilfrid*. It was in the fall of 1843 that Newman preached his famous sermon, "The Parting of Friends," and retired to Littlemore. Faber looked to Newman for leadership and guidance so much so that Ronald Chapman says "All his life Faber wanted Newman to make decisions for him, which Newman was not prepared or able to do."[13] There is definitely something to this. Newman was received into the Catholic Church on October 9, 1845, and Faber followed was his little community of thirteen on November 17. "Newman was wise, slow to move, careful, thoughtful—all that Faber was not. He needed Newman as a guide, to protect him from himself."[14] In 1847, Faber was ordained to the priesthood and the following year, along with his community, he joined the Oratory of St. Philip Neri, which Newman had introduced into England.

The relationship between Newman and Faber was certainly not an easy one. There are always difficulties living in community, including a certain element of competitiveness. The difficulties became such, however, that Faber established a branch of the Oratory in London, initially in King William Street and then from 1854 at its present location on the Brompton Road, now known popularly as the Brompton Oratory. Although Faber was the superior of the Brompton Oratory, he constantly referred everything to Newman in the Birmingham Oratory, exacerbating the relationships between the two communities of St. Philip Neri, and especially between Newman and himself. As Hilda Graef has it, "[The London Oratorians] were a very emotional group, who threw themselves with reckless abandon into all that was most popular in Roman Catholicism and could not have enough of miracles and little devotions."[15] This was not Newman's way. Ronald Chapman writes:

---

13. Chapman, *Father Faber*, 101.

14. Chapman, *Father Faber*, 117. Chapman goes on to say, "If Newman had not become a Catholic, or had Faber venerated Pusey instead, it is probable he would have remained an uneasy Anglican for the rest of his life."

15. Graef, *God and Myself*, 110.

From the 1850s onwards there was much less intimacy between Faber and Newman. They now wrote infrequently. . . . The most likely explanation is that Faber had outgrown his dependence on Newman and had begun to be annoyed at the elder man's cautious criticism. Gossip seems to have been incautiously repeated. But whatever irritation Faber may have felt, at bottom he still loved and revered Newman.[16]

Both Faber and Newman were writers. Faber roamed far and wide in his writing, commenting on mystical authors, writing lives of saints and not always with a commonsensical critique, and composing many hymns, which were very popular, even if at times somewhat saccharine. His devotional books and hymns has led one historian to describe him as "the guiding spirit of Victorian popular Catholicism."[17] More needs to be said. Acquainted with Faber's entire corpus of work, Chapman refers to it fundamentally as "a cosmology of love."

> It is the vision not the message which is important. Faber, too, was trying to communicate the incommunicable—the fire of love he saw everywhere, in the life of the ordinary worldly Catholic, in the life of the saint, in the Blessed Sacrament, in the life of our Lady, in our Lord's life, in creation. He is at times repetitive, vulgar, silly. He wholly lacked the reticence of the prose stylist. But every now and again we see what he saw. That is his achievement. A lot can be forgiven and forgotten because of it.[18]

Perhaps it is best expressed in a hymn composed in 1862 that became very popular across the denominational divides:

> There's a wideness in God's mercy,
> like the wideness of the sea.
> There's a kindness in God's justice,
> which is more than liberty.

---

16. Chapman, *Father Faber*, 263.

17. Gilley, "Vulgar Piety and the Brompton Oratory, 1815–1860," 15. There is no doubt about the popularity of Faber's hymns. However, in recent years, some historians have cautioned about overestimating the popularity of Italianate devotions in England, the kind of devotions with which Faber is associated. Thus, Heimann writes: "the statistics of church-based devotions, far from corroborating the notion of a Roman or Ultramontane triumph in devotional matters, indicate that native Italian practices met with a marked lack of enthusiasm from the mass of Catholics in England, although they always had a few admirers" (*Catholic Devotion in Victorian England*, 44).

18. Gilley, "Vulgar Piety and the Brompton Oratory, 1815–1860," 313.

There is no place where earth's sorrows
are more felt than up in heaven.
There is no place where earth's failings
have such kindly judgment given.

For the love of God is broader
than the measures of the mind.
And the heart of the Eternal
is most wonderfully kind.
If our love were but more faithful,
we would gladly trust God's Word,
and our lives reflect thanksgiving
for the goodness of our Lord.

"Faber was ill again in the spring of 1863, fatally it was said. But ever since his conversion, if not before, he had been having visual illnesses. In 1845, he had received the Last Sacraments and risen suddenly from his bed, cured. Death-bed scenes occurred almost every year. So it was no wonder that Newman said to Ambrose, 'How many times has Fr. Faber been a-dying'"[19] Faber, however, did die in 1863. At the funeral Mass Newman and St. John came from the Birmingham Oratory, and representing the archdiocese of Westminster was Msgr. Henry Edward Manning. In the difficult relationships between Newman and Manning, Meriol Trevor, the author of a massive two-volume biography of Newman, favors her subject. However, she is both fair and insightful as she writes in the following paragraph:

> Newman has been considered hard-hearted and unforgiving in his attitude to Faber. But forgiveness is not a simple act of oblivion. In human relationships, confidence, once broken, can be built up again, but it is different in kind from the confidence that has never been broken. And it must be the work of both sides; trust is mutual. But even in his extremity Faber did not offer Newman the chance to establish confidence again, since he never openly admitted any feelings or ask for forgiveness. He only offered the opportunity for an act of kindness, and this he received.[20]

---

19. Trevor, *Newman, Light in Winter*, 300.
20. Trevor, *Newman, Light in Winter*, 308.

FROM THE ORATORY: EDWARD CASWALL (1814-78)

"Caswall shares with Frederick William Faber not only the role of hymn writer, but also the distinction of being one of the earliest members of Newman's Oratorian community in Birmingham."[21] He took his BA at Oxford 1836 and was ordained a priest in the Church of England in 1839. December 21, 1841 saw him married to Louisa Walker. It is not entirely clear if Caswall was influenced by Newman during his time at Oxford, although it is very likely that he heard Newman preach—along with the many others who came to listen to him—at the University Church of St. Mary. What we do know is that serving as a priest in the southwest of England he had begun to read the *Tracts for the Times* in the early 1840s. It seems that his pastoral work did not bring him a great deal of satisfaction, and that many of his parishioners were rather indifferent to religion. This has led Caswall's biographer, Nancy de Flon, to suggest that "Caswall's experience of what he regarded as the lifelessness of the Church of England proved to be a significant factor influencing him to reconsider the relative positions of the Established and the Roman Churches and ultimately helping to convince him of the validity of the latter's claims."[22]

Whether that was the case or not, Caswall began to keep a journal, a journal that was never published and remains in the archives of the Birmingham Oratory. It was entitled initially "Thoughts on the English Church" and runs to some 630 pages until he was received into the Catholic Church on January 18, 1847. The journal records a variety of thoughts about the church of his birth and baptism in the Roman Catholic Church, thoughts he had about a number of his friends going over to Rome, as well as notes that he took from various books he was reading at the time. Newman's 1845 *Essay on the Development of Christian Doctrine* played a significant role here. As with so many of his friends, the journey Romewards was fraught with tension and difficulties in all kinds of ways, including with his family. He and his wife Louisa, after visiting Catholic institutions and attending Catholic services in Ireland and in Italy, were received into the Catholic Church in January 1847.

During the summer of 1849 a cholera epidemic broke out in England. The Caswalls were staying in Torquay at the time, a favorite vacation town in the southwest of England. On the morning of September 14, Edward

---

21. De Flon, *Edward Caswall*, 1.
22. De Flon, *Edward Caswall*, 1.38.

went out to Mass and when he returned Louisa had been stricken with cholera and died the same day. Newman celebrated the Requiem Mass for Louisa. Nancy de Flon writes: "For the remaining twenty-eight years of his life, Caswall kept not only the newspaper obituary and his intimately personal account of and response to the event but also a pencil portrait of Louisa sketched when she was a very young woman."[23] After spending some time discerning his future with Newman, he joined the Oratory as a novice on Good Friday 1850. Caswall made over a large sum of money, nine thousand pounds as well as one thousand for Masses to be celebrated in his wife's memory, to Newman, which paid for the building of a new Oratory at its present site in Edgbaston, Birmingham.[24] On December 21, 1850, the anniversary of his marriage to Louisa, Caswall was ordained as a sub-deacon. The Oratorian community moved into their new Oratory in the spring of 1852, and on September 18 that year Edward Caswall was ordained a priest. Newman was taken up between 1854 and 1859 with the Catholic University of Ireland in Dublin and his absence from the Birmingham Oratory was obviously going to be a challenge. He chose Edward Caswall to be the superior of the Oratory at this time.

Obviously, as superior of the Oratory, Caswall was responsible for the minutiae of the daily running of the religious house—schedules, finances, planning, etc. He fulfilled these duties superbly. He also threw himself into the work of education, planning, and raising money for a school at the Oratory itself as well as mission schools in the general area of the West Midlands. Add to that his general pastoral work as a priest, celebrating the sacraments and preaching. His pastoral work did not end there. During his earlier visit to Ireland with Louisa, experiencing Catholic religious services and institutions, he noted that the liturgy was celebrated in Latin making it unintelligible to the majority of the laity. Now that he was a priest he threw himself into translations from Latin to English, having had an excellent training as a classicist at Oxford. "A major motivation for his translations was a wish to compensate for the inaccessibility of the Latin ritual by making available, in the vernacular, a significant portion of the Roman Catholic liturgical tradition that laypersons could read and pray in private."[25] Caswall was in his own way a gifted poet and he authored many hymns that made their way into popular use.

23. De Flon, *Edward Caswall*, 1.108.
24. Gilley, "Vulgar Piety and the Brompton Oratory, 1815–1860," 270.
25. De Flon, *Edward Caswall*, 151.

Needless to say, Caswall and Newman would have been in regular conversation at the Oratory. When Newman published in 1870 his *Essay in Aid of a Grammar of Assent*, it was widely acclaimed. Not all the Oratorian fathers would have been equally engaged with this difficult book, but Caswall was. Some seven years later, and as it happened one year before Caswall died, Newman explained to his friend what the essence of the book was about, and Caswall noted the following comment on the flyleaf of his copy: "Object of the book twofold. In the first part shows that you can believe what you cannot understand. In the second part that you can believe what you cannot absolutely prove."[26] Caswall remained intellectually engaged and was not just a man of practical affairs.

A newspaper obituary, otherwise unidentified, from the archives of the Birmingham Oratory describes Fr. Edward Caswall as follows:

> He was an untiring worker [who] threw himself heartily into the parochial duties assigned to him. . . . Among the poor and sick, into whose sorrows he freely entered, he was a welcome and frequent visitor. His gentle genial ways won the hearts of all, and his charity was limited only by his means. Nothing could exceed his fondness for little children, unless it were the delight they found in his company. . . . If he had a fault it was that of optimism. He looked at everything from its best side, discovered virtues invisible to people of weaker faith, and was always slow to believe in the wickedness of human nature.[27]

WAS JOHN HENRY NEWMAN GAY?

Everyone reads between the lines at least some of the time, and when it comes to John Henry Newman, some people read between the lines most of the time. It is a statement of fact that Newman had many lifelong male friends both at Oxford and at the Birmingham Oratory. It is a statement of fact that he was attracted to the celibate life from very early on, and frowned at times when some of his clergyman friends in the Church of England got married. It is a statement of fact that after the death of Ambrose St. John, Newman altered his will so that he might be laid to rest finally in the same grave as Ambrose, Ambrose undoubtedly being the companion he loved most in the latter part of his life. That Newman was chaste no one disputes,

---

26. Cited in Strange, *Newman 101*, 29.
27. Cited in de Flon, *Edward Caswall*, 205–6.

but from facts such as these some have concluded that Newman was a gay man. One has to acknowledge that in principle this is possible. The point was put to Ian Ker, the Newman scholar who published in 1988 the most recent biography of Newman, running to 768 pages, and a raft of other books on various aspects of Newman's life and theology. Ker responded that on the basis of all the evidence with which he was acquainted over decades of Newman study, he believed that Newman was heterosexual.[28] Ultimately, while there is no way finally to know, Ker's judgment must be taken with great seriousness by any open-minded person.

CONCLUSION

In one of his sermons, Newman wrote these words: "In seasons of unusual distress or alarm, when men's minds faint for fear, then [the Christian] will have a natural power over the world, and will seem to speak, not as an individual, but as if in him was concentrated all the virtue and the grace of those many Saints who have been his lifelong companions."[29] Friendship, especially lifelong friendship, is a very precious thing. Newman lived a very long life, spanning almost the entirety of the nineteenth century, 1801–90. During the course of this long life and in the most varying of circumstances and contexts he made many friends. In this chapter and the prior one, we have looked at just a few of his friends—Keble, Froude, Pusey, St. John, Faber, Caswall. As he affected so many people during his life, so his close friends affected him. That is the very nature of friendship. I do not think it is too much to say that in Newman was concentrated all the virtue and grace of the saintly people who had been his lifelong friends and companions.

28. See Cornwell, *Newman's Unquiet Grave*, 2.
29. Przywara, *The Heart of Newman*, 293–94.

6

Newman's Women!

> *Joyce Sugg has searched out much information about Newman's mostly forgotten women and their lives make fascinating reading.*
>
> Meriol Trevor[1]

IN OUR OPENING QUOTATION, Meriol Trevor is entirely accurate: the Newman scholar Joyce Sugg has indeed searched out much pertinent information about the women in Newman's life and has provided an outstanding account to which this chapter is much indebted. Newman's openness to and encouragement and support of his women friends must be set alongside his own almost monastic nature. Owen Chadwick writes of this: "Newman was a monk by nature as well as by grace. Born in 1801 and sent to a boarding-school at the age of seven, he lived his remaining eighty-two years in male communities: schools, two Oxford colleges, a 'monastery' at Littlemore, a college at Rome, and the Oratory at Birmingham."[2] He certainly was no misogynist, even if he understandably shared some of the cultural ideas of his time about women. He may have felt a personal call to celibacy but he esteemed marriage and was kind and supportive to the women in his life.

---

1. Trevor, "Preface," in Sugg, *Ever Yours Affly.*
2. Chadwick, *Newman, A Short Introduction*, 6.

THE WOMEN OF THE FAMILY

John Henry Newman's parents, John and Jemima Newman, had six children: John Henry, Charles, Harriet, Francis, Jemima, and Mary, all born between 1801 and 1809. The children were all brought up together in various homes that reflected the increasingly difficult financial circumstances of the elder John Newman. The boys were sent away to school when the time came, and the girls were largely educated at home. "There is no doubting the importance in Newman's development of the women in his family, grandmother, mother, aunt, sisters. Life in a boys' school and then at Oxford (exclusively male) never eradicated those first impressions."[3] That is probably true of most families, but in this particular family the oldest sibling took a special interest in contributing all that he could to his sisters' education. He contributed not only to their education but also after his father's bankruptcy in 1822 when he had gained his fellowship at Oriel College Oxford, he did all he could to send money home for the support of the family, and most especially after the death of his father in 1824.

Mrs. Jemima Newman was a religious woman, but in the conventional sense of the word. She was no enthusiast. When John and Francis were both students at Oxford, on one occasion John wrote to his mother and told her that both of them intended to take Holy Communion every two weeks. Mrs. Newman thought this excessive, though she was not opposed. In 1825, the year after her husband died and a few months after John Henry's ordination as priest, Mrs. Newman and the girls arrived in Oxford for several months. During this time he celebrated the Eucharist for them and both Jemima and Mary received holy communion from him for the first time. Newman cared for his sisters in every possible way.

> Probably he loved and admired Mary most, having more than once a presentiment that this most attractive girl would not be with them long. This feeling is not based on evidence of decline, of physical weakness, but it was strong, reinforced perhaps by a sense of the fragility of life as he attended his parishioners' death beds. He had a special feeling for Harriet too, the nearest in age. In one of his most open utterances he wrote to her "I cannot say how I love you. No calamity I think, could occur to me here so great, as to lose your love and confidence. Four of all my brothers and

---

3. Sugg, *Ever Yours Affly*, 11.

sisters (from one cause or another) you alone know my feelings and respond to them."[4]

When Newman had care of the parish at Littlemore, just outside of Oxford, his mother and sisters helped in the practical running of the place. They cooked food and took meals to the poor and needy of the parish. They helped with the general instruction of children and especially with their religious education. This came to an end after the sudden death in 1836 of Mrs. Newman and the marriages of Jemima and Harriet. Both sisters married two brothers, John and Thomas Mozley. Mrs. Newman died three weeks after Jemima's marriage to John Mozley, a union of which she approved because John ran the family printing and banking business in Derby and because of the obvious "gentility" of the Mozleys.[5] Tom Mozley, husband to Harriet, was a clergyman in the Church of England, and John Henry helped him get a living through Oriel College that gave the newly married couple at least some income. Tom and Harriet Mozley and their daughter Grace went on vacation to Normandy in 1843. They were exposed to Catholicism in a way that they had not been accustomed to, visiting churches, and noting the devotion of very ordinary Normandy Catholics. This made quite an impression on them, and Tom returned home and shortly thereafter wrote to his wife, who was still in Normandy, that he was going to become a Catholic. Sheridan Gilley describes the incident:

> Tom Mozley was swept off his feet by the fervent peasant Catholicism of Normandy, left Harriet in Caen and came home to become a Roman Catholic. Newman went straight down to his vicarage to persuade him to postpone the decision for two years, but the ignorant Harriet, who came back from Caen to find Tom all but a papist, blamed her brother . . . for the near loss of her home and means of livelihood, and never forgave him.[6]

Tom was talked out of it. Harriet's relationship with John came to an end in 1843 so that, as Sheridan Gilley notes, "it was left to Jemima to bear in patience with him and to remain, with Mary dead and Charles, Francis, and Harriet all estranged from him, the loan loving sibling of the family."[7]

---

4. Sugg, *Ever Yours Affly*, 22.
5. Gilley, *Newman and His Age*, 157.
6. Gilley, *Newman and His Age*, 225.
7. Gilley, *Newman and His Age*, 225.

At this time, of course, Newman was moving closer and closer to the Catholic Church, something that both Jemima and Harriet found very difficult. Jemima wrote to John Henry in 1844 or early in 1845, attempting to dissuade him as it were from what seemed the inevitable step he was taking, "I cannot help feeling a repulsion from that church which has so many stains upon her."[8] Jemima remained in touch with John after his reception into the Catholic Church but she never invited him to visit her growing family. Correspondence with Harriet was much more limited. Tom Mozley gave up his work as a clergyman for a time and became a journalist, writing for the *Times* of London, and in that capacity he reported on the First Vatican Council. Harriet died rather suddenly in 1852, just forty-eight years of age. Newman wrote at the time to a friend whom the family had known a long time: "I daresay I have spoken severely of [Harriet] to my sister Jemima before now—but I am not aware that I have ever felt unkindly. Poor Harriet, what a change from what it was when you first knew us! What a world this is."[9] One can hear great sadness in these words and perhaps also regret. Jemima, "the last and fondest of his sisters," died on December 25, 1879. The Mozley family, according to Sheridan Gilley, were upset "by a seeming coldness in [Newman's] grief, and by telling them that he would say Mass for her soul."[10] Was his grief cold? Newman was not particularly accustomed to displaying his emotions. Might it be the case that with this "last and fondest" gone, he was frozen in grief?

ELIZABETH BOWDEN

One of John's best friends at Oxford in the early days was John Bowden, a wealthy young man whose father was a director of the Bank of England. Apparently, he was so close to John that after he had married his wife Elizabeth, he sometimes addressed her as "Newman." Consumption or tuberculosis was a very serious health issue in the nineteenth century. John Bowden succumbed to this illness and in 1844, the year before his conversion, Newman went to visit him knowing that he did not have long to live. "[Newman] described for Keble the little scene at night when Bowden was carried upstairs by two servants, his wife going ahead with a candle, the invalid joking about his 'procession' and making sure that his friend, at

8. Cited in Sugg, *Ever Yours Affly*, 50.
9. Cited in Sugg, *Ever Yours Affly*, 52.
10. Gilley, *Newman and His Age*, 418.

the foot of the stairs, saw that she looked at him as he went. He died in September and Newman's grief was compounded with his own doubts and distresses."[11]

Newman remained close to Elizabeth Bowden and before and after he joined the Catholic Church they remained in touch through letters in which he was able to express confidentially his joys and sorrows, and she became ever more sympathetic to Catholicism. Elizabeth's brother-in-law, an army man, impressed upon her that becoming a Catholic would be a foolish decision. John, as always indeed, was sensitive to the situation and wrote to Elizabeth as follows: "But as to your being driven about hither and thither, by opposite disputants, I cannot bear to think of it. It is meant kindly, but for me, I am not capable of stunning you with arguments, or stifling you with folios, or subduing you by an urgent tone or a confident manner."[12] Newman never pressurized anyone into becoming a Catholic. Elizabeth became a Catholic in July 1846 and her younger children followed her, but not her oldest son John. He was seventeen and at Eton College. Newman insisted that no pressure should be brought to bear on this young man and that he should be allowed to find his own way. Eventually John Bowden the younger joined his mother and siblings in the Catholic Church.

MARIA ROSINA GIBERNE

Maria Rosina Giberne was a close friend of the Newman family. She receives a fine description from the pen of Joyce Sugg:

> He was a handsome, striking brunette, with a tall figure, a fine bust. She was a young Juno, calculated to turn the heads of the men; she knew her powers and expected flattery.... Her outstanding characteristic was her tendency to strong, romantic feeling (which might be for a man or for a woman), gushing out, a river that was forever overflowing its banks. Her feelings seem to have been very like those of any adolescent, real enough but immature, difficult to canalise, expressed with artifice fervor.[13]

---

11. Sugg, *Ever Yours Affly*, 56.
12. Cited in Sugg, *Ever Yours Affly*, 58.
13. Sugg, *Ever Yours Affly*, 25–26.

She certainly turned Francis Newman's head and he proposed marriage to her, but she declined. Instead, she set her hopes on a young army officer who went out to India and who unfortunately died out there. In his will he left all his money to Maria so that she was independently wealthy—perhaps a better investment than Francis Newman!

When Maria first met John Henry she thought him a little stiff and rigid, but they were to become good friends, lifelong friends, and Maria lived almost as long as he did. She was with the family the evening before young Mary Newman died, probably from appendicitis, and her presence was a great comfort to them all. Maria became an ardent follower of the Tractarians, and often engaged in distributing the tracts. This made her rather dangerous in the eyes of some. "She still moved in evangelical circles and was a temptation to young ministers because of her good looks and lively air and also because of the attraction of the forbidden, since her Tractarian convictions would render her dangerous."[14]

Maria followed Newman into the Catholic Church in 1845, two months after Newman himself. She continued to remain very close to "the Father," the term she often used for him. After Newman set up the Oratory in Birmingham, he informed her regularly of all the details concerning not only the Oratory but also the parish. Other members of the Oratory stayed regularly in touch with Maria, as if she were part of the larger Oratory family. She was of particular assistance to Newman at the time of the Achilli trial. An ex-Dominican, Giacinto Achilli, had been condemned in Rome for his sexual transgressions. He became a Protestant and was touring England lecturing against Catholics and for Protestantism. Newman began to write against him and, to cut a long story short, was had up for libel. In order adequately to defend himself, he needed to bring to England some of those Italian women who had been seduced by Achilli. The problem was how to bring these women to England to give witness at the trial. The solution to the problem was Maria Giberne! She traveled to Italy, and brought some of the women back to England to assist in Newman's defense.[15]

After speculating about joining various religious orders of women, Maria joined the Visitation nuns at a convent in France, at Paray-le-Monial. She took the religious name of Sister Maria Pia, undoubtedly out of her devotion to the Pope, Pius IX. Newman wrote to her in one letter as follows:

---

14. Sugg, *Ever Yours Affly*, 78.

15. The entire escapade is wonderfully described by Joyce Sugg in *Ever Yours Affly*, 84–98.

"My dear Sister M. P., Not Member of Parliament, or much presented, or miserably placed, but Maria Pia."[16] Her stay in this convent was not without difficulty—Sheridan Gilley says that she "failed her novitiate"—and eventually she transferred to the Visitation convent in Autun in 1863 where she made her final vows. Newman and his fellow Oratorians continued to look after her financially.[17]

In 1875, when Fr. Ambrose St. John who had also been a close friend of Maria's died, Newman wrote to her:

> What a faithful friend he has been to me for 32 years! Yet there are others as faithful. What a wonderful mercy it is to me that God has given me so many faithful friends? He has never left me without support at trying times. How much you did for me in the Achilli trial, (and at other times), and I have never thanked you, as I ought to have done. This sometimes oppresses me, as if I was very ungrateful. You truly say that you have seen my beginning, middle and end. Since his death, I have been reproaching myself for not expressing to him how much I felt his love—and I write this lest I should feel the same about you, should it be God's will that I should outlive you. I have above-mentioned the Achilli matter, but that is only one specimen of the devotion, which by word and deed and prayer, you have been continually showing towards me most unworthy. . . . I hope I don't write too small for your eyes.[18]

Maria died in December 1885.

MARIA PUSEY

Maria Pusey was the wife of Edward Bouverie Pusey, about whom we have already heard, in Joyce Sugg's terms "the gentle wife." Newman was fond of her. Along with her husband she gave up entertaining so that the money saved could go to building churches. She also sold her jewelry so that the money could be given to charity. When she died prematurely in 1839 Newman attempted to console Pusey, and along with John Keble insisted to him that her death was not God's judgment on his Christian witness.

---

16. Cited in Sugg, *Ever Yours Affly*, 219.
17. Gilley, *Newman and His Age*, 330.
18. Sugg, *Ever Yours Affly*, 223.

CONCLUSION

There were many other women in John Henry Newman's long life—spiritual directees, nuns, aristocratic ladies, authors, and so forth. This brief chapter gives some indication of his devotion to his women friends. All of his friends kept up with him and he remembered them in his prayers and in his celebrations of the Eucharist. "Once he thought of writing an account of the ladies he had known, putting them together in what he called a 'galaxy.' The idea was dropped—but the notion itself shows his regard for his faithful women. They did not shine as identical stars and some of them were small luminaries but his word, galaxy, describes them very well."[19]

---

19. Sugg, *Ever Yours Affly*, 299.

7

Vatican I, 1869–70

Every Council is a complex and unpredictable event whose consequences run far beyond the substance of its formal decisions and decrees. No human construct is timeless, and neither an ecumenical Council of the Catholic Church, nor even that church itself, stands above the slippage, flux, and confusion of the tide of history, which carries us toward a future we cannot predict, and do not control.

Eamon Duffy[1]

We stand at a distance of just a hundred and twenty years from the first Vatican Council. Not so much the opening of the archives, as the healing perspective of time, has enabled students to perceive that greatest controversy of modern Christian history in more judicious and less partisan frames of mind. The infighting seems now as irrelevant and as wearisome as the infighting over the Council of Florence or the Council of Constance.

Owen Chadwick[2]

INTRODUCTION

THE QUOTATIONS THAT OPEN this chapter from church historian Eamon Duffy and Duffy's doctoral supervisor Owen Chadwick could not be more

1. Duffy, "The Staying Power of Christianity," 70.
2. Chadwick, *Spirit of the Oxford Movement*, 311.

accurate. Beginning with Duffy, the dense and detailed, messy and complex historical situation of the church must be acknowledged again and again. Fresh light is thrown on every angle of the past as historians continue their studies. Going on to Owen Chadwick, he is right about the healing perspective of time and the irrelevance of the infighting surrounding the first Vatican Council. Quite simply everything has changed with Vatican II (1962–65) and was in the process of change before it. There has been an enormous change of consciousness about all social and ecclesiastical structures throughout the world. Probably for the first time the peoples of the world were beginning to realize that they had certain inalienable rights about their political governance. The Catholic Church could not expect to be immune from this growing realization. Add to this the fact that the last reforming council of the church before Vatican I had been the Council of Trent, and before that the Council of Constance (1414–18). "From [the Council of Constance] forward the relationship of Pope to Council became uneasy, to the point that at times the popes feared councils as if they were avenging angels."[3] Constance had deposed three claimants to the papacy and then proceeded to elect a new pope, Martin V. Conciliarism—the doctrine that supreme authority in the church lies with a council—now became an issue, and an issue that never went away entirely. Trent had met to respond to some of the issues of the Protestant Reformation in the sixteenth century. In a rapidly changing world after the French Revolution, the time was ripe for a new council.

"Vatican I was the Catholic answer to the *many* revolutions affecting the nineteenth century."[4] Among these revolutions we may count not only the French Revolution, but also the American Revolution, the Industrial Revolution, and the Scientific Revolution. Each in its own fashion created or was seen by man to cause problems for the church, and the Council was the Catholic answer to these problems. There are those who interpret Vatican I with such a hermeneutic of suspicion that it seems to be an expression of "stifling despotism" on the part of Pius IX and his cronies, "trying to get away with the dogma of papal infallibility."[5] While there is a grain of truth in that perception of the Council, in the fact that the Pope and his close allies were keen on having the dogma proclaimed, it is hardly adequate. It certainly does not take into account the many revolutions noted above,

3. O'Malley, *Vatican I: The Council and the Making of the Ultramontane Church*, 4.
4. Fitzer, *Romance and the Rock*, 5.
5. Hales, *Pio Nono*, 293.

with the exception of the American Revolution all European issues and challenges.

> [Vatican I's] plans, debates and documents reflected preoccupation with Europe's nineteenth-century problems: the impact of the Enlightenment and French Revolution, the influence of Kant and Hegel, nineteenth-century continental liberalism. The Italian *Risorgimento* was quite literally at the gates of Rome. A thousand years of papal sovereign rule in central Italy were in their final twelve months. Since Pius VII's time, a succession of popes had set official Catholicism's face squarely against the political, social, and intellectual temper of the times. The Vatican Council was designed by Pius IX to set the seal on that opposition.[6]

As early as 1864 Pope Pius IX wished to call an ecumenical council, and finally in June 1868 this wish was announced publicly in the papal bull *Aeterni Patris*.[7] There had been no ecumenical council since the Council of Trent in the sixteenth century and for Pius never was a council more necessary than at this time. The bull of convocation included such matters as "clerical life and its needs, providing new safeguards for Christian marriage and the Christian education of youth, taking up in this new age the ancient problems of the relations of Church and State and providing appropriate guidance, so as to promote peace and prosperity in the national life everywhere."[8]

On June 29, 1868, Pope Pius IX promulgated the bull *Aeterni Patris*, fixing the date for the opening of the Council the next year. It seems to have been the case that the Pope, at least in the beginning, did not have a very clear and precise program for the upcoming Council. He would have been aware of the central role of councils in the history of the church, and undoubtedly "he hoped that the new Council would strengthen the church so it could better cope with the numerous attacks being made upon it."[9] The Council opened on December 8, 1869 and suspended its sessions on September 1, 1870. About eight hundred cardinals, patriarchs, archbishops, bishops, abbots, and religious superiors participated, and it is estimated that about 80,000 people were tightly packed into the basilica of St. Peter's for the opening event. Poorer bishops and vicars apostolic from missionary

---

6. Hennessey, SJ, *American Catholics*, 168.
7. Coppa, *Cardinal Giacomo Antonelli and Papal Politics*, 149.
8. Hughes, *The Church in Crisis*, 299, slightly adapted.
9. Coppa, *Pope Pius IX*, 156–57.

territories, many of whom had been created by the Pope, were lodged at Pius's own expense in Rome. This gave rise to his witty remark, appreciated only in Italian: "I don't know whether the Pope will emerge from this Council fallible or infallible [*fallibile od infallibile*], but it is certain that he will be bankrupt [*fallito*]."[10]

This was the first general council of the church in which bishops assembled in Rome from every continent. It must be recalled that at the Council of Trent in the sixteenth century the world was still in the process of being opened up geographically. It is also interesting and of note that the presence and participation of English-speaking bishops in Vatican I was substantive, some 120 taking part.[11] Historical generalizations are seldom very accurate, but in terms of an overview we may say that there were two basic groups at the Council—the ultramontanist group, desirous of supreme authority in the church for the pope and of total Catholic allegiance to that authority, and the liberal group, who wished to promote a closer relationship between the church and modernity, "although, to be fair, the variety of positions along the ideological spectrum dispute the idea of a monolithic 'left' or 'right.'"[12]

Even a cursory awareness of the standard English-language histories of Vatican I indicates some of the major problems.[13] These ranged from such practical issues as the dissemination of texts in good time for them to be read and digested by the bishops, acoustics in St. Peter's Basilica, the tedium of debate around procedural protocols, groups of bishops meeting along party lines, and so forth. Above all there was the question of papal infallibility, which was always understood to be there, but did not formally surface on the council floor for several months.

Two doctrinal constitutions were promulgated, *Dei Filius* (April 24, 1870), dealing with reason and faith, and *Pastor Aeternus* (July 18, 1870), defining the primacy and infallibility of the pope. Thirty-five theologians were invited from outside Italy. Most of them were ultramontane in outlook, but Ignaz von Döllinger and John Henry Newman were far from

---

10. Hales, *Pio Nono*, 295.

11. Hales, *Pio Nono*, 296.

12. Bellitto, *The General Councils*, 117.

13. Butler, OSB, *The Vatican Council, 1869–1870*; Hennessey, SJ, *First Council of the Vatican, the American Experience*; O'Gara, *Triumph in Defeat: Infallibility, Vatican I, and the French Minority Bishops*. Butler's and Hennessey's volumes are particularly valuable because they are laced with citations from correspondence from the participants at the Council.

ultramontanism. In point of fact, Döllinger was vetoed by the Archbishop of Munich, Cardinal Reisach, and Newman did not accept the invitation for a number of reasons: his health, his dislike of ecclesiastical politics, and the fact that he was working on his book *An Essay in Aid of a Grammar of Assent*. While he was at work on his book, his fellow priest and former friend Henry Edward Manning was hard at work promoting a conciliar definition of papal infallibility, and a very wide-ranging conciliar definition at that. Manning held an extreme view of papal infallibility.

HENRY EDWARD MANNING (1808–92)

No account of Vatican I, especially for Anglophone readers, could be adequate without some account of the ultramontane bishop Henry Edward Manning. Bishop Manning is often contrasted with Newman and few have penned this contrast in such an interesting way as Owen Chadwick.

> Two Oxford men, two Anglican clergymen; both converted to the Roman Catholic Church during the wave of 1843–1851; and then going their separate ways, the one to public affairs, hierarchy, power, the forefront of the Catholic fight, the purple, place, papal favor, and grandeur; the other to a monk's cell, retreating from the fight, solitary and unpretentious, a critic of hierarchy, oppressed by hierarchy, suspect to Rome, shabby in his cassock, as underground as possible; quiet meditator versus high ecclesiastic and politician.[14]

Chadwick's contrast may be somewhat overdrawn but it is not inaccurate. Henry Edward Manning has not been served well by his early biographers, Lytton Strachey and Edmund Sheridan Purcell. The former attacks him most unjustly in his *Eminent Victorians*, where he is presented as "a relentless power-seeker flourishing in an age of humbug."[15] Purcell's biography, while not as acid as Strachey's portrait, sets out to show Manning in a most unfavorable light. The picture painted in this chapter is hopefully more balanced and has to do largely with Manning as a propagandist

---

14. Chadwick, "Newman and the Historians," in his *Spirit of the Oxford Movement*, 158.

15. Strachey, *Eminent Victorians*. The book has been reprinted many times. The quotation describing Manning is from Michael Holroyd, cited in Gilley, "New Light on an Old Scandal: Purcell's Life of Cardinal Manning," in Bellenger, *Opening the Scrolls*, 166.

for papal infallibility especially at Vatican I, but some details of his life are necessary.

The youngest son of William Manning, a member of Parliament, Henry Edward Manning was educated at Harrow. Thomas Bokenkotter offers a summary description of those secondary schooling years: "He spent his teenage years at Harrow, a public school noted for its brutal discipline, where little attention was given to religion and much to sports, at which he proved to be quite adept. The same talent no doubt showed up in his accuracy at stone-throwing in the pitched battles the boys fought with the local townsfolk. . . . The qualities that were later to be so prominent in his character soon became apparent: a steely determination to achieve a goal, self-confidence and self-control, and the ability to make the most of his talents and opportunities."[16] Although not entirely expected, he gained a first in classics at Balliol College Oxford. However, his father fell into bankruptcy and Manning's circumstances changed very quickly. His hope to move into politics collapsed.

Although students of Manning sometimes debate his motives, in 1832 he decided to seek ordination in the Church of England, and was elected to a fellowship at Merton College Oxford. Manning plunged himself into reading what he called "acres of Anglican writers," from the Caroline divines with their high church ecclesiology and sacramental theology, to more liberal Protestant authors. At this time he dined on a number of occasions with the up-and-coming John Henry Newman of Oriel College Oxford, and began to confront what one scholar has called "the doctrinal chaos in Anglicanism."[17]

The following year, 1833, he went as curate to John Sargent, rector of Lavington. He was moving more and more closely to the high church theology of the Tractarians of the Oxford Movement, and his developing high church views are well summarized by Thomas Bokenkotter: "In 1834 he was converted to belief in the real presence of Jesus in the consecrated bread and wine, and established daily Matins and Evensong in his parish."[18] Though he did not yet know it, Manning was becoming more and more Roman, and given his personality, upbringing, and circumstances, perhaps even more Roman than the Romans themselves. In May 1833, he succeeded Sargent as rector, and later in that year he married Caroline, Sargent's

---

16. Bokenkotter, *Church and Revolution*, 174–75.
17. Bokenkotter, *Church and Revolution*, 177.
18. Bokenkotter, *Church and Revolution*, 179.

daughter, but she died very suddenly in 1837. He told Newman at the time: "All I can do now is keep at work. There is a sort of rush into my mind when unoccupied I can hardly bear."[19] Although he was never at this time committed to celibacy in the way that Newman was, he never sought someone to replace his beloved Caroline. His Romeward tendencies continued to develop in April 1838 when he made the first of his twenty-two trips to Rome.

In 1841, Manning became Archdeacon of Chichester. Though originally evangelical in his theological orientation, he was now firmly allied with the high church Tractarians and authored No. 78 in the *Tracts for the Times*.[20] A recent biographer has put the case persuasively that Manning was in terms of theology an autodidact. "Theologically, the Anglican Manning was very much a self-taught man.... He had no teacher to direct his steps, nor did he look for one. His ideas were not shaped in the hotbed of intellectual intercourse that was Tractarian Oxford; rather, they germinated and grew up in Lavington, the fruit of study and silent contemplation."[21] Of course he was informed by the theology of the Tractarians, but due to his pastoral concerns and remoteness from the center in Oxford he was not involved in the day-to-day cut and thrust of theological exchange. He was certainly influenced by John Henry Newman's *Essay on the Development of Christian Doctrine* of 1845, but even having read it and having been largely convinced by its argument in favor of Rome he still had to make his own way, and that was gradual.[22] Newman wrote to Manning: "I think the Church of Rome the Catholic Church, and ours not part of the Catholic Church because not in communion with Rome."[23] After Newman was received into the Catholic Church, Manning wrote to him in a very warm fashion: "Only believe always that I love you. If we may never meet again in life at the same altar, may our intercessions for each other, day by day, meet

---

19. Cited in Gray, *Cardinal Manning*, 64.

20. This is what Manning wrote in a letter in 1850 to Samuel Wilberforce, Bishop of Oxford, who was also Manning's brother-in-law, about his theological-sacramental beliefs in 1833 when he arrived in Lavington: "When I came to Lavington in 1833 I believed, as I always did, in Baptismal Regeneration: I had no view of the Sacrament of the Body and Blood of Christ: and no idea of the Church." This letter is cited from Pereiro, *Cardinal Manning*, 10. It provides some indication of Manning's gradual movement away from evangelicalism to a more Catholic sensibility.

21. Pereiro, *Cardinal Manning*, 329.

22. Pereiro, *Cardinal Manning*, especially 67–74, highlights the contours of Manning's pilgrimage to Rome vis-à-vis Newman's *Essay*.

23. Gray, *Cardinal Manning*, 93.

in the court of Heaven."[24] He was not always to feel so warmly disposed towards Newman.

After Newman became a Catholic in 1845, a number of Anglicans looked to Manning as a leader of the Oxford Movement, but it was not to be. One of the better-known Anglican theologians of that time, Frederick Denison Maurice, said of Manning, "His power with the clergy is very great, greater certainly than that of any man living."[25] The straw that broke the camel's back for Manning was undoubtedly the Gorham judgment, in which the Judicial Committee of the Privy Council found in favor of an Anglican clergyman, George Gorham, who had been refused installation as a vicar by the Bishop of Exeter because he did not accept the traditional doctrine of baptismal regeneration. The Privy Council—a secular court—controversially overruled the Bishop's decision. Manning was received into the Catholic Church in 1851 in the Jesuit church of Farm St., London, and two months later he was ordained a priest by Archbishop Nicholas Wiseman. In 1857, he was made Provost of the Westminster Metropolitan Chapter, and he succeeded Wiseman as Archbishop of Westminster in 1865. A rapid rise through the ecclesiastical ranks!

> Converts such as Newman and Manning who came barging into the church at full tilt were at odds with [the traditional Catholic] mentality in many ways, and the old Catholics resented their attitude of intellectual superiority, their enthusiasm for things Roman, and their ostentatious piety. "Where old English priests had eschewed even black coats, convert priests gloried in sporting Roman collars and in parading in cassocks and birettas."[26]

Manning and Newman make an interesting contrast, captured nicely by Sheridan Gilley: "Manning's private and personal influence in his way and in his own day was just as great as Newman's, but as it belonged to the realm of deeds and to the spoken rather than the written word, so it died with those who have known him, whereas heart still speaks to heart wherever Newman finds readers."[27] There is something in this careful judgment about the influence of both men. Manning was very definitely a man of action, while Newman turned the carefully crafted word. Manning was a man of the people, one who constantly thought about and protested about

---

24. Gray, *Cardinal Manning*, 106.
25. Cited in Gray, *Cardinal Manning*, 129.
26. Bokenkotter, *Church and Revolution*, 188.
27. Gilley, "Newman and the Convert Mind," 8.

the social evils of his times, in the manner of Charles Dickens the novelist and Frederick Denison Maurice the Anglican theologian.[28]

Manning, however, came to distrust Newman and even to think of him as dangerous, as one who exemplified a somewhat independent English Catholicism with an Oxford accent. Newman's Catholicism for Manning was insufficiently certain and bold.[29] Both of them believed in papal infallibility, but while Newman thought the definition was both unnecessary and unwise and might discourage conversion to the Catholic Church, Manning was convinced that far from having an adverse reaction in England, such a definition would bring Anglicans flocking over to Rome. What Manning wanted was "downright, masculine, and decided Catholics—*more* Roman than Rome, and more Ultramontane than the Pope himself."[30] For Manning, "Ultramontanism is Catholic Christianity."[31] As a man of action, Manning set himself wholeheartedly to do all in his power to achieve the highest expression of his ultramontanism through his promotion of the definition of papal infallibility. When all is said and done, it makes a great deal of sense. Manning had left the Church of England at considerable cost to himself because of what he saw as a lack of doctrinal and traditional orthodoxy expressed in an authoritative and hierarchical structure. "He was convinced that the papacy was the only bulwark against the faith-destroying forces of rationalism and atheism."[32]

Before returning to the Vatican Council, we get perhaps another insight into Manning by recalling that he shared a platform with none other than John Henry Newman's brother, Francis Newman. On October 22, 1867, at a meeting in the Manchester Free Trade Hall, Francis Newman and Archbishop Manning found themselves sharing similar views on the

---

28. See McClelland, *Cardinal Manning*, 214. McClelland's book thoroughly documents Manning's concern for the poor through government action as well as charitable concern, both as an Anglican and then later as a Catholic bishop. These concerns long anticipated his participation in the settlement of the London Strike of 1889, for which he is well known, and it is alleged influenced Pope Leo XIII in his encyclical *Rerum Novarum*.

29. Sheridan Gilley makes the point that Manning's biographer, Edmund Purcell, in a biographical sketch of Newman in 1881 praised Newman to the skies and denigrated his enemies, "among them by implication Manning." See Gilley, "New Light on an Old Scandal," 170. Gilley goes on to say that this "attempt to use Newman as an instrument against Manning was one which was to recur."

30. Cited in Hastings, *A History of English Christianity 1920–1990*, 147.

31. Pereiro, *Cardinal Manning*, 255.

32. Bokenkotter, *Church and Revolution*, 191.

social problems caused by alcohol. Manning knew the problems alcohol caused, not least among his large and growing Irish immigrant flock in London, and so he allied himself with the tirade of some fervent Protestants, including Francis Newman, "against the enormous success of the trade in intoxicating drink." When Francis Newman wrote to his brother John about his enthusiasm for Manning on this issue, thinking this might be something both brothers shared in common, John replied: "As to what you tell me of Archbishop Manning, I have heard that some also of our Irish bishops think that too many drink-shops are licensed. As for me, I do not know whether we have too many or too few."[33] This was not Francis's hoped-for reply. Newman knew about drink and its problems but did not wish to associate himself with the views of Manning and his brother. After all, he lived in industrial Birmingham, and his first church in that sprawling industrial conurbation was in a former gin distillery.

IGNAZ VON DÖLLINGER AND LORD ACTON

Two opponents of the definition of papal infallibility were the Bavarian priest and church historian Ignaz Döllinger (1799–1890) and the English lay Catholic historian Lord Acton (1834–1902). Döllinger had been ordained priest in 1822 and from 1826 until 1873 he was a professor of church history in Munich. Newman met him in the company of Ambrose St. John in the Chapel Royal at Munich en route back to England from Rome late in 1847. Earlier in life Döllinger leaned in an ultramontane direction, but through personal research and friendship—especially with John Henry Newman and Lord Acton—he distanced himself from ultramontanism, and was fundamentally opposed to the definition of papal infallibility that was being argued for at Vatican I in 1870. As Owen Chadwick has it, "He was a church historian who believed that history disproved the infallibility of the Pope."[34] The anonymous author of the article on Döllinger in *The Oxford Dictionary of the Christian Church* ends his contribution with these words: "His capacity for work was almost limitless and his personal life simple. He was also a great teacher."[35] It is an accurate description of the man himself, and his best-known pupil was the Englishman, Lord Acton.

---

33. Cited in Willey, *More Nineteenth Century Studies*, 47.
34. Chadwick, *A History of the Popes 1830–1914*, 192.
35. Cross and Livingstone, *The Oxford Dictionary of the Christian Church*, 416.

Vatican I, 1869-70

John Emerich Edward Dalberg Acton was born at Naples. His father died when he was only one, and his mother saw to his education, first at Paris with the somewhat Gallican Abbé Dupanloup, who was later to become Bishop of Orleans and a player at Vatican I, and then at Oscott College, Birmingham, where he was taught by Nicholas Wiseman, who would become Cardinal-Archbishop of Westminster, and then at Munich, as a pupil of Döllinger. While a professor of canon law and church history at the University of Munich, Döllinger enhanced his income by taking in pupil-boarders of whom Acton, arriving in 1850, was the most famous. Döllinger was to be his master-teacher. "Acton found the father he had never known, and Döllinger discovered the son whom as a celibate priest he could not beget."[36] Summarizing the relationship between the two men, Thomas Howard writes as follows: "Polyglots both, men of serious faith and immense learning, the two kept alive their friendship—albeit not without some tensions and differences of opinion—through correspondence and visits until Döllinger's death in 1890."[37]

Döllinger became involved in German politics and for a while lost his post at the University of Munich. When he was reinstated, he gave over his time more strictly for the study of theology and church history. One fine example of his historical research was his 1853 book *Hippolytus and Kallistus*. The work came about as a result of the discovery in 1842 of a manuscript entitled "Philosophumena." Döllinger weighed carefully the claims for authorship and came down on the side of the third-century Roman presbyter Hippolytus who had found himself at odds with Pope Zephyrinus (198–217) and Pope Callistus (217–222). When the monograph came to print Döllinger found his reputation further enhanced and underscored because of his evenhanded historical methodology. Other historical and theological works flowed from his pen and his growing reputation found him in contact and in correspondence with scholars and leaders in other Christian traditions, for example, Edward B. Pusey of Oxford, Cardinal Nicholas Wiseman of Westminster, William Gladstone, the English prime minister, and Alfred Plummer, an Anglican theologian and historian.

Not long after Montalembert spoke at the Malines Conference in 1863, Döllinger gave a more powerful speech at a congress of Catholic theologians at Munich, "The Past and Present of Catholic Theology." In this speech, he set out his understanding of historical theology, underscoring

---

36. Chadwick, *Acton and History*, 4.
37. Howard, *The Pope and the Professor*, 92.

the importance of academic freedom for Catholic scholars researching the past. Döllinger argued that Catholic theology must be transformed by an essentially historical approach, especially as this was developing in German universities. Acton shared his teacher's perspective, but a position that seemingly advocated history over the timelessness of Catholic dogma was bound to provoke a negative reaction from Rome. That negative reaction came in the form of a Papal Brief, *Tuas Libenter*, to the Archbishop of Munich in December 1863, but it was not published until March of the following year. The "Munich Brief," as it has come to be known, condemned any kind of scholarly research by Catholics that seemed to sit loosely to ecclesiastical authority. While Döllinger was not condemned by name, the nature of the theological-historical enterprise as he understood it clearly was. Döllinger's ongoing historical work and his developing ecclesiastical-political awareness made him an ever more steadfast opponent of ultramontanism and so also of the definition of papal infallibility at Vatican I. His opposition to papal infallibility made him reach out to others whom he took to be of a similar mind on the issue, and especially John Henry Newman, who thought such a declaration inopportune. Döllinger wrote to Newman in March 1870:

> In my opinion, and probably in yours too, the situation of the Catholic Church has not been more dangerous in the last four centuries than it is at present. At such a time the true sons and friends of the church ought to be communing together.... Every one of us, who are the theologians of the church, should cast the weight of his testimony, whatever it may be, into the scales of the balance. Your position in the church is such a high one, that silence becomes a snare for thousands. It will be said: *qui tacet, consentit* [he who is silent, consents]. And yet it is impossible that you should be of one mind with [Archbishop] Manning.... Among the theologians of Germany, except a few disciples of the Jesuits, there is not one man of some note who does not abhor and deprecate this new dogma of personal infallibility, which is to be forced upon us. Of course I don't pretend to judge the reasons which you may have had to remain silent up to this moment. But I think the crisis is so near, that those reasons must now have lost their weight. Neutrality in such a case is too near akin to lukewarmness, but if you speak out, then let "the trumpet give a clear and certain sound" and believe such a splendid opportunity to do signal service to the cause of the church will not be offered again.[38]

38. Dessain, *Letters and Diaries of John Henry Newman*, 84.

Newman's response was not what Döllinger had hoped for. Newman was far from naïve about the goings-on of church councils in history, and yet at the same time he believed that God was working through them.

Acton too was an outright opponent of ultramontanism and all that went with it. With his formation and historical training under the tutelage of Döllinger, and as a nineteenth-century representative of the English Cisalpine tradition, a man with an enormous range of knowledge, and a defender of liberal views, Acton was strongly opposed to Pope Pius IX's *Syllabus of Errors*. He attacked ultramontanism "as a form of Catholic escapism into the teaching of the church as the sole foundation and test of all certain knowledge."[39]

Lord Acton actually attended Vatican I as a layman, attempting to influence bishops and others against the definition of papal infallibility. "Acton was at the center of the anti-infallibilist activities. Albert du Boys, a confidant of [Bishop] Dupanloup, noted in his memoirs that some fifteen or twenty North American prelates, among them Kenrick [Archbishop of St. Louis] and Connolly [Archbishop of Halifax], frequented Acton's salon and met there with their German counterparts."[40] Acton and his associates were, of course, unsuccessful. Döllinger was excommunicated in 1871 for refusing to accept the decree on infallibility, but, while Acton continued to be suspect in ultramontane circles, there was never any excommunication. Suspicion of Acton, while understandable, seems undeserved in this regard. What Acton wanted was a vibrant Catholic intellectual life, a life that was marked by critical scholarship and genuine serious discernment, perhaps especially on the part of the laity. That is a good much to be desired. Newman wanted much the same thing. However, Newman's approach was much less pugnacious than Acton's. "Whereas Newman had a great deal of sympathy with Catholics like Acton, he was repelled by the autocratic and intellectually fearful positions espoused by Manning and by many members of the episcopacy."[41]

Many people regretted the excommunication of Döllinger, including Pope Leo XIII, and various efforts were made to effect a reconciliation between him and Rome. A strenuous effort in this regard was made by Sir Peter le Page Renouf (1822–97) and his wife during the 1880s. Both of them had been long-time friends and admirers of Döllinger. Renouf was a most

---

39. Hill, *Lord Acton*, 145.
40. Hennessey, SJ, *American Catholics*, 46.
41. Anderson, *The Great Catholic Reformers*, 178.

distinguished Egyptologist and had been engaged by Newman to teach in his Catholic University. Their efforts came to nothing, not least because Döllinger thought that he would have to renounce his basic historical and theological points of view, and not just his opposition to the papal dogma of infallibility.[42]

DEI FILIUS

The initial sessions of the Vatican Council were given over to the Dogmatic Constitution *Dei Filius*, which had to do with revelation and faith.[43] The initial *schema*, prepared largely by the Roman theologian Johannes Franzelin, SJ, was judged too long, too technical, and too hostile to the modern world and so it was returned for revision. The revision was undertaken by another Roman theologian, Johannes Kleutgen, SJ, and eventually this was promulgated as the Constitution *Dei Filius* on April 24, 1870.

In the accurate words of Philip Hughes, "The ten pages of text of this Constitution are so closely knit as to defy summary," but a summary must be attempted here.[44] The opening section of the Constitution reiterates Christ's presence to and in the church, guarding and assisting the church into all truth. Chapter 1 is entitled "On God the Creator of All Things." God is distinct from the world and creates not out of necessity, but freely, to manifest his perfection. Chapter 2 is "On Revelation." Its opening sentence reads: "The same holy mother church holds and teaches that God, the source and end of all things, may be known [*cognosci posse*] with certainty from the consideration of created things, by the natural power of human reason." This is a natural knowledge of God. It is important to be clear what the Constitution actually said—that it is "possible" for natural reason to know God's existence and attributes. It is important to acknowledge what the Constitution did not say. In the words of Gerald McCool, "Although the Constitution declared that natural reason had the ability to know God's existence and attributes, it did not determine whether, in point of fact, natural reason ever did so. . . . The Constitution confined itself to the declaration that natural knowledge of God was possible in principle. It did not affirm

---

42. See Howard, *The Pope and the Professor*, 215.

43. A useful summary may be found in McCool, *Catholic Theology in the Nineteenth Century*, 216–40.

44. Hughes, *The Church in Crisis*, 304.

that purely natural knowledge of God had ever been achieved in fact."[45] The Constitution goes on to insist that God has made himself known also in a "supernatural way," in the Scriptures and lastly by his Son (Hebrews 1:1–2). Chapter 3 is "On Faith." Faith accepts what God reveals, and that acceptance is based not on "the natural light of reason" but on "the authority of God himself." Faith is a gift of God. The chapter also defends the reasonableness of the act of faith, insisting on this against the Fideist tradition of Protestant pietism. The Constitution maintains that "it was God's will that there should be linked to the internal assistance of the Holy Spirit outward indications of his revelation, that is to say divine acts, and first and foremost miracles and prophecies, which clearly demonstrating as they do the omnipotence and infinite knowledge of God, are the most certain signs of revelation and are suited to the understanding of all."[46] The insistence on these outward signs of revelation as well as the internal assistance of the Holy Spirit is undoubtedly responding to those theologians of the nineteenth century who emphasized the interiority of Christian experience over against all external manifestations of revelation, perhaps especially Friedrich Schleiermacher. Chapter 4, finally, is "On Faith and Reason." The conviction of the Constitution is that since God is the source of both our intelligence/reason and revelation/faith, there can be no real disagreement between reason and faith. Rather, faith and reason are mutually supportive.

PASTOR AETERNUS

At least at the outset, there was no pressure on the Council participants to rush through important matters and to steamroll towards the definition of papal infallibility. There was full and, from the comments of the participating bishops, sometimes frustratingly repetitious debate.

The *schema* on the church could have been much finer. The scholar of nineteenth-century theology Michael Himes points out: "The Roman School's incarnational ecclesiology laid the theological groundwork and colored the actual language of *Pastor Aeternus*, but unfortunately neither its patristic richness nor its systematic vision is reflected in the document."[47] The patristic richness of the Roman School of theology owed something to the influence of Tübingen theologian Johann Adam Möhler, but it was

45. McCool, *Catholic Theology in the Nineteenth Century*, 219.
46. Tanner, *Decrees of the Ecumenical Councils*, vol. 2, 807.
47. Himes, "The Development of Ecclesiology," 61.

not to make its way into the actual text of the document.[48] It was not only the theology of the document that was lacking in richness. The atmosphere among the prelates was quickly concentrated around the acerbic issue of papal infallibility. Different groups formed around the question of papal infallibility, with the majority, in fact, being in favor of some kind of definition. Real debate took place, though it is not obvious from a cursory reading of the finished text of *Pastor Aeternus*. "The text as we have it fails to show any marks of the sweat—rather, stains of the blood—that was shed as it was being composed. It is the product of a conflict between ecclesiologies."[49]

Both in Rome and in the background were the extremist ultramontanes who advocated for the most comprehensive possible definition. William G. Ward, a convert from Anglicanism, for example, desired that all papal pronouncements be considered infallible. Some bishops came very close to sharing Ward's perspective, the most notable being Archbishop Manning of Westminster, who used excessive language of the pope, such as "the incarnation of the Holy Spirit." It was not only the bishops who entered the lists on the issue of papal authority. The French Catholic layman and ultramontane Louis Veuillot, editor of the paper *The Universe*, wrote to the effect that the pope carries through the very thought of God, and, because of that his directions must be completely followed. The Jesuit paper in Rome, *Civiltà Catolica*, said: "When the Pope thinks, it is God who is thinking in him."[50] While leaving open the element of ecclesiological truth found in these expressions, this is surely hyperbole. Those who endorsed such points of view were the "infallibilists."

A minority group was opposed to defining infallibility at the Council, the "anti-infallibilists." This group included many of the French bishops, coming from a tradition of Gallicanism, sometimes perhaps unconscious and at other times quite conscious, headed by Archbishop Georges Darboy of Paris and Bishop Felix Dupanloup of Orleans. Margaret O'Gara describes Bishop Dupanloup's activities both before and at the Council in

---

48. Himes writes: "Möhler's thought played a role in the ecclesiology of the influential Roman school. The principal figures of the school—Giovanni Perrone (1794–1876) and Carlo Passaglia (1827–1887), their students Johannes Baptist Franzelin (1816–1886) and Clemens Schrader (1820–1875), and Franzelin's and Schrader's student Matthias Joseph Scheeben (1835–1888)—were all, like Möhler, influenced by patristic study and sought to place the treatment of the church within a wider systematic theology" ("The Development of Ecclesiology," 59).

49. Kerr, "Vatican I and the Papacy 1: A Proud Appellation," 170.

50. These citations are from Margaret O'Gara, *Triumph in Defeat*," 70.

these words: "Before the Council, Dupanloup had begun extensive correspondence with Rome, with other bishops, and with foreign theologians. Soon after arriving at Rome, he plunged into a series of feverish organizing activities, using his residence as a base of operation."[51] Dupanloup wrote to Pius IX late in April 1870:

> Most Holy Father, my name is not pleasing to you; I know it, and it is my sorrow. But for all that, I feel myself authorized and obliged, in the profound and inviolable devotion of which I have given so many proofs to Your Holiness, to open my heart to you at this moment. . . . I would think I was betraying the Holy See and the church if, knowing what I know, and foreseeing what I foresee, I did not utter a word of warning to Your Holiness . . . while there is yet time to spare the church and the Holy See from evils that may become disasters for all Christendom during long ages.

Dupanloup, as well as the other French bishops, may not simply be disregarded as marked by a false, Gallican ecclesiology that expressed itself in bitter opposition to papal infallibility. They had the good of the church at heart, and from their perspective infallibility was the wrong course to take. This was a matter of conscience. Pius replied to Dupanloup early in May:

> Venerable Brother, your name is no less pleasing to us now than in the past, nor do we love you less, or esteem less than formerly the gifts that God has bestowed upon you. . . . Return, brother, I pray you to that golden simplicity of little ones; cast away prejudiced opinions, which may obscure the holiness of your character, and which may make, if not pernicious, certainly useless for the church those great gifts of intellect, alacrity, eloquence, with which God has so liberally endowed you for the extending of his Kingdom.[52]

The tone is somewhat patronizing, to be sure, but it is not without its kindness and concern, as much for Dupanloup himself as for the church.

The reasons for the French opposition are complex, but certainly important are the Gallican tendencies of the earlier eighteenth and nineteenth centuries, when most of the French bishops at Vatican I were in seminary formation. Gallicanism, by and large, exemplifies a certain pride in French Catholicism, advocating a decentralized church, with great respect for the independence of the local diocesan community. Some of these "Gallican" French bishops not only maintained their opposition to infallibility during

---

51. O'Gara, *Triumph in Defeat*, 31.
52. Butler, *The Vatican Council*, 2:40–42.

the Council's proceedings, but left Rome before the final vote was taken on July 18, so that they would not, in conscience, have to vote against it. Some American bishops sided with the French party also, most notably Archbishop Kenrick of St. Louis. Then there were the "inopportunists," those who regarded it inopportune to promote a definition. Representative of this group was Archbishop Martin Spalding of Baltimore and many of the Austrian and German bishops.

Alec Vidler points out that there was ample opportunity for discussion of the matter at the Council and that the inopportunists were not simply browbeaten into submission. He writes: "No doubt there was much intrigue behind the scenes, but no more than is customary, and perhaps inevitable, in ecclesiastical assemblies."[53] These are sage remarks. If we had a complete record of the proceedings of every church council, we would see in varying degrees similar intrigue, as the advocates of different theological positions made their positions clear and also tried to influence others. This is the way of conversation and debate, and there simply is no short-circuiting the process. Archbishop Manning gives us some idea of the intrigue behind the scenes. He tells us that the inopportunists "met often, and we met weekly to watch and counteract. When they went to Pius IX we went also. It was a running fight."[54] Eamon Duffy's judgment about these extreme infallibilists is surely accurate when he says: "Manning and his associates wanted history without tears, a living oracle who could short-circuit human limitation. They wanted to confront the uncertainties of their age with instant assurance, revelation on tap."[55] As things turned out, the extreme infallibilists did not get what they wanted.

In early January 1870, the infallibilists got together five hundred signatures petitioning for a definition, since the original schema on the church did not explicitly include it. The opposition managed to get only 136 signatories for a counter-petition. As a result of the majority request, a chapter on infallibility was added to the schema on the church. A new constitution on the church, not including the definition of papal primacy and infallibility, was announced on April 29. Debate continued from May until the middle of July. On May 9, at the insistence of a number of bishops, there was an addition made to the effect that the jurisdiction of the papacy did not in principle conflict with the jurisdiction of the episcopate. While

---

53. Vidler, *The Church in an Age of Revolution*, 156.
54. Purcell, *Life of Cardinal Manning*, 2:453.
55. Duffy, *Saints and Sinners*, 299.

this principle was never denied, it was found most uncomfortable by the extremist ultramontanes. The best theologian of the English episcopate, William Clifford, made a speech insisting that virtually any statement made by the Council about papal authority was bound to cause some degree of misunderstanding unless it was presented within the more general framework of a statement on authority in the church as a whole. He was hissed at by some of the audience in the aula. On June 18, the Dominican theologian Cardinal Filippo Maria Guidi, Archbishop of Bologna and an ardent infallibilist, made the emphatic point from the podium in the Council aula that it was not the pope who was infallible but his teaching. He argued that a condition of infallibility was its prudent exercise, in consultation with the worldwide episcopate. Guidi himself was an infallibilist. However, he was keen to state the tradition that the pope was no isolated monarch, but rather was first among the bishops. When Guidi descended from the podium after his speech, he was embraced by members of the minority, who appreciated his conciliatory perspective. Pius felt betrayed and summoned Guidi, and this is the famous occasion on which Pius said to him: "I am the church! I am the tradition."[56] Basing himself on the three-volume work on Pope Pius IX by the Italian church historian Giacomo Martina, SJ, the late Archbishop John Quinn adds to the normal account of Pius's outburst: "Maintaining his calm, Guidi replied that everything he had said was based on St. Thomas and on Bellarmine. With this, the Pope himself calmed down and said, 'Certainly, before deciding the Pope must take counsel,' and went on to say that he himself had in fact asked the opinion of the bishops prior to the definition of the Immaculate Conception." Quinn continues: "The unpremeditated outcry of the Pope is not a sign that he was unbalanced so much as that he was living under tremendous pressure. Furthermore, the Pope was reacting to a verbal report of his staff. He had not yet read the actual speech before seeing Guidi."[57]

The preamble to the actual text of *Pastor Aeternus* often is overlooked, and yet it is very important for an adequate interpretation of the decree, as Fergus Kerr, OP, comments: "The preamble of 'Pastor Aeternus' sets the doctrine touching the institution, perpetuity, and nature of the Petrine primacy very firmly in the context of preserving the unity of the episcopate

---

56. Butler, *The Vatican Council*, 2:96–98.

57. Quinn, *Revered and Reviled*, 83. Martina's three-volume biography was published by Rome's Gregorian University Press in the 1980s, and has not been translated into English.

within a church which has been founded to perpetuate the saving work of redemption."[58] Chapters one and two of *Pastor Aeternus* define "a primacy of jurisdiction over the whole Church of God," given to St. Peter and to his successors, the popes. This primacy of jurisdiction is "over all others" in matters of faith and morals, and also in matters of discipline and government. As it stands, this kind of language suggests that the bishops are nothing more than papal representatives. In chapter three of the document, however, we read: "So far is this power of the Pope from being damaging or obstructive to that ordinary and immediate power of episcopal jurisdiction by which bishops, who have been set by the Holy Spirit to succeed and hold the place of the apostles, feed and govern each his own flock, as true pastors, that their power, precisely, is asserted, strengthened, and protected by the supreme and universal pastor." In other words, the bishops are not mere papal mouthpieces but succeed to the place of the apostles, and the pope's role is to assert, strengthen, and protect the pastorate of the bishops. The understanding of papal primacy is that its role is to maintain and support and never to weaken or threaten the integrity of local churches.[59]

In terms of papal infallibility, a formula on its nature and extent that came from Cardinal Paul Cullen of Dublin, who had nominated Newman as rector of the Catholic University, was finally accepted by a majority of the conciliar fathers. This formula fell short of what the more rigorous ultramontanes wanted. Nonetheless, it won the day and was incorporated into the Constitution, *Pastor Aeternus*, which was adopted formally on July 18 by a vote of 433 to two.

It is in chapter 4 of the Constitution that we find the definition of infallibility:

> We teach and define as a divinely revealed dogma that when the Roman Pontiff speaks from the chair (*ex cathedra*), that is, when, in the exercise of his office as shepherd and teacher of all Christians, in virtue of his supreme apostolic authority, he defines a doctrine concerning faith or morals to be held by the whole church, he possesses, by the divine assistance promised him in blessed Peter, that infallibility which the divine Redeemer willed his church to enjoy in defining doctrine concerning faith or morals. Therefore, such definitions of the Roman Pontiff are of themselves, and not by the consent of the church, irreformable.

58. Kerr, "Vatican I and the Papacy 1: A Proud Appellation," 169.

59. John Quinn's comments on this particular issue are helpful. See his *Revered and Reviled*, 35–54.

The definition is complex and sounds very strong indeed, almost giving the pope free reign in matters doctrinal and moral. It demands some theological comment by way of clarification. The last sentence, "Therefore, such definitions . . . irreformable," is couched in this way to reject the position adopted by the 1682 assembly of French bishops, the Gallican Articles. These articles insist that for definitions of the pope to be binding they must have the consequent assent of the church. The concordat with Napoleon in 1801 added another strand to this Gallicanism. The clergy of France, now salaried by the government and thus to some extent influenced by the government, were caught in the tension between national interests and the international interests of the church. One historian draws the conclusion: "It was these political conditions that necessitated the dogma of papal infallibility for the same reason that the political conditions of the eleventh century necessitated the papal decree on lay investiture: The liberty of the church was at stake."[60]

Here in the text of *Pastor Aeternus* the implication seems to be that such consequent assent is unnecessary since the prior consultation with the episcopate would have taken place, thus making consequent assent redundant. It was generally assumed that no pope would proceed with an infallible definition without consulting the church, as in fact Pope Pius IX had done prior to his definition of the dogma of the Immaculate Conception of the Blessed Virgin Mary in 1854. As E. E. Y. Hales wrote: "It was, indeed unthinkable that [the pope] should do otherwise. But no wording to this effect was put into the definition."[61] That is exactly correct. If the popularly misconceived position of the pope as wrapped up in his own autonomous infallibility were in fact the correct understanding and interpretation, it would nullify the episcopate. Bishop Connolly of Nova Scotia certainly had it right when he remarked in his very un-Ciceronian Latin that "*iuxta schema, omnes episcopi ecclesiae aequivalent zero,*" "according to this scheme, all the bishops of the church are equal to zero."[62]

Theological clarification from the pens of theologian and commentators is abundant, but the viewpoint of F. X. Lawlor in the former edition of the *New Catholic Encyclopedia* (and reissued in the enlarged second edition) is especially clear on this important point. Lawlor writes:

---

60. Bokenkotter, *A Concise History of the Catholic Church*, 326.
61. Hales, *Pio Nono*, 309.
62. Cited in Sweeney, "The Forgotten Council," 163.

The pope's juridic autonomy does not entail discommunity or isolation; his juridic independence is never a solitary independence. He always acts as part of the Body, in the sense that he always acts within a meta-juridic community of life, based on the fact that the Spirit assumes a continuum of faith both lived and taught between the Roman Pontiff and his fellow believers in the church and his fellow bishops in the episcopate.[63]

It would be difficult to better this clarification.

Critics of papal infallibility point to the fact that this way of understanding is not formally explicit in the text of *Pastor Aeternus*. While that may be true, the theological datum and context explicated by Lawlor, and indeed accepted probably by the majority of Catholic ecclesiologists, give a sense of balance. Without this balancing context, papal infallibility loses its fundamental *raison d'être*, service of the church. It is this service to the church, a service in, with, and for the church that is the very hallmark of papal infallibility. The point has been grasped so well by Garrett Sweeney when he writes:

> Far from overwhelming every other authority, the papal prerogative remained obstinately dormant: to be aroused (if indeed it was then aroused) only for a brief moment in 1954 the definition of the Assumption. But this restraint can be interpreted neither as accidental nor as due to papal distrust of its own powers. It must be seen rather as the observance of built-in obligations never indeed defined, but recognized explicitly by the Conciliar Fathers as limiting the action of the papacy to rare and exceptional locations.[64]

Having acknowledged the importance of these hermeneutical principles for understanding papal infallibility, it still seems clear that this is far from the popular understanding. At the popular level, and included here is the perception of many of the clergy, there is much misunderstanding, captured accurately by one historian as follows:

> Once the council was over, misunderstanding was widespread. Most people understood it to have defined not the irreformability of papal definitions but papal infallibility, not the infallibility of the church as the basis of papal teaching authority, but papal teaching authority as the source of infallibility, and not the right and

---

63. Lawlor, "Infallibility," 7:450. The same basic perspective is provided by Quinn, *Revered and Reviled*, 55–78.

64. Sweeney, "The Forgotten Council," 163–64.

responsibility of the bishops to govern and teach their dioceses, but the power of the Pope to teach and direct everyone, starting with the bishops.[65]

THE PROMULGATION OF PASTOR AETERNUS

The Revd Thomas Mozley, Anglican priest, brother-in-law of John Henry Newman, and correspondent for the London *Times*—and, moreover, who knew no Italian or French and was dependent on hearsay for most of his reportage—describes the thunderstorm during which the vote was taken on *Pastor Aeternus*.

> The storm, which had been threatening all the morning, burst now with the utmost violence, and to many a superstitious mind might have conveyed the idea that it was an expression of divine wrath, as "no doubt it will be interpreted by numbers," said one officer of the Palatine Guard. And so the "placets" [positive votes] of the fathers struggled through the storm, while the thunder pealed above and the lightning flashed in at every window and down through the dome and every smaller cupola, dividing if not absorbing the attention of the crowd. "Placet," shouted his Eminence or his Grace, and a loud clap of thunder followed in response, and then the lightning darted about the baldachino and every part of the church and the conciliar hall, as if announcing the response.[66]

Critics took this as a sign of God's anger. Not Archbishop Manning, who said, "They forgot Sinai and the Ten Commandments."[67]

Sixty-one fathers submitted written protests against the definitions and left wrong on the eve of the solemn promulgation, although they accepted it once it had been passed. The two bishops who voted against it, Luigi Riccio of Caiazzo, Italy, and Edward Fitzgerald of Little Rock, Arkansas, accepted the definitions right away.

---

65. Heft, "From the Pope to the Bishops," 61.
66. Cited in Butler, *The Vatican Council*, 2:123.
67. Cited in Duffy, *Saints and Sinners*, 301.

CONCLUSION

The day following the definition of infallibility, war was declared between Prussia and France, effectively bringing the Council prematurely to an end. The French needed all their military, and so the French garrison in Rome, guaranteeing papal independence and protection, was withdrawn almost immediately. Within a month King Victor Emmanuel invaded the Papal States. Rome fell to his troops on September 20, and Pius became the "prisoner" of the Vatican. On October 20, Pius IX issued an apostolic letter suspending the Council indefinitely.

No bishop left the church over the papal definitions. By the end of 1870, almost all the French bishops who had opposed infallibility had accepted it, and signified that acceptance by letter to the Pope, by a pastoral letter, or by some other means of promulgating the conciliar decree in their individual dioceses.[68] Dom Cuthbert Butler says of the anti-infallibilist bishops, "It is not to be supposed that the submission of faith came automatically or easily.... There was a period of hesitation and interior struggle and conflict that had to be battled through, before Catholic principle came out victorious over private judgment."[69] While extreme ultramontanes like Archbishop Manning sought the most aggressive interpretation of *Pastor Aeternus*, not every bishop thought or acted in this way. The English bishops, for example, did not issue a joint pastoral letter on Vatican I until their Low Week meeting of 1875, five years later. What they came up with on that occasion was essentially an acknowledgment of the rights of local bishops. A bishop was not simply a papal vicar.

Although no bishop left the church, a number of theologians were excommunicated or left the church of their own accord. The German theologian Johann Friedrich left and with his followers formed the schismatic group known as the Old Catholics. Ignaz Döllinger, the German theologian, historian, and friend of the late Johann Adam Möhler, and teacher of Lord Acton, could not accept the definition of infallibility, despite the gentle encouragement and sensitivity of his ordinary, Archbishop Gregor von Scherr of Munich, and so incurred excommunication.

It is sometimes suggested that Pope Pius IX promised preferment to those who engineered and lobbied for the definition of papal infallibility, but this seems most implausible. No one was made a cardinal for three

---

68. Butler, *The Vatican Council*, 2:171.
69. Butler, *The Vatican Council*, 2:187.

years after the Council, and then it was roughly equal between pro- and anti-infallibilist bishops. Archbishop Manning, for example, "to whom the pope was most indebted, and who had succeeded Cardinal Wiseman in 1865 as Archbishop of Westminster, was not elevated to the purple until 1875."[70]

Nonetheless, something happened at Vatican I in terms of infallibility that was not especially healthy or wholesome. A broad-based failure throughout the entire Catholic world to understand the intricacies of the issue led to an excessive focusing on the papacy, and to regarding ordinary papal teaching as bordering on infallibility, if not, indeed, latently infallible. Again, Garrett Sweeney with a sense of humor puts it right: "There may at least be a suspicion that the faithful have been trained for a hundred years to shop for nothing but Instant Infallibility from a permanently Infallible Pope, and now find that the stock has been sold out and the shelves are bare." Sweeney was writing in the wake of the encyclical *Humanae Vitae* in 1968. How might the situation be ameliorated?

> Can a recovery of the history of Vatican I help towards a renewal of this devotion to the Chair of Peter? Negatively: yes—in so far as it clears away misconceptions and allows it to be seen that infallible definitions are the least important role of a teaching papacy. History bears out the teaching of Vatican I but such definitions are the last desperate resort of the faithful when all other means of authentification have failed.[71]

Bishop Ullathorne, Newman's own bishop in England, desired him to go to Rome as a consultor on the commission that was preparing for the Vatican Council. Newman, of course, did not go to the Council. He was working on his major work *The Grammar of Assent*, which was published in March 1870. Five years later he would bring out another publication with the title *Letter to the Duke of Norfolk*. This letter, addressed to the premier Catholic layman of England, was intended to sort out some of the confusion that surrounded infallibility. It was Newman's response to a pamphlet of Gladstone against the papacy entitled *The Vatican Decrees in Their Bearing on Civil Allegiance*. Newman is very clear that he believes in infallibility, and infallibility that touches religion only and not science, and an infallibility that safeguards theological truth. In that very precise sense, authority can never usurp the place of the individual conscience. Newman

---

70. Hales, *Pio Nono*, 312.
71. Sweeney, "The Forgotten Council," 172–73.

once wrote famously: "If I am obliged to bring religion into after-dinner toasts (which indeed does not seem quite the thing) I shall drink—to the Pope if you please—still to Conscience first, and to the Pope afterwards."[72] Newman really did not have any doubts about papal infallibility, but he was concerned about its conciliar definition, especially because of the misunderstandings to which it could give rise. He wrote to one who was troubled by the definition as follows, indicating the importance of historical perspective: "If you look into history, you find popes continually completing the acts of their predecessors, and councils too—sometimes only half the truth is brought out at one time—I doubt not a coming Pope, or a coming Council, will so explain and guard what has now been passed by [the] late Council, as to clear up all that troubles us now."[73]

As Ian Ker points out, "This is a remarkable prophecy of the Second Vatican Council."[74]

---

72. Newman, *Difficulties of Anglicans*, 261.
73. Cited in Strange, *Newman 101*, 53.
74. Ker, *Newman on Vatican II*, 74–75.

8

Newman the Poet

Faith can be stifled by mere prose: it needs some touch of poetry to find its fire.

Michael Paul Gallagher, SJ[1]

Religious communication generally must overcome a long addiction to the discursive, the rationalistic, and the prosaic.

Amos Wilder[2]

In November 1828, Newman wrote an essay on poetry for a periodical, *The London Review*. In that essay, entitled "Poetry with Reference to Aristotle's Poetics," we find the following passage:

> With Christians, a point of view of things is a duty—we are to color all things with hues of faith, to see a divine meaning in every event, and a superhuman tendency.... It may be added, that the virtues peculiarly Christian are especially poetic—meekness, gentleness, compassion, contentment, modesty, not to mention the devotional virtues; whereas the router and more ordinary feelings are the instruments of rhetoric more justly than of poetry—anger, indignation, emulation, martial spirit and love of independence.[3]

---

1. Gallagher, SJ, *Dive Deeper*, 1.
2. Wilder, *Theopoetic: Theology and the Religious Imagination*, 1.
3. Cited in Tristram, *John Henry Newman, Autobiographical Writings*, 246.

Every Christian then, for Newman, is a sort of poet, and Newman himself certainly was, being a man of imagination and metaphor. He wrote poetically. "Supremely literary among English theologians of the nineteenth century, Newman had no aptitude for the abstractions of metaphysics, the severe disciplines of syllogistic logic, the arid prose of stock theological manuals. His preference across the entire corpus of his writing is for feeling, concrete language, irony, satire, the dynamism of metaphor."[4]

Very few of the many words penned by John Henry Newman have been set to music. Three compositions, however, have become universally popular in the Christian world: "Lead, Kindly Light," "Firmly I Believe and Truly," and "Praise to the Holiest in the Height." The first stands on its own. The other two are taken from "The Dream of Gerontius." These two poetic pieces, "Lead, Kindly Light" and "The Dream of Gerontius" represent the very best of Newman as a poet. Indeed, apropos of "Lead, Kindly Light" Hilda Graef opines that "All the spirituality of the maturing Newman is in these lines."[5]

At the time of his Mediterranean trip with Hurrell Froude and his archdeacon father, Newman was not in a good place. Historian Hilary Jenkins is helpful in describing his situation:

> Newman was scarred by his experience of life. . . . We can recognize major deprivations, first, he had been deprived of his childhood happiness at Ham when the family suffered from his father's bankruptcy; second he had been brutally deprived through the death of his much loved sister Mary; third, he had felt deprived of his chosen career at Oriel in the defeat of his tutorial policy, which he bitterly resented. . . . The fact that these sadnesses were borne in a Christian manner and did not embitter him in the conventional sense may be the obverse of a pattern confirming his rejection of life as essentially desolate.[6]

A very bleak description, and perhaps too bleak on Jenkins's part. However, there seems little doubt that Newman went through a period of desolation at the time of the Mediterranean journey, even if he could not quite put those words of Jenkins on it. He needed rest and recovery from the ordinary trials and tribulations of life. He was as we should say today seriously

---

4. Cornwell, *Newman's Unquiet Grave*, 173.
5. Graef, *God and Myself*, 45.
6. Jenkins, "The Meaning of the Lyra Apostolica and the Genesis of 'Lead, Kindly Light,'" 134.

depressed. He needed a breathing space to find himself and to re-direct the course of his life. The external journey of the voyage might hold out hope for an internal journey of self-rediscovery and renewal.

THE MEDITERRANEAN JOURNEY

On December 8, 1832, Newman left Falmouth in England with his close friend Hurrell Froude and his father, Archdeacon Froude, for a journey to the Mediterranean, a journey that was to last some seven months. Hurrell Froude was ill, an illness from which he would never recover, but the medical wisdom of the time recommended a warmer climate. He invited Newman along, as his best friend. It was Newman's first trip outside England. It brought them into very close encounters with Catholicism, eliciting from him both positive and negative thoughts of the church. Louis Bouyer, the French Oratorian, writes so descriptively of Newman's attitude to the mainly Catholic Mediterranean people's offensiveness:

> Revolting filth, beggars pushing their way everywhere, sloth, dishonesty—all these shocked [him] as they were calculated to shock any average Anglo-Saxon and tourist. Nevertheless, [he] did not fail to detect innumerable evidences of kindliness and humanity. But the basis of their religion seemed on the whole to be a form of idolatry that had virtually no connection whatever with righteous living.[7]

Newman was conflicted about Catholicism. He appreciated the historic expression of Catholicism throughout his travels in the churches, monasteries, art, and so forth, but found the popular religious expression of the faith repulsive. He thought of Catholic devotions in his typical English way as superstitious. He was scandalized that priests roaring with laughter in the confessionals in Naples.

During his months abroad, Newman wrote many letters to his family and friends, letters that are not particularly significant, describing as they do the various places he visited and experiences he had, typical tourist letters. However, he also wrote verse, and the verse was more revealing of the inner journey that Newman was undertaking. There were many such verses that have come to be known collectively as the *Lyra Apostolica*. The English literary critic Roger Sharrock makes an interesting remark of these

---

7. Bouyer, *Newman, His Life and Spirituality*, 135.

Mediterranean poems: "The steady flow of poems on the Mediterranean journey may have been partly due to an effort to relieve the tedium of a long voyage. But once Newman got into the vein there is no doubt that a serious part of his mind became engaged by the contemplation of a distant England under the sway of liberalism"[8] With more time on his hands than he had ever experienced before, Sharrock implies, Newman turned to writing poetry. The poems provide commentary on how he saw the state of the Church of England now that he was geographically removed. The church, due to forces both within and without, was undergoing a forced process of liberalism, but more of that later when we turn to comment on "The Pillar of the Cloud." At the same time, the poems provide a sort of window into Newman's soul. "The verses . . . are significant in revealing the spiritual purification and development he underwent which gave meaning to the entire journey, ending in a conviction that God had a work for him to do in England."[9]

Both at the actual time and later through a series of recountings of what had occurred, Newman came to understand the fearful experience of the illness that befell him in Sicily and his recovery as a providential sign that he must re-order the course of his life.[10] But that did not happen immediately. On April 9, his companions, the Froudes, left to return to England, but Newman remained behind. He wanted to re-visit Sicily on his own, though his friends had cautioned against it. After a few days in Naples, he sailed for Sicily.

He arrived at Messina on April 21 with his Neapolitan servant Gennaro. On April 30, he experienced a fever, but felt better the next day so that he set off again, arriving at the town of Leonforte on May 3. There he succumbed in all probability to typhoid. The servant accompanying Newman, Gennaro, thought his master was on the point of death. Confined to bed with the illness, Newman found himself constantly saying to himself, "I have not sinned against the light." This sinning against the light may have been immediately a self-reflection on not taking the advice of the Froudes about the Sicilian trip. Could it have been more?

Just before leaving Oxford to join the Froudes for the trip, Newman preached a sermon, his ninth University sermon, entitled "Willfulness, the Sin of Saul." It was fresh in his mind. Was Newman willful? He thought of

---

8. Sharrock, "Newman's Poetry," 50–51.
9. Blehl, *Pilgrim Journey, John Henry Newman 1801–1845*, 114.
10. Turner, *John Henry Newman*, 153.

the disrespect he had expressed towards his superior, the Provost Edward Hawkins of Oriel College, with whom he had seriously disagreed over educational and theological matters to the point where Hawkins disallowed him any more students. Newman thought he might have received Holy Communion unworthily because he cherished in his heart a measure of resentment against Hawkins, who effectively had deprived him of his tutorship at Oxford: "At the time I was deeply impressed with a feeling that it was a judgment for profaning the Lord's Supper, in having cherished some resentment against the Provost for putting me out of the tutorship."[11] Could there have been more?

Feeling somewhat better, he set off with Gennaro from Leonforte, but, after walking about seven miles, he collapsed. Subsequently, Newman was taken to a house and cared for over the next three weeks both by a local medical doctor and Gennaro, with the latter sleeping in the same room as Newman who feared being left alone. As the crisis passed, Newman longed for the light of day, and when it came through the shutters in the room, he responded, "O sweet light, God's best gift."[12] Finally, when the fever was spent, Newman moved on by carriage towards Palermo. He was still very weak and unable to walk on his own and about May 26 or 27 found him "profusely weeping, and only able to say that I could not help thinking God has something for me to do at home."[13] It was time to go home.

On June 13, Newman sailed from Palermo on an orange boat bound for Marseilles. The boat found itself in a calm in the Straits of Bonifacio, and it was here at sea on June 16 that Newman wrote his "The Pillar of the Cloud." After arriving at Marseilles on June 27, he traveled through France, across the English Channel, and arrived back in England on July 8. It is fanciful to delve too deeply into Newman psychology, but the Newman scholar Joyce Sugg, in a popular little book, may have captured the heart of the "something more" that failed him when she says: "He went down even further into his past actions and motives, and saw his own 'utter hollowness.' The fever was not clouding his mind at that moment; indeed, he felt that he was seeing himself more clearly than ever before. He was sorry and ashamed."[14]

---

11. Tristram, *John Henry Newman, Autobiographical Writings*, 122.
12. Blehl, *Pilgrim Journey, John Henry Newman 1801–1845*, 125.
13. Tristram, *John Henry Newman, Autobiographical Writings*, 122.
14. Sugg, *Snapdragon: The Story of John Henry Newman*, 57.

"THE PILLAR OF THE CLOUD"

The title of the poem comes from the Book of Exodus. Hilary Jenkins, echoing the sentiments of the consensus of Newman scholars, says: "It is a peculiarity of Newman's literary genius that he should write such clear poetic prose and be such a bad poet.... The prose can sing, the choice of words seems to be ordained, but the verse so often falls flat."[15] The one exception Jenkins notes to this judgment of Newman's poetry in the *Lyra Apostolica* is this poem entitled "The Pillar of the Cloud," best known in English from its opening line, "Lead, Kindly Light." It is Newman's "one immortal song."[16] The poem was so personal to Newman that it seems never to have been sung in the Birmingham Oratory during his lifetime.

> *Lead, kindly Light amid the encircling gloom*
> *Lead Thou me on!*
> *The night is dark, and I am far from home—*
> *Lead Thou me on!*
> *Keep Thou my feet; I do not ask to see*
> *The distant scene—one step enough for me.*
> *I was not ever thus, nor pray'd that Thou*
> *Shouldst lead me on.*
> *I loved to choose and see my path, but now*
> *Lead Thou me on!*
> *I loved the garish day, and spite of fears,*
> *Pride ruled my will; remember not to past years.*
> *So long Thy power hath blest me, sure it still*
> *Will lead me on,*
> *O'er moor and fen, o'er crag and torrent, till*
> *The night is gone;*
> *And with the morn those angel faces smile*
> *Which I have loved long since, and lost awhile.*

STANZA 1

In this first stanza, Newman asks God, the "kindly Light," to lead him on. "Lead Thou me on," occurs three times in the poem. It is a prayer trusting in God's kindly providence, to lead Newman on through the tumult of life. He

---

15. Jenkins, "The Meaning of the Lyra Apostolica and the Genesis of 'Lead, Kindly Light,'" 117.

16. Honan, "Newman's Poetry," 92.

acknowledges that he is far from home. He looks for small steps forward, "one step enough for me." Home is England, yes, but home is also heaven. Life is like a dark journey, like the journey of the ancient Hebrews from slavery in Egypt to their "homeland" flowing with milk and honey. In the Book of Exodus, we read: "The LORD went in front of them in a pillar of cloud by day, to lead them along the way, and in a pillar of fire by night, to give them light, so that they might travel by day and by night" (Exodus 13:21). And so, Joyce Sugg comments: "We are like the Israelites released from Egypt, struggling on through the wilderness towards the promised land, weary and homesick, but at peace because God is leading us."[17]

He names the darkness in which he finds himself, "the encircling gloom." This is a complex issue, reflecting Newman's illness and undoubted depression but perhaps also his fear of what he called "Liberalism," "the mechanical, mathematical, ecologically disastrous spirit of a disenchanted new order."[18] This new order, descended from the 1789 French Revolution with its proclamation of "liberty, equality, fraternity," had disastrous results as far as Newman was concerned. Gloom, as Newman saw it, abounded socially, politically, and religiously. Liberalism affected religion and the church. A liberal religious spirit wasn't broad that would even be willing to concede Catholic Emancipation in 1829! The great educationist, Thomas Arnold, headmaster of the Rugby School, had called for a comprehensiveness in religion, a coming together of all the denominations, but of course, without Roman Catholics and Quakers. Newman saw this "ecumenical" proposal as monstrous. He was afraid that in this temper the Church of England might very well be disestablished, finally demonstrating the victory of liberal thinking to the detriment of the church and its witness in the nation. Life as he understood and experienced it was gloomy indeed. What was the next step for the church? What was the next step for himself? Newman did not know, but he knew that, as in Exodus, in the "pillar of cloud" and the "pillar of fire" the Lord was going in front of him.

STANZA 2

Having trustingly asked God to lead him on, Newman now confesses his sins. Past years had demonstrated perhaps a degree of complacency with

17. Sugg, *Snapdragon: The Story of John Henry Newman*, 61.
18. Jenkins, "The Meaning of the Lyra Apostolica and the Genesis of 'Lead, Kindly Light,'" 126.

his life, especially his life in the church. Newman was well known. He had cut quite an impressive figure at Oxford. He loved "the garish day." He was proud. Hilda Graef points out what might have been ailing Newman. "There are temptations of the spirit, an inordinate longing for fame, for surpassing everyone else in one's work, coupled with equally inordinate depressions if anything goes wrong, if one does not reach the top of the ladder. It seems that young Newman was aware that this pride was his chief personal temptation."[19] The Sicilian illness, however, had laid him low. Newman seems to confess in the words "I was not ever thus" that he was not always able to see God's holy yet mysterious presence in his life, inviting him to flourish through a gentle but confident submission, a submission that in its very submitting is far from passive. Newman was marked by a constant and vivid sense of living in God's presence, but his Sicilian illness brought about a match-deepened awareness of this presence. This is how the Newman scholar Roderick Strange puts it: "[Newman's] perilous condition brought about a revelation of divine presence.... His declining fortunes... may all have combined, even in him whose sense of God's presence was so vivid, to dim his awareness of that presence. The illness revived it."[20]

STANZA 3

This last stanza has been described as "magically beautiful."[21] Now, aware of God's providential presence as never before, he moves into the unknown future with confident hope. The "kindly Light" will continue to lead him on. This is realist verse. Newman had traveled on a mule through the mountains of Sicily, a tough and dangerous journey over "moor and fen, crag and torrent." The physical dangers were all too real, not least his illness. But God has been with him, and God will lead him on "till the night is gone." That "night" is the gloom of the first stanza—the circumstantial gloom of the Church of England and his own existential gloom. He is full of hope as he waits for the night to pass and the "morn" to arrive.

The loss in death of his sister Mary had a powerful impact on Newman. They shared a strong and intimate bond in the family. Some weeks after Mary's very sudden death, Newman wrote these words of his experience during a horseback journey, the short ride between Oxford and the village

19. Graef, *God and Myself*, 19.
20. Strange, "'A Strange Providence': Newman's Illness in Sicily," 127.
21. Honan, "Newman's Poetry," 92.

of Cuddesdon, just north of the city. In a letter to his sister Jemima of May 10, 1828, he wrote: "Dear Mary seems embodied in every tree and hid behind every hill. What a veil and curtain this world of sense is! Beautiful, but still a veil!"[22] Louis Bouyer thinks that Mary was in Newman's mind when he penned the last two lines of the poem, that she was the first of "those angel faces, loved long since and lost awhile."[23] It may also be the case that he was thinking, too, of the home he first remembered, the garden at Ham, "where as a child he thought that angel faces were all around him."[24]

So many others in Victorian England found real solace in this poem, including Queen Victoria herself to whom it was read as she lay dying. It may be, thinks Hilary Jenkins, that the last words she heard on earth were:

So long Thy power has blest me, sure it still
Will lead me on.

Mrs. Tait, wife of the Anglican Bishop of London and later Archbishop of Canterbury, lost five children in death in 1856. Beneath the framed picture of her children were the words:

And with the morn those angel faces smile,
That I have loved long since and lost awhile.[25]

"The Pillar of the Cloud" was set to music by John B. Dykes (1823–76) thirty-two years after it was written. It is simply splendid. Newman in point of fact attributed the popularity of the poem to Dykes's musical rendition. While there is something in that, it nonetheless remains true that the poem captivates because it *is* John Henry Newman. Not only is it Newman, but it is also ourselves, as we allow it to penetrate our thoughts before God, the kindly Light, who is leading us too through life "till the night is gone."

"THE DREAM OF GERONTIUS"

I believe that the very best way into "The Dream of Gerontius" is to listen to the entirety of the Sir Edward Elgar composition with the text of "The

---

22. Cited in Jenkins, "The Meaning of the Lyra Apostolica and the Genesis of 'Lead, Kindly Light,'" 119.
23. Bouyer, *Newman, His Life and Spirituality*, 217.
24. Sugg, *Snapdragon: The Story of John Henry Newman*, 61.
25. Jenkins, "The Meaning of the Lyra Apostolica and the Genesis of 'Lead, Kindly Light,'" 117–18.

Dream" in front of you. If this chapter leads the reader to Elgar's music, to Newman's text, and then to personal prayer the author will be well pleased.

> There is a presence that walks the road of life with you. This presence accompanies your every moment. It shadows your every thought and feeling. On your own, or with others it is always there with you. When you were born, it came out of the womb with you, with the excitement at your arrival, and nobody noticed it. Though this presence surrounds you, you may still be blind to its companionship. The name of this presence is death.[26]

These are the words of the Irish philosophical-theologian and poet, John O'Donohue. The sentiments expressed in the words initially may sound strange, but they should not be alien to the Christian. Think, for example, of St. Francis of Assisi, who speaks of death as "Sister Death." In "The Canticle of Brother Sun," Francis wrote: "Praised be You, my Lord, through our Sister Bodily Death." Of course, we do not always get on terribly well with our siblings. Sister Death may be one of the siblings we should like to keep at as far a distance as possible. But it isn't possible. A time will come, morning or evening, day or night, when each of us will have to die. The great insight of St. Francis is that death is "neither an enemy to be overcome nor a fate to be accepted but rather a friend, a kinsman, to be received with all courtesy."[27] It is about making death a friend, strange though the language sounds. Making death a friend is of great benefit and importance. "To continually transfigure the faces of your own death ensures that at the end of your life, your physical death will be no stranger, robbing you against your will of the life that you have had; you will know its face intimately. Since you have overcome your fear, your death will be a meeting with a lifelong friend from the deepest side of your own nature."[28] This is part of what John Henry Newman was writing about in his epic poem, "The Dream of Gerontius."[29] It is his vision of what death and what happens afterwards ought to be like for a Christian.

While Newman's vision in the Dream is enormously hopeful, as we shall see, it is not a romantic vision. He realizes all too well the ambiguity that surrounds death and dying, but equally well he refuses to concede

---

26. O'Donohue, ODC, *Anam Chara*, 187.
27. O'Donoghue, ODC, *The Holy Mountain: Approaches to the Mystery of Prayer*, 142.
28. O'Donohue, ODC, *The Holy Mountain: Approaches to the Mystery of Prayer*, 187.
29. The text of the "Dream" is public domain, and is available in a wide variety of sources.

ultimacy to that ambiguity. Newman's Gerontius moves from an understandable fear to serenity and joy. That is the way it should be, especially for a Christian. Nevertheless, one can understand this fundamental ambiguity about death and dying. On the one hand, it is the end of life as we know it in this world, the severing of relationships, business left undone. One author, speaking of the Shoah and its devastation, writes: "[Those who died in the Holocaust] were torn from mistakes they had no chance to fix; everything unfinished. All the sins of love without detail, detail without love. The regret of having spoken, of having run out of time so to speak. Of hoarding oneself. Of turning one's back too often in favour of sleep."[30] On the other hand, Christians believe that death is the portal through which we go home to the Father's house, our entry point into full communion with God.

In 1864, Newman wrote his *Apologia pro Vita Sua*. The book is autobiographical in style and provides an account of Newman's growth and development in his spiritual and religious life. It was a turbulent period in Newman's life, and he seems to have had a vivid sense of his own impending death. This is the context in which "The Dream of Gerontius" was written. It was written over a period of three brief weeks and was published in the periodical *The Month* in May and June 1865. Newman's method was to labor over his prose, revising and revising and revising. This text, however, seems to have sprung from deep in his soul, having taken root there over the years. A friend of Newman's, Thomas William Allies, had attended an acted performance of the "Dream" in Liverpool, at a teacher-training college, and he wrote to tell Newman about it. This is how Newman describes the writing of the "Dream" by way of reply to Mr. Allies: "On the 17th of January last it came into my head to write it. I cannot really tell how, and I wrote on till it was finished, on small bits of paper."[31]

It describes the time, if time is indeed the right word, between dying and coming before God in judgment. It paints a picture of the ideal Christian death, with the dying man being surrounded and supported in his final agony by his friends. Newman's gift for lasting friendships is well known. However, there may be another nuance to this picture. It may be literally quite true. All around the wall near Newman's bed in the Oratory in Birmingham were pictures of his friends.

---

30. Michaels, *Fugitive Pieces*, 147.
31. Dessain, et al., *Letters and Diaries*, vol. 22, 72.

The poem is about the dying of an elderly Christian, Gerontius. The word *geron* in Greek means "an old man." The poem begins with these extraordinarily moving words:

> *Jesu, Maria—I am near to death,*
> *And thou art calling me; I know it now.*
> *Not by the token of this faltering breath,*
> *This chill at heart, this dampness on my brow,*
> *Jesu, have mercy! Mary, pray for me!*
> *'Tis this new feeling, never felt before,*
> *Be with me, Lord, in my extremity!*
> *That I am going, that I am no more.*

Gerontius has been sick before, but this is a new feeling "never felt before." The moment of dying is described as follows:

> *As though my very being had given way,*
> *As though I was no more a substance now,*
> *And could fall back on nought to be my stay . . .*
> *And drop from out this universal frame*
> *Into that shapeless, scopeless, blank abyss,*
> *That utter nothingness, of which I came.*

Newman's description is so vivid and so intense in this passage of the "Dream," that it leads one to surmise that perhaps he had an experience—an experience of mortality, or some kind of spiritual experience—that enabled him to reach this expression in the poem. This description of emptiness is followed by the prayers of the assistants, those at his bedside, and then Gerontius makes his statement of faith:

> *And I hold in veneration,*
> *For the love of Him alone,*
> *Holy Church, as His creation,*
> *And her teachings, as His own.*
> *And I take with joy whatever*
> *Now besets me, pain or fear,*
> *And with a strong will I sever*
> *All the ties which bind me here.*

This is a powerful confession of faith, which ties together his love of God with his love of the church and her teachings. He emphasizes that he "takes with joy" whatever now he is to experience. Finally, and this is very strong language, he severs "all the ties which bind him here." It is indeed a very powerful confession of his Christian faith. Yet it does not save him from the terror of death. Gerontius goes on to say:

> *For now it comes again,*
> *That sense of ruin, which is worse than pain,*
> *That masterful negation and collapse*
> *Of all that makes me man.*

His very existence, his humanity is collapsing, is being negated, as it were, by his dying and death. He is, in his own words, "falling through the solid framework of created things." Once again, the assistants pray for Gerontius, he commends himself into the hands of God, like Jesus in St. Luke's Gospel—"into thy hands I commend my spirit"—and the priest prays that wonderful prayer for the dying: "Go forth upon thy journey, Christian soul! Go from this world! Go, in the name of God." Hearing this confident prayer, Gerontius dies. Immediately the text continues as follows:

> *I went to sleep; and now I am refreshed.*
> *A strange refreshment: for I feel in me*
> *An inexpressive lightness, and a sense*
> *Of freedom, as I were at length myself,*
> *And ne'er had been before. How still it is!*

The soul of Gerontius leaves this world, and is aware of leaving this world:

> *So much I know, not knowing how I know,*
> *That the vast universe, where I have dwelt,*
> *Is quitting me, or I am quitting it.*

At this point, the soul feels companionship. He is not alone. His guardian angel is helping him move forward, and has come to take his soul home to the house of God.

> *Someone has me fast*
> *Within his ample palm.*
> The soul of Gerontius speaks to his guardian angel:
> *Why have I now no fear at meeting [God]?*
> *Along my earthly life, the thought of death*
> *And judgment was to me most terrible . . .*
> *Now that the hour is come, my fear is fled . . .*
> *Now close upon me, I can forward look*
> *With a serenest joy.*

At this point the demons come into play, demons described as having "an animal vulgarity" as they jeer at the passing of Gerontius. Whatever one makes of these demons, it may at least be claimed that they stand for the final residue of fear, doubt, and ambiguity in the face of death.

As his natural fear of dying and death is left behind, his guardian angel carries him forward towards God, and his experience is one of joy. There is no fear. Gerontius now hears "The First Choir of the Evangelicals" singing that marvelous hymn:

> *Praise to the Holiest in the height,*
> *And in the depth be praise:*
> *In all His words most wonderful;*
> *Most sure in all His ways!*

Gerontius now enters the house of judgment. The judgment, however, comes from one whose best name is Love. There is no room for fear. Once again he hears the hymn from "The Second Choir of Evangelicals," and "The Third Choir of Evangelicals," "Praise to the Holiest in the height." His guardian angel explains to him that these evangelical choirs "sing of thy approaching agony." What agony is being spoken of here? It is the agony of seeing the God who is Love with a simultaneous recognition that one is so unlovely.

> *What then—if such thy lot—thou seest thy Judge . . .*
> *Thou wilt be sick with love, and yearn for him . . .*
> *There is a pleading in his pensive eyes*
> *Will pierce thee to the quick, and trouble thee.*
> *And thou wilt hate and loathe thyself; for though*
> *Now sinless, thou wilt feel that thou hast sinn'd*
> *As never thou didst feel; and wilt desire*
> *To slink away, and hide thee from his sight . . .*
> *The shame of self at thought of seeing Him—*
> *Will be thy veriest, sharpest purgatory.*

These words immediately bring to my mind the eucharistic words of the priest poet George Herbert:

> *Love bade me welcome*
> *Yet my soul drew back guilty of dust and sin.*

I am unclear if Newman was aware of this poem, but whether he was or not, the sentiments are identical. The pain of purgatory is not some external pain inflicted upon the soul. The pain of purgatory is the recognition in the presence of Love that one is not lovely. The pain of purgatory is the intense pain of regret that one has not lived a life of love.

The intensity of purgatorial regret is expressed by Newman through Gerontius in the following words spoken by the soul to his guardian angel:

> *Take me away, and in the lowest deep*
> *There let me be,*
> *And there in hope the lone night-watches keep . . .*

The soul desires to move away out of a most profound sense of utter unworthiness from the presence of the God who is Love. "Take me away . . . let me be." The guardian angel who has accompanied Gerontius thus far recognizes the importance of this cleansing moment, this most intense moment of deepest regret. Gerontius feels his sinfulness. It is an immediate feeling on coming into God's loving presence. The soul is learning that

> *The flame of Everlasting Love*
> *Doth burn ere it transform.*

"Purgatory," as Paul McPartlan rightly has it, "is the state of grace where the process of *Christification* can be perfected."[32] It is heaven's door, not hell's threshold. Nonetheless, it takes time, as it were, to be cleansed. The angel says to the soul:

> *Softly and gently, dearest, sweetest soul,*
> *In my most loving arms I now enfold thee,*
> *And, o'er the penal waters, as they roll,*
> *I poise thee, and I lower thee, and hold thee.*
> *And carefully I dip thee in the lake . . .*
> *Farewell, but not forever! brother dear,*
> *Be brave and patient on thy bed of sorrow;*
> *Swiftly shall pass thy night of trial here,*
> *And I will come and wake thee on the morrow.*

The guardian angel also tells the soul that it will be nursed and tended by angels during this purgatorial moment. It will not be left alone. Purgatory is described in this section of the "Dream" almost like a mystical state. What is the time that it takes for this cleansing to occur? "Time" seems a strange word to use now that time is over for the soul who has left this life. This time of cleansing is best understood as instantaneous. Coming before the God who is nothing but unconditional Love, one comes to understand

---

32. McPartlan, "Go Forth, Christian Soul," 248.

that one has been anything but unconditional love in the living of one's life. That is the "moment" of cleansing pain, the pain of regret, the searing pain of recognizing that one cannot return to the pilgrimage on earth to undo what one ought not to have done. Nothing could hurt more, but the hurt is the consequence of the final realization that God is Love. The passage also sounds like the rite of baptism—the soul is dipped into the lake of baptism, as it were, before being finalized as Body of Christ, in God.

Newman lived through the First Vatican Council (1869–70), but the Second Vatican Council (1962–65) has been called Newman's Council. The revised liturgical rites of the church that flowed from that council have, for the most part, been well received by the faithful throughout the world. If we leaf through the Rites for the Commendation of the Dying, we find a horizon of understanding that is truly Catholic, and so truly Newman's, as it were. In writing the "Dream," Newman reworked an ancient Latin prayer, the *Profiscere*, the first words of which are: "Go forth, Christian soul." The new rite includes a formulation of this prayer. But before we get to it, we need to acknowledge the beginning of the rite. The rite says this: "One or more of the following short texts may be recited with the dying person. If necessary, they may be softly repeated two or three times." Here are some of those short scriptural texts:

> "Who can separate us from the love of Christ?" (Romans 8:35).
> "Whether we live or die, we are the Lord's." (Romans 14:8).
> "We have an everlasting home in heaven." (2 Corinthians 5:1).
> "We shall be with the Lord forever." (1 Thessalonians 4:17).
> "We shall see God as he really is." (1 John 3:2).
> "Though I walk in the shadow of death, I will fear no evil, for you are with me." (Psalm 23:4).

The rite continues with further readings from Scripture and moves into the Litany of the Saints, recalling Gerontius's prayer at the beginning of the "Dream": "Jesu, Maria—I am near to death . . . Jesu, have mercy! Mary, pray for me!" Then come the quite magnificent words of the Prayer of Commendation, words used "at the very cusp of the divide between life and death":

> "Go forth, Christian soul, from this world
> In the name of God the Almighty Father,
> Who created you,
> In the name of Jesus Christ, Son of the living God,
> Who suffered for you,
> In the name of the Holy Spirit,

> Who was poured out upon you,
> Go forth, faithful Christian.
> May you live in peace this day,
> May your home be with God in Zion,
> With Mary, the Virgin Mother of God,
> With Joseph, and all the angels and saints."

This prayer, "Go forth, Christian soul" is the gentle nudging that may be needed to move forward from this world and to sail into the presence of God.

After death has occurred, the ritual offers various prayers among which the following may be found:

> Saints of God, come to his/her aid!
> Come to meet him/her, angels of the Lord!
> Receive his/her soul and present him/her to God the Most High.
> May Christ who called you, take you to himself;
> May angels lead you to Abraham's side.

These beautiful prayers are essentially the same prayers that are reflected in the "Dream" by Newman. They indicate to us all too clearly that while there is an understandable element of fear in the unknown reality of death and dying, fear is not the final thing. Rather, a quiet hopeful confidence of coming into God's lovely presence is the final thing. This is the meaning of Newman's "Dream of Gerontius."

SIR EDWARD ELGAR AND THE DREAM OF GERONTIUS

Why not just read the text? Why listen to the musical composition of Sir Edward Elgar? Does the music add anything to this text? I am no musician. But Newman himself said: "I always sleep better after music. . . . Perhaps thought is music."

However, I find these words of a theologian reflecting on what music does to us particularly persuasive:

> To listen seriously to music and to perform it are among our most potent ways of learning what it is to live with and before God. . . . In this "obedience" of listening and following, we are stretched and deepened, physically challenged as performers, imaginatively as listeners. The time we have renounced, given up, is given back to us as a time in which we have become more human, more real,

even [or especially] when we can't say what we have learned, only that we have changed.[33]

The claim is being made that listening seriously to music changes us. We are made different by the music. We are stretched and deepened. We are made more human. Too few things in life stretch and deepen us. Music has the capacity to do this. Being aware of the text, and listening to Elgar's composition of *The Dream of Gerontius* seems to me a uniquely privileged moment of grace. Grace is God reaching out to us, in this case reaching out through word and music. We are changed.

Sir Edward Elgar composed the oratorio *The Dream of Gerontius* in 1900. It was composed for the Birmingham Music Festival and its first performance took place in Birmingham Town Hall on October 3, 1900. Birmingham then as now is a very ordinary city, an industrial center, a city of ordinary working people. There is something entirely appropriate about the first performance of *The Dream of Gerontius* taking place in Birmingham. Birmingham Town Hall is about three miles from the Birmingham Oratory on the Hagley Road, founded by Newman, and in which he composed the "Dream." Birmingham was a far cry from the elegance of Oxford and its university. Yet it was in Birmingham that Blessed John Henry Newman lived, prayed and worshiped, ministered to the people, and died. It was in the industrial city of Birmingham that John Henry Newman opened a church in what had been previously a gin distillery. He cared for the very ordinary people of Birmingham. When invited by the rather pompous Monsignor George Talbot to preach a series of Lenten sermons to his genteel English congregation in Rome, advising Newman that he "would have a more educated audience of Protestants than could ever be the case in England," Newman replied curtly: "Birmingham people have souls, and I have neither taste nor talent for the sort of work which you cut out for me: and I beg to decline your offer." It was one of the best literary snubs in English. Arguably it was for the ordinary Christian folk that "The Dream of Gerontius" had been written.

---

33. Williams, *Open to Judgment: Sermons and Addresses*, 248.

9

Newman the Preacher

There is no question that the English sermon had never before and has never since attained such psychological intensity and subtlety as in Newman.

Ian Ker[1]

The Oxford sermons may lack some of the accuracy and experience of Newman's more weighty works, but nothing he wrote has more freshness and originality.

H. Francis Davis[2]

INTRODUCTION

"THE ESSENTIAL NEWMAN WAS a preacher, and he followed the patristic tradition of making sermons the primary vehicle for theology."[3] Many associated Newman with his major theological works, for example, his *Essay in Aid of a Grammar of Assent* or his *Essay on the Development of Doctrine*, but these came later in his life. Long before these formal explorations in theology developed, Newman was a preacher. Newman's premier twenti-

---

1. Adapted from Ker, *The Achievement of John Henry Newman*, 95.
2. Davis, "Introduction," 9.
3. Rutler, "Newman, John Henry," 345.

eth-century biographer, Ian Ker, writes: "Newman may have thought that teaching was his real vocation and that his principal intellectual mission was the philosophical defense of religious belief, but the fact is that during at least the Anglican half of his life, he probably spent more time composing sermons than writing anything else."[4] Very interesting language! Newman spent more time composing sermons than anything else, and although his collected sermons could never be regarded as a systematic theology as we understand that term today, they do contain almost all of Christian theology.[5] Today it is more "ecclesiastically correct" to speak of homilies rather than sermons. But what about the language of "composition"? "Compose" probably suggest someone who works in music, such as Beethoven, Bach, or the Beatles. When Ian Ker uses the verb "compose" of Newman's homiletic labor, he is trying to convey something of the complexity and excitement of the task. Hours of preparation following upon years of philosophical and theological foundation, finding just the right words so that you can, under God's grace, make the right sound to resound in the hearts of God's people. That's what "composing homilies" is about. Many of Newman's sermons were published. At present, there are thirty-six volumes of his collected works. Eight volumes are given over to his *Parochial and Plain Sermons*. In point of fact, however, these *Parochial and Plain Sermons* constitute only about one third of the pastoral sermons he wrote as an Anglican. He published two volumes of sermons as a Catholic, *Sermons Addressed to Mixed Congregations* and *Sermons Preached on Various Occasions*. After his death, a small volume of sermons was published as *Catholic Sermons of Cardinal Newman*, some of which were preached in the Cathedral of St. Chad, Birmingham. If the liturgy is primary theology, then the liturgical homily—what Newman called a "sermon"—surely must feature as a normative and regular form of theology. This does not mean, of course, that the homily is the place for heavy-duty theological analysis. While the homily ought not to be a tract in Christian doctrine or morality, it cannot be composed without saturation in Scripture, doctrine, moral theology, philosophy, literature, and the multiple disciplines that go into the making of a preacher. Such considerations lead historian Owen Chadwick to pronounce that "the sermons at St. Mary's, Oxford, were the most important publication, not only of his Protestant days, but of his life."[6]

4. Ker, "Vatican I and the Papacy 1: A Proud Appellation," 74.
5. See Bouyer, *Newman's Vision of Faith*, 17.
6. Chadwick, *Newman, A Short Introduction*, 18. Robinson, "Preaching," 242,

The Irish Benedictine Placid Murray believes that these *Plain and Parochial Sermons* of Newman "can hardly be surpassed as liturgical preaching."[7] For Newman, liturgical preaching was a means to an end, to draw the hearers into a fuller sense of communion with God, and to develop their sense of mission and witness in daily life. But, before we move more fully into Newman's understanding of liturgical preaching, Murray also reminds us of human-considered preaching very broadly. This is what Newman wrote about preaching:

> In Scripture to preach is to do the work of an evangelist, is to teach, instruct, advise, encourage in all things pertaining to religion, in any way whatever. All education is a kind of preaching—all catechizing, all private conversation—all writing. In all things and at all times is a Christian minister preaching in the scriptural sense of the word ... and in all matters and pursuits of this world as truly, though not as directly as when engaged in religious subjects.[8]

There is a continuum among all education, catechizing, conversation, and writing. All Christians, in living out the witness of their baptism, are engaged in preaching, but there is a special commission to preach given to the ordained.

THEOLOGY OF PREACHING

Newman offers his theology of this ordained ministry of preaching in an essay of 1855 entitled "University Preaching," which is included in his book *The Idea of a University*. For the sake of brevity and clarity we might summarize his views in three central points. First, the key idea and the central object of the preacher must be only one thing, "the spiritual good of the hearers." "As a marksman aims at the target and its bull's-eye, and at nothing else, so the preacher must have a definite point before him, which he has to hit." Following St. Paul's line of thought in the first letter to the Corinthians, Newman believes that questions of display and rhetoric and delivery and so forth are not the primary issue. The primary issue must be and must be only having one object and going after it, this "spiritual good."

---

writes: "Tracts were the natural way of initiating a popular movement and arousing the interest of the people. Preaching was another way. In both endeavors, Newman proved himself to be a master strategist."

7. Murray, *Newman the Oratorian*, 31.

8. Cited from Murray, *Newman the Oratorian*, 37.

He cites St. Paul to the effect that "the kingdom of God is not in speech, but in power." "Talent, logic, learning, words, manner, voice, action, are all required for the perfection of a preacher; but 'one thing is necessary,'—an intense perception and appreciation of the end for which he preaches, and that is, to be the minister of some definite spiritual good to those who hear him." But the spiritual good must be something definite, not some vague or general spiritual good. To keep focus on this definite spiritual good, Newman says: "I would go the length of recommending a preacher to place a distinct categorical proposition before him, such as he can write down in a form of words, and to guide and limit his preparation by it, and to aim in all he says to bring it about, and nothing else." In other words, maintain one key central point in the homily. Newman is talking about focus and clear direction of thought. He is not opposed, of course, to the development of this one point, but such development as is undertaken should not detract from the point that is being laid down. One must be able to see the wood and not just a number of trees, however fascinating such trees may be. With a definite object in mind, then, the preacher should

> study it well and thoroughly, and first make it his own, or else have already dwelt on it and mastered it, so as to be able to use it for the occasion from an habitual understanding of it; and that then he should employ himself, as the one business of his discourse, to bring home to others, and to leave deep within them, what he has, before he began to speak to them, brought home to himself. What he feels himself, and feels deeply, he has to make others feel deeply.[9]

The preacher must have brought the message, this one definite spiritual message home to himself before he shares it with his congregation.

Second, the preacher should be aware of his audience. There is no preaching in general for Newman. In *The Idea of a University*, he continues: "A hearer is included in the very idea of preaching; and we cannot determine how in detail we ought to preach, till we know whom we are to address." Newman recognizes, needless to say, that the great themes of the Christian tradition remain the same for everyone, but here he is advocating that the preacher know his audience, so that he can tailor what he has to say in such a fashion that it will be heard and understood. Newman provides an example from the New Testament to illustrate his point, St. Paul in the Acts of the Apostles: "To the Jews he quotes the Old Testament; on the

---

9. Newman, *The Idea of a University*, 406, 408, 411–12, 413.

Areopagus, addressing the philosophers of Athens, he insists, —not indeed upon any recondite doctrine, contrariwise, upon the most elementary, the being and unity of God; —but he treats it with a learning and depth of thought, which the presence of that celebrated city naturally suggested."[10]

Preaching to worshiping Jews in their synagogues, and preaching to a philosophic club are different. They are different not because the philosophers are superior to the worshipers, nor because the worshipers are less wise than the philosophers, but because the audience is different. Essentially this is but a variation on Newman's key and opening point. Preaching should be aimed at a definite spiritual good to be effective, and if it is to achieve this definite spiritual good, the preacher needs to know his definite audience.[11]

Third, is the issue of writing out a homily. This is disputed territory in the academy of homiletics! Should a preacher preach with a written text or not? Newman knows full well that there are different practices here, and he is respectful of practices that differ from his own, but he lays down quite clearly the importance of a written text. "These remarks, as far as they go, lead us to lay great stress on the preparation of the sermon, as amounting in fact to composition, even in writing, and *in extenso*." Homilies should be written down, in Newman's judgment. Why? Here is his answer: "I think that writing is a stimulus to the mental faculties, to the logical talent, to originality, to the power of illustration, to the arrangement of topics, second to none. Till a man begins to put down his thoughts about a subject on paper he will not ascertain what he knows and what he does not know; and still less will he be able to express what he does know." Writing out the homily enables real clarity of thought to emerge, as one struggles with the ideas, reaches for lucidity, striving for the spiritual good of the hearers and oneself. Newman offers another reason, and it is that writing out the homily may prevent a preacher from wandering all around the theological and spiritual world, moving like a free spirit through a free association of ideas, so that each homily becomes a virtual encyclopedia. Needless to say, Newman puts it more felicitously:

> Such a practice [as writing] will secure them against venturing upon really *ex tempore* matter. The more ardent a man is, and the greater power he has of affecting his hearers, so much the more will he need self-control and sustained recollection, and feel the

---

10. Newman, *The Idea of a University*, 415, 419.
11. See Robinson, "Preaching," 243.

advantage of committing himself, as it were, to the custody of his previous intentions, instead of yielding to any chance current of thought which rushes upon him in the midst of his preaching. His very gifts may need the counterpoise of more ordinary and homely accessories, such as the drudgery of composition.

Self-control, sustained reflection, avoiding the constant temptation of yielding to any chance thought that crosses one's mind, and, notice Newman's own phrase, "the drudgery of composition." Preaching is hard work, exciting work, but hard work. Composition in preaching flows only from the disciplined habits of prayer, study, and word-crafting.

Having committed his homily carefully to writing, however, Newman does not think that it ought to then to be read. For him a read sermon is a dead sermon. "While, then, a preacher will find it becoming and advisable to put into writing any important discourse before hand, he will find it equally a point of propriety and expedience not to read it in the pulpit. . . . If he employs a manuscript, the more he appears to dispense with it, the more he looks off from it, and directly addresses his audience, the more will he be considered to preach. . . . Preaching is not reading, and reading is not preaching."[12]

Having outlined all that goes into homily preparation, it might be interesting to discover what Newman himself was like as a preacher.

NEWMAN THE PREACHER

Newman was appointed vicar of St. Mary's in 1828, the church of the University of Oxford. The church was full when Newman preached with, it is estimated, between five hundred and six hundred undergraduates and graduates, as well as others.[13] The others would have included local shopkeepers, merchants, and numerous university servants. Newman preached from the pulpit of St. Mary's for the next sixteen years at the afternoon service at 4 PM on Sundays and feast days. The Victorians were interested in buying and reading volumes of sermons, and Newman's sold very well indeed, not least because they were recognized even then as "undoubted classics of Christian spirituality."[14]

---

12. Robinson, "Preaching," 421, 422–23, 424.
13. Middleton, "The Vicar of St. Mary's," 131.
14. Ker, "Vatican I and the Papacy 1: A Proud Appellation," 75.

What would it have been like to listen to Newman preach? Almost universally his hearers witnessed to the power of his preaching. One who heard him often, J. A. Froude, spoke of the psychological penetration of Newman's preaching: "He seemed to be addressing the most secret consciousness of each of us—as the eyes of a portrait appear to look at every person in a room."[15] That is no small accomplishment, the sense that the preacher is speaking directly to one. Froude's description of Newman preaching is worth hearing at greater length: "I had then never seen so impressive a person. I met him now and then in private; I attended his church and heard him preach Sunday after Sunday. . . . He was . . . the most transparent of men. He told us what he believed to be true. He did not know where it would carry him. . . . Newman's mind was world-wide. He was interested in everything."[16] Another contemporary, the famous Matthew Arnold of Rugby, had this to say of Newman the preacher: "Who could resist the charm of that spiritual apparition, gliding in the dim afternoon light through the aisles of St. Mary's, rising into the pulpit, and then, in the most entrancing of voices, breaking the silence with words and thoughts which were a religious music—subtle, sweet, mournful."[17] Notice immediately this remark about musical composition that so frequently comes to mind when thinking of Newman as a preacher. Theologically, Matthew Arnold was at some considerable distance from Newman, so that this description is quite an accolade. The University Church of St. Mary would have been quite dark, creating something of a receptive atmosphere, accentuated by the gas lamp and the shadowy outline of the preacher. With little natural light, with very little to distract, the ambience of the church led to a great concentration on the preacher and what he had to say.

Not everyone who heard Newman preach, of course, was impressed and entranced like Froude and Arnold. For example, in 1838 a sectarian preacher from Philadelphia, John Alonzo Clark—enormously suspicious of Catholics and on the lookout for "the cloven hoof of Popery," but interested in contemporary approaches to preaching—was advised to go to Oxford to hear Newman preach. His reaction to a sermon at St. Mary's from the celebrated preacher was not quite the same as Froude and Arnold. He describes

---

15. Froude, *Short Studies on Great Subjects*, 186.
16. Froude, *Short Studies on Great Subjects*, 246.
17. Cited in Middleton, "The Vicar of St. Mary's," 131.

Newman as "[a] thin, sallow-looking man... cold in the pulpit as an icicle," and the sermon as "exceedingly dull and uninteresting."[18]

The late homilist Walter J. Burghardt, SJ, who has published volumes of his own homilies as well as a handbook on preaching, writes of Newman's skills and word-crafting:

> In my early Jesuit days, it was not so much Newman's ideas that captivated me as his mastery of language. The words he chose always seemed so right; he could sustain the periodic sentence; and the language was instinct with love. And so we young Jesuits imitated him, not to plagiarize *but to get his feel for words, for style, for the ordering of a clause, a sentence, a paragraph, ... how to use language with reverence, with care, with discrimination, with feeling.*[19]

This in no way demands a use of words designed to impress. The Oratorian fathers who were Newman's colleagues in Birmingham noted that he spoke in the pulpit much as he spoke in ordinary occasions.[20] If there is a continuum of education, conversation, and formal preaching, one would expect there to be some continuum in the care with which words are used. Newman constantly exercised such care. The careful choice of words, the seeking after just the right expression in the pulpit, echoed the no-less-careful choice of words in conversation, in letter writing, and indeed in his theological writing. It has been reckoned that the average length of Newman sermons was fourteen pages, which took about forty-five minutes to deliver.[21]

Apparently, the practice was quite well established in England at the time—and experience of contemporary homiletic services by some of the ordained suggests that it has by no means disappeared—of reading the sermons prepared by someone else, perhaps published sermons, at the Sunday service. Newman almost never did this. In point of fact, he only ever read sermons written by another on three occasions, all sermons prepared by his close friend Hurrell Froude. One month after Froude's death in 1836, he tells us that he "read one of dear H.F.'s sermons [on his birthday] being the

---

18. Cited in DeLaura, "'O Unforgotten Voice,'" 82.
19. Burghardt, SJ, *Preaching: The Art and the Craft*, 193.
20. Griffiths, "Newman: The Foolishness of Preaching," 66.
21. Murray, *Newman the Oratorian*, 31.

first not my own I ever read in my life."[22] He read two others that year. This is Newman's grief preaching, not a model for imitation.[23]

There is an inescapable sense in which preaching is autobiographical. Our own experience, our own lives, our reading and education, the movies we see, the newspapers we read—all are necessary grist to the preaching mill. Overt autobiographical comment is another thing. Though it is impossible at times not to see connections between his preaching and the events of his own life, self-reference did not enter much into Newman's sermons. "What is truly startling and distinctive in his sermons is the absence of the pronoun 'I.' It appears in 'The Parting of Friends,' for instance, only in biblical quotations and through the formulaic phrase 'my brethren'; in this sermon, delivered on the most piercing occasion in his life to that time, Newman appears as 'one' and 'he.'"[24] "One" and "he" rather than "I," the third person rather the first person. Instead of dwelling on the events of his own life, Newman tends to interpret that life through Scripture, the liturgy, and the doctrine of the church. He inhabits the language of Scripture, liturgy, and doctrine so that he speaks out of this language.

"The Parting of Friends," his final sermon as a priest of the Church of England, delivered in the church of Littlemore on September 25, 1843, is particularly powerful. It would be almost another two years before he was received by the Italian Passionist, Dominic Barberi, into the Catholic Church, but there was a general sense that he was on his way. Many wept in the church, as they intuited Newman's farewell. His concluding words to his Anglican companions and friends are moving indeed:

> And O, my brethren, O kind and affectionate hearts, O loving friends, should you know anyone who's lot it has been, by writing or by word-of-mouth, in some degree to help you thus to act; if he has ever told you what you knew about yourselves, or what you did not know; has read to you your wants or feelings, and comforted you by the very reading: has made you feel that there was a higher life than this daily one, and a brighter world than that you see; or encouraged you, or sobered you, or opened away to the inquiring, or soothed the perplexed, if what he has said or done has ever made you take interest in him, and feel well inclined towards him; remember such a one in time to come, though you hear him not,

---

22. Gornall, *Letters and Diaries of John Henry Newman*, vol. 5, 267.
23. See Griffiths, "Newman: The Foolishness of Preaching," 65.
24. Griffiths, "Newman: The Foolishness of Preaching," 67.

and pray for him, that in all things he may know God's will, and at all times he may be ready to fulfill it.[25]

Beautiful and moving words, yet laconic in their autobiographical reference! At the end of the sermon, Newman took off his academic hood and threw it over the altar rails of the church, indicating, it seemed, that he had ceased to be a preacher and teacher in the Church of England.

SOME ASPECTS OF HIS CONTENT

Like the great patristic liturgical preachers, Newman emphasized the holiness of the Christian life. "We dwell in the full light of the gospel, and the full grace of the sacraments. We ought to have the holiness of Apostles. There is no reason except our own willful corruption, that we are not by this time walking in the steps of St. Paul or St. John, and following them as they followed Christ."[26] This is no abstract holiness that Newman commends. His sermons were and are practical and concrete, and very realistic. "Nothing is more difficult than to be disciplined and regular in our religion. It is very easy to be religious by fits and starts, and to keep up our feelings by artificial stimulants; but regularity seems to trammel us, and we become impatient. . . . Is not holiness the result of many patient, repeated efforts after obedience, gradually working on us, and first modifying and then changing our hearts?"[27]

The real problem, as Newman saw it, is self-deception, and so his purpose as a preacher is to lead his congregation "to some true notion of the depths and deceitfulness of the heart, which we do not really know."[28] Human beings, even the most religious, are so often inconsistent.

> If we look to some of the most eminent saints of Scripture, we shall find their recorded errors to have occurred in those parts of their duty in which each had most trial, and generally showed obedience most perfect. Faithful Abraham through want of faith denied his wife. Moses, the meekest of men, was excluded from the land of promise for a passionate word. The wisdom of Solomon was

---

25. Newman, *Sermons on Subjects of the Day*, 409.
26. Newman, *Parochial and Plain Sermons*, 1:13, 82.
27. Newman, *Parochial and Plain Sermons*, 1:11, 252.
28. Newman, *Parochial and Plain Sermons*, 1:27–28, 35, 172.

seduced to bow down to idols. Barnabas again, the son of consolation, had a sharp contention with St. Paul.[29]

Ian Ker considers that the theme of consistency and inconsistency was almost an obsession for Newman, but might that so-called obsession be nothing more than a pastoral consequence of the studied observance of human fragility?[30]

One of his most engaging sermons is entitled "The Danger of Accomplishments." In this sermon, Newman complains about reading novels, which is, in some degree, problematic. "We have nothing to do; we read, are affected, softened or aroused, and that is all; we cool again, —nothing comes of it."[31] This certainly could be a problem, reading being understood as an essentially passive activity. But what if something does actually come of it? It may be that the reading of literature, of novels, introduces the reader into a very rich world of imaginative experience that invites some degree of personal transformation. We know that Newman liked to read Trollope and Eliot, astute interpreters of human nature. So it would seem that he would approve of such novels and movies as enlarge our capacity for empathy with others and invite us to a deeper compassion for the vulnerabilities of the human condition.

---

29. Newman, *Parochial and Plain Sermons*, 1:46–47.
30. Ker, "Vatican I and the Papacy 1: A Proud Appellation," 89.
31. Newman, *Parochial and Plain Sermons*, 2:371.

10

Looking Back

We are, in fact, each of us, intolerably complex: confused, bewildered, bombarded by discordant signals and demands, subject to conflictual desires and motives, unstable moods and fragile loyalties; driven by insecurity and ineffectively smothered fear.

Nicholas Lash[1]

As I attempt to look back over *John Henry Newman and His Age*, I find Nicholas Lash's description above of "each of us," of myself, so very accurate. That being so, one's looking back at Newman and his age cannot be an entirely free and clear looking back, but rather a looking that is clouded by the complexity that each of us is. With that disclosure, a risk is taken, the risk that what one finds in the Newman retrospective will necessarily manifest something of oneself, but the risk is worth taking.

Let's begin the retrospective with some words of Owen Chadwick, that outstanding twentieth-century English and Anglican church historian who had a way with words second to none. He has a wonderful paragraph that opens an essay entitled "Newman and the Historians" that runs like this:

> The historians were late getting at Newman. They only get at people when they are dead. Newman took a long time to die. He retreated from the world into a monastery in 1842. He lived for

---

1. Lash, "On Learning To Be Wise," 358.

another forty-eight years; quiet, retired, prayerful, unpretentious, a bit scruffy. He appeared from behind the veil three times: once to libel, or rather not to libel but to be convicted of libeling, a very libeling ex-Dominican; once to defend himself, not in a law court, against a libel; and once to become a cardinal, the first cardinal the English people enjoyed having since they had a Reformation. Historians like people who do things: who conquer Gaul, or fornicate on Capri, or evangelize the East, or are beheaded. They have not much to say about people who do nothing; and the class of people who do nothing consists, *inter alia*, of practically all dons, and practically all monks. Dons do nothing but sit at their desks and toy with paper. Monks do practically nothing but get on their knees and be silent or vocal before God. In two chunks of life, Newman was a professional academic, and after he resigned his academic posts he remained donnish in cast of mind, even though after the age of seventy he refused the offer of a professorship. And in all his life from 1842 to the end, if not before, he was a sort of monk. That left history with thin materials.[2]

Well, one might argue with Chadwick on this point and that in this intense and humorous paragraph, but Chadwick then goes on to point out what a treasure trove for the historian are the letters that Newman wrote, some trivial, some very revealing and important, and all archived and very many now published. The letters and journals and the legion of secondary studies provide a window into the religious attitudes of the Victorians and much more importantly, of course, a powerful window into the soul of John Henry Newman himself.

Looking back on Newman's life and times, on the material contained in these brief chapters, it is reasonable to ask what are the major lessons that may be learned from this engagement with John Henry Newman and his age. Much will depend, of course, on who is reading the book, what questions she or he entertains, what presuppositions are brought to the reading, and so forth. In this concluding retrospective chapter, I would like to focus on six major lessons.

Lesson 1 has to do with the complexity of the human person. Each one of us represents the coming together of all kinds of circumstances—historical, personal, psychological—and most especially in our immediate families. There is no exception. Maturing means coming to terms as best one can with one's complexity. Newman is now for Catholics "Blessed" John

---

2. Chadwick, "Newman and the Historians," in his *Spirit of the Oxford Movement*, 154.

Henry Newman, on his way to becoming "St." John Henry Newman, an icon for us within the communion of saints, "in Christ." That does not mean, however, that either Newman is from the human point of view perfect, or that his family was perfect. His father was a poor businessman and failed in business, a failure that generated not just hardship for the family but great shame, shame that Newman continued to carry at least in his earlier years. There was the usual rivalry among the children of the Newman family and each went her/his own way: John, on his way to sainthood; Francis on his own idiosyncratic enthusiastic religious path; Charles, unable to hold a job and look after himself, and moving far away from the family geographically and religiously; Jemima, who had great hopes for her older brother but who after his conversion to Catholicism did not allow Newman to visit any of her children at home; Harriet, more extreme than Jemima, who never communicated with her older brother after his conversion; and Mary, so close to Newman's heart and who died so very young. A complicated and somewhat messy family, and in that sense like most families. Psychotherapist Mary Pipher writes: "We can't hate our families without hating ourselves. . . . Life makes most of us unhappy. . . . While families are imperfect institutions, they are also our greatest source of meaning, connection and joy."[3] I think Newman would find himself in agreement. Familial challenges he had aplenty, but he seems never to have given up on his family. He tried to be supportive in so many ways—financially, personally, through visits, through writing at times agonized letters. Striving for holiness out of messy circumstances is the Christian way. The very complexity of the Newman family should offer the contemporary reader, especially in the church, both reassurance and hope.

Lesson 2. When a person moves from one religious tradition to another, he or she does not leave the first tradition behind but, in so many ways, stands on its shoulders to look ahead and to move forward. Newman left the Anglican Communion, yes, but so much of it remained in his years as a Catholic. Pluses and minuses are the stuff of conversion. One gains and one loses. Owen Chadwick writes:

> When Newman left the Church of England, he thought himself repudiated by that church. He had tried to wind up his church, which refused, he imagined, to be wound. In truth, if he could have known it, he had won. The Church of England would look back upon the days of Newman's Oxford Movement as days to

---

3. Pipher, *Letters to a Young Therapist*, 28–29.

which it spiritually owed a permanent debt. For the Church of England the loss was disaster.[4]

The pluses and minuses of religious conversion, of Christians moving from one tradition to another, should not fuel ecclesial triumphalism but reach out towards ecumenical gift exchanges, gift exchanges that are mutually enriching. Theologian Paul D. Murray writes: "Receptive ecumenical awakening is properly a matter of the heart before it is a matter of the head; a matter of falling in love with the experienced presence and action of God in the people, practices, even structures of another tradition and being impelled thereby to search for ways in which all impediments to closer relationship might be overcome."[5] Looking back at Newman's life and career, at his friendships and at his challenges, helps us, I believe, to be more receptively ecumenical, "to fall in love with the experienced presence and action of God in the people, practices, and structures of the Anglican Communion." That perspective does not, of course, eliminate differences, differences in interpretation of Scripture, doctrine, and tradition. Difference, however, is not divisiveness.

Lesson 3 is the absolute importance of history for accuracy of understanding. Newman especially valued the study of history for the understanding of theology. One contemporary church historian puts it like this: "Perhaps his most valuable insight was that history, which reveals both the triumphs and the failures of the church, was not something that Catholics should fear. By framing his agenda in terms of the teachings of the fathers and doctors of the church, he was able to demonstrate his loyalty to the church, even as he criticized some of the doctrinal stances promulgated by the magisterial hierarchy."[6] History liberates from ill-conceived or ill-informed presuppositions and in theology these can mistakenly be taken to be the teaching of the church. A long and deep historical perspective helps us to be freed from the tyranny of our own ignorance and naïveté. Newman's approach to theology exemplifies the greater accuracy that is emergent from close attention to the study of the history of the church.

Lesson 4. There is a technicality to any discipline, including the discipline of theology. But at the same time the deepest things may be expressed in relatively uncomplicated, if not exactly simple, language. One

---

4. Chadwick, *Newman, A Short Introduction*, 77.
5. Murray, "Receptive Ecumenism and Catholic Learning," 15.
6. Anderson, *The Great Catholic Reformers*, 179.

long-standing Newman scholar of the mid-twentieth century indicates Newman's simple and concrete use of language.

> It is rarely that Newman writes in technical language. This has certain apparent disadvantages. It makes him in some respects less exact. I say "in some respects"; for reality is so complex and beyond expression that nearly all exact formulations of it have no more than a tidy outward appearance of exactness. They remain inexact as statements of reality. Concrete reality, as Newman is forever reminding us, does not fit into any neat statements or categories. Not that we can do without technical words and even exact definitions. Even Newman uses them. But he uses them with far less confidence than the scholastic.[7]

Too much theology has been obscured in scholastic terminology and concepts. Newman offers us both in his preaching and teaching an alternative and more persuasive form of theological expression and understanding.

Lesson 5. The Catholic Church today is polarized, perhaps especially in the United States—liberal versus conservative, orthodox versus heterodox, and on it goes. If it is impossible to grasp with accuracy the interiority of another, and perhaps even our own interiority, then we can learn from Newman to avoid these crude caricatures of one another. "[Newman] was a highly complex and subtle thinker who refused to see issues in black and white alternatives. He was both radical and conservative, a reformer but also a traditionalist."[8] Needless to point out, of course, being a highly complex and subtle thinker means being an excellent listener, especially when one is not particularly open to the one who is speaking. Newman was an excellent listener. He had his own positions on all manner of things and was prepared to argue for them, but by all accounts he gave primacy to listening.

Lesson 6. Newman at prayer. John Henry Newman said his prayers. He had been taught how to pray as a child, had prayed regularly, found in his boarding school a discipline not only of study but of prayer, prayed as an undergraduate at Oxford and attended the liturgical services, prayed as a Tractarian and as the pastor of the University Church of St. Mary in Oxford, and then prayed for the last forty-five years of his life as a Roman Catholic. That is what a Christian does. If prayer is the raising up of the

---

7. Davis, "Introduction," 12.
8. Ker, *Newman on Vatican II*, 3.

mind and heart to God, Newman had always done this, both as an Anglican and as a Catholic.

Theology and the life of prayer cannot be separated, distinguished yes, but never separated. The one flows into the other. That has been one of the great hallmarks of the Christian tradition. That is how it was for Newman as a theologian. Louis Bouyer writes comparing Newman favorably and ecumenically in this regard with great theologians of the tradition. The passage is worth quoting at some length:

> Of Newman must be said what was already true of those theologians of the first generation of what we call "Christian humanists"—like Erasmus, Bartolomeo Carranza, Morrone or Pole, or later Petau and Thomassin—all Catholics—or Anglicans like Hooker and his heirs, the Caroline Divines, or even Lutherans of the same period and tendencies, like Johann Gerhard: I mean that for all these as for Newman, who in this followed their example, the rediscovery of the great Fathers of the Church, especially the Greek Fathers, led to a fresher look at the Bible and created in their time a "new" way of doing theology that had in fact been that of all the early Christians. For these, theology and spirituality could never be divorced—nor even distinguished—from one another. We should even say more: Newman, along with the Christian humanists of the Renaissance, followed the vision represented by the Christian thinker known as Pseudo-Dionysius. However saturated this Father might be by philosophy, for him "mystical theology" would not have meant some "scientific" theology applied to mysticism but the mystical experience itself, as constituting the highest possible knowledge of God.[9]

It is a very fine statement. It situates Newman very clearly as a prayerful theologian, perhaps even in Bouyer's terms as a mystical theologian, never letting theology and prayer become alienated one from the other.

As Newman made his way theologically and prayerfully throughout his life, he was taken by the prayers and spiritual exercises of the great Anglican Bishop Lancelot Andrewes (1555–1626). Bouyer finds Andrewes a fine example of being prayerfully theological and theologically prayerful. "Stupefyingly erudite, but even more cultivated than erudite, he was nonetheless a pastor unreservedly devoted to his flock, and, to cap all, practiced a spirituality of inner contemplation that approached mysticism."[10]

---

9. Bouyer, "Introduction," xv–xvi.

10. Bouyer, *Orthodox Spirituality and Protestant and Anglican Spirituality*, 117.

Much the same could be said of John Henry Newman and, in point of fact, Newman translated and adapted Andrewes's collection of prayers and devotional exercises, and use them every day before and after the celebration of the Eucharist.

If one were to seek a brief way of expressing the nucleus of Newman's prayer-filled theological life, I think it would be captured in his phrase *sola cum Solo*, "all on one's own (with God)." Of course, by "alone" Newman means something like "personally present in the presence of God." He does not mean, because he cannot mean, being *entirely on one's own* with God. For he knows that no one can be entirely "alone" in some isolationist sense. Each of us is peopled by the generations that have gone before us and by those among whom we live—a statement of fact. But, if one is to be sustained as a Christian and to help sustain others, there must be times of aloneness with God, alone before the Mystery, alone adoring the Mystery. Newman could not have been who he was, both as an Anglican and as a Catholic, without this constancy of *sola cum Solo*. Newman's sense can be picked up in these few sentences from his *Meditations and Devotions*: "By nature and by grace Thou art in me. I see Thee not in the material world except dimly, but I recognize Thy voice in my own intimate consciousness. I turned around and say Rabboni. One ever thus with me."[11]

Newman's appreciation of the Eucharist traverses both halves of his life, as an Anglican and as a Roman Catholic. As an Anglican, Newman accepted the central aspect of eucharistic doctrine, the real presence of Christ—in point of fact, Newman speaks of having as an Anglican "an absolute and overpowering sense of the Real Presence"—and the Eucharist as sacrifice.[12] However, as an Anglican and along with most Anglicans of his time, he did not accept the doctrine of transubstantiation because it seemed to be a rational explanation of what is in essence mysterious. While he accepts the Eucharist as sacrificial, there is no articulation of sacrificial theology as such, and he is content to affirm that the eucharistic sacrifice is not a new sacrifice, but rather "a mysterious representation of [Christ's] meritorious sacrifice in the sight of Almighty God."[13] There is no speculation with how the Eucharist is sacrificial, but its ontological connection with

---

11. Newman, *Meditations and Devotions*, cited in H Francis Davis, "Newman's Influence in England," in Coulson and Allchin, *The Rediscovery of Newman*, 227.

12. Newman, Letter to Henry Wilberforce, quoted in Murray, *Newman the Oratorian*, 43.

13. Newman, *Lectures on the Doctrine of Justification*, cited in Härdelin, "The Eucharist in the Theology of the Nineteenth Century," 83.

Christ's unique sacrifice on the cross is underscored. Newman's movement into the Catholic Church involved obviously an ascent to the eucharistic doctrine of that church. It comes, therefore, as no surprise that he did not write a great deal about the Eucharist. The grammar of eucharistic doctrine had been clearly set out in the decrees of the Council of Trent, and Catholic theologians saw it as their task to teach, to preach, and to clarify this doctrine. That Newman did, on an ad hoc basis. However, on the personal level he had a deep appreciation of the Eucharist, not only in public liturgical celebration but also in his private devotional practice. This was something that developed after he became a Catholic. Dom Placid Murray points out with reference to a number of Newman texts that as an Anglican he had little or no idea of the eucharistic presence in the Reserved Sacrament.[14] This was to change enormously in the direction of a really intense devotion. In one of his letters in 1846 to Mrs. John Bowden, a letter written from Milan, Newman writes finely of the Blessed Sacrament and what it means to him: "Here a score of churches which are open to the passer-by . . . in each of which . . . the Blessed Sacrament is ready for the worshiper even before he enters. There is nothing which has brought home to me the unity of the church, as the Presence of its Divine Founder and Life wherever I go—all places are, as it were, one."[15] Unity and catholicity through the Eucharist blend together in this comment, and the sheer physical presence of so many Catholic churches compared with England made a very deep impression on him. A later letter to the same Mrs. Bowden has Newman telling her that "an intense devotion to the Blessed Sacrament will overcome every trial."[16] Mrs. Bowden herself was received into the Catholic Church in July 1846. In this letter, Newman is revealing the depths of his own soul. He found solace and comfort before the Blessed Sacrament.

When all is said and done, Newman can only be understood as a saint for both churches, his own Church of England and the Catholic Church. His theology and his spirituality and in fact everything about him come to him from both communions. Even as he felt the call to move into full communion with the Catholic Church, he never felt entirely at home there, nor did he feel that he was abandoning everything he had received from the Anglican Communion. Perhaps we might say that he was caught in the "between"—between Anglicanism and Catholicism. That "between" is the

---

14. Murray, "Receptive Ecumenism and Catholic Learning," 48.
15. Dessain, *The Letters and Diaries of John Henry Newman*, vol. 11, 254.
16. Dessain and Blehl, *The Letters and Diaries of John Henry Newman*, vol. 14, 307.

uncomfortable space of ecclesial separation. If we are genuinely to honor Newman's witness today, it may be in trying to overcome the "between," in working together to overcome such barriers as remain "between" both churches so that Anglicans and Catholics may break bread at the one table of the Lord.

Appendix

Going Further

THE BIBLIOGRAPHY ATTACHED TO this short book is long. What now follows is the author's selection from this bibliography of those items that have helped more than others in the attempt to understand *John Henry Newman and His Age*.

The shortest of short and popular introductions is Joyce Sugg, *Snapdragon: The Story of John Henry Newman* (Huntington, IN: Our Sunday Visitor, 1982). Joyce Sugg has been a lifelong student of Newman and this straightforward introduction to the man is a delight.

Owen Chadwick, *Newman, A Short Introduction* (Oxford: Oxford University Press, 1983).

There are many Newman biographies. My favorite is the two-volume work, running to well over one thousand pages, of Meriol Trevor: *The Pillar of the Cloud* (London: Macmillan, 1962), *Newman, Light in Winter* (London: Macmillan, 1962). These volumes are superbly written. Trevor researched these at the Birmingham Oratory before annotated Newman editions were made. Add to these her much briefer synthesis *Newman's Journey* (Glasgow: Collins, 1974).

Ian Ker, *John Henry Newman, A Biography* (Oxford: Oxford University Press, 1988).

For those interested in a deeper appreciation of Newman's theology, Ian Ker and Terrence Merrigan, eds., *The Cambridge Companion to John Henry Newman* (Cambridge: Cambridge University Press, 2009) offers a very useful set of essays on different aspects of Newman's theology.

Hilda Graef, *God and Myself: The Spirituality of John Henry Newman* (London: Peter Davies, 1967).

This is a very fine study of Newman's spirituality, clearly and straightforwardly written, and guaranteed to hold one's attention, described by Owen Chadwick as "the best book on Newman's idea of devotion and the life of prayer."[1]

Finally, an excellent thematic anthology of Newman's writings has been put together by Erich Przywara, SJ, ed., *The Heart of Newman* (San Francisco: Ignatius, 1997). There are earlier editions of this work, but this is probably the most easily accessible.

---

1. Chadwick, *Newman, A Short Introduction*, 80.

Bibliography

Adams, Byron. "Elgar's Later Oratorios: Roman Catholicism, Decadence and the Wagnerian Dialectic of Shame and Grace." In *The Cambridge Companion to Elgar*, edited by Daniel Grimley and Julian Rushton, 81–105. Cambridge: Cambridge University Press, 2004.

Allchin, A. M. "Pusey. The Servant of God." In *Pusey Rediscovered*, edited by Perry Butler, 366–90. London: SPCK, 1983.

———. "The Theological Vision of the Oxford Movement." In *The Rediscovery of Newman*, edited by John Coulson and A. M. Allchin, 50–75. London: SPCK, 1967.

Allitt, Patrick. *Catholic Converts: British and American Intellectuals Turn to Rome*. Ithaca, NY: Cornell University Press, 1997.

Anderson, C. Colt. *The Great Catholic Reformers*. New York-Mahwah: Paulist, 2007.

Aubert, Roger. "Pius IX, Pope, Blessed." In *New Catholic Encyclopedia*, 2nd ed., 11:385. Detroit: Thomson Gale in association with the Catholic University of America, 2003.

Barr, Colin. *Paul Cullen, John Henry Newman and the Catholic University of Ireland*. Leominster, UK: Gracewing, 2003.

Battiscombe, Georgina. *John Keble: A Study in Limitations*. New York: Knopf, 1964.

Bellitto, Christopher M. *The General Councils: A History of the Twenty-one Church Councils from Nicaea to Vatican II*. Mahwah, NJ: Paulist, 2002.

Blehl, Vincent. *Pilgrim Journey, John Henry Newman 1801–1845*. New York-Mahwah: Paulist, 2001.

———. *Realizations: Newman's Own Selections of His Sermons*. Collegeville: Liturgical, 2009.

Bokenkotter, Thomas. *Cardinal Newman as an Historian*. Louvain: Publications Universitaires de Louvain, 1959.

———. *Church and Revolution*. New York: Doubleday, 1998.

———. *A Concise History of the Catholic Church*. Rev. ed. New York: Doubleday, 2004.

Borsch, Frederick H. "Ye Shall Be Holy: Reflections on the Spirituality of the Oxford Movement." In *Tradition Renewed: The Oxford Movement Conference Papers*, edited by Geoffrey Rowell, 64–77. Allison Park, PA: Pickwick, 1986.

Bouyer, Louis. "Introduction." In John Henry Newman, *Prayers, Verses, and Devotions*, xv–xvi. San Francisco: Ignatius, 1989.

———. *Newman, His Life and Spirituality*. New York: Kenedy and Sons, 1958.

———. *Newman's Vision of Faith*. San Francisco: Ignatius, 1986.

———. *Orthodox Spirituality and Protestant and Anglican Spirituality*. London: Burns and Oates, 1969.

Bibliography

Brendon, Piers. *Hurrell Froude and the Oxford Movement*. London: Elek, 1974.
Brilioth, Yngve. *The Anglican Revival: Studies in the Oxford Movement*. London: Longmans Green, 1933.
———. *Eucharistic Faith and Practice*. London: SPCK, 1969.
Brown, Stewart J., Peter B. Nockles, and James Pereiro, eds. *The Oxford Handbook to the Oxford Movement*. Oxford: Oxford University Press, 2017.
Burghardt, Walter J. *Preaching: The Art and Craft*. Mahwah, NJ: Paulist, 1987.
Butler, Cuthbert. *The Vatican Council 1869–1870*. 2 vols. Westminster, MD: Newman, 1962.
Butler, Perry, ed. *Pusey Rediscovered*. London: SPCK, 1983.
Callahan, Annice. *Karl Rahner's Spirituality of the Pierced Heart: A Reinterpretation of Devotion to the Sacred Heart*. Lanham, MD: University Press of America, 1983.
Carlen, IHM, Claudia, ed. *The Papal Encyclicals*. 5 vols. Ann Arbor, MI: Pierian, 1990.
Chadwick, Owen. *Acton and History*. Cambridge: Cambridge University Press, 1998.
———. *Catholicism and History*. Cambridge: Cambridge University Press, 1978.
———. *Freedom and the Historian, An Inaugural Lecture*. Cambridge: Cambridge University Press, 1969.
———. *From Bossuet to Newman*. 2nd ed. Cambridge: Cambridge University Press, 1987.
———. *A History of the Popes 1830–1914*. Oxford: Oxford University Press, 1998.
———. "John Henry Newman." In *Great Spirits 1000–2000*, edited by Selina O'Grady and John Wilkins, 151–54. Mahwah, NJ: Paulist, 2002.
———. *Newman: A Short Introduction*. Oxford: Oxford University Press, 1983.
———. *The Spirit of the Oxford Movement*. Cambridge: Cambridge University Press, 1990.
———. *The Victorian Church*, Vol. 1. London: Hymns Ancient and Modern, 1966.
Chapman, Ronald. *Father Faber*. Westminster, M.D.: Newman, 1961.
Congar, OP, Yves. "Church History as a Branch of Theology." In *Church History in Future Perspective*, edited by Roger Aubert, 85–96. New York: Herder and Herder, 1970.
Cooke, Bernard, ed. *The Papacy and the Church in the United States*. Mahwah, NJ: Paulist, 1989.
Coppa, Frank J. *Cardinal Giacomo Antonelli and Papal Politics in European Affairs*. Albany, NY: State University of New York Press, 1990.
———. *The Papacy, the Jews, and the Holocaust*. Washington, DC: Catholic University of America Press, 2006.
———. *Politics and the Papacy in the Modern World*. Westport, CT: Praeger, 2008.
———. *Pope Pius IX*. Boston: Twayne, 1979.
Cornwell, John. *Newman's Unquiet Grave*. New York: Continuum, 2010.
Coulson, John, and A. M. Allchin, eds. *The Rediscovery of Newman*. London: SPCK, 1967.
Cross, F. L., and E. A. Livingstone, eds. *The Oxford Dictionary of the Christian Church*. 2nd ed. New York: Oxford University Press, 1974.
———. *The Oxford Movement and the Seventeenth-Century Background*. London: SPCK, 1933.
Cummings, Owen F. "A Century of Near Eastern Languages at University College Dublin." *Doctrine and Life* 58 (2008) 30–36.
———. *Eucharist and Ecumenism: The Eucharist across the Ages and Traditions*. Eugene, OR: Pickwick, 2013.
———. *Eucharistic Doctors*. Mahwah, NJ: Paulist, 2005.

BIBLIOGRAPHY

———. *Prophets, Guardians and Saints, Shapers of Modern Catholic History*. Mahwah, NJ: Paulist, 2007.
Daley, SJ, Brian E. "The Church Fathers." In *The Cambridge Companion to John Henry Newman*, edited by Ian Ker and Terrence Merrigan, 29–46. Cambridge: Cambridge University Press, 2009.
Davis, Charles, ed. *English Spiritual Writers*. London: Sheed and Ward, 1961.
Davis, H. Francis. "Introduction." In *The Heart of Newman*, arranged by Erich Pryzwara, 9–16. San Francisco: Ignatius, 1997.
———. "Newman and Thomism." In *Newman Studien IV*, edited by Heinrich Fries and Werner Becker, 157–69. Nürnberg: Glock und Lutz, 1957.
Dawson, Christopher. *The Spirit of the Oxford Movement*. London: St. Austin, 2001.
De Flon, Nancy. *Edward Caswall*. Leominster, UK: Gracewing, 2005.
DeLaura, David J. "'O Unforgotten Voice': The Memory of Newman in the Nineteenth Century." *Renascence* 43 (1991) 81–104.
Dessain, Charles S. *John Henry Newman*. London: Darton, Longman and Todd, 1966.
———. "John Henry Newman: A Brief Biographical Sketch." In *Newman Studien X*, edited by Fries, Heinrich and Werner Becker, hg., 21–25. Heroldsberg bei Nürnberg: Glock und Lutz, 1978.
———. "Newman's Spirituality." In *English Spiritual Writers*, edited by Charles Davis, 136–60. London: Burns and Oates, 1961.
Dessain, Charles S., and Vincent F. Blehl, eds. *The Letters and Diaries of John Henry Newman*, Vol. 15. London: Nelson and Sons, 1964.
Dessain, Charles S., and Thomas Gornall, SJ, eds. *The Letters and Diaries of John Henry Newman*, Vol. 25. Oxford: Oxford University Press, 1973.
———, eds. *The Letters and Diaries of John Henry Newman*, Vol. 26. Oxford: Clarendon, 1974.
Duffy, Eamon. "The Age of Pio Nono: The Age of Paul Cullen." In *Cardinal Paul Cullen and His World*, edited by Dáire Keogh and Albert McDonnell, 47–60. Dublin: Four Courts, 2011.
———. *Saints and Sinners: A History of the Popes*. Rev. ed. New Haven: Yale University Press, 2001.
———. "The Staying Power of Christianity." *The New York Review of Books*, June 2013, 70.
———. *Ten Popes Who Shook the World*. New Haven: Yale University Press, 2011.
Dulles, Avery. *John Henry Newman*. New York: Continuum, 2002.
Fitzer, Joseph, ed. *Romance and the Rock: Nineteenth Century Catholics on Faith and Reason*. Minneapolis: Augsburg, 1989.
Forrester, David. "Dr. Pusey's Marriage." In *Pusey Rediscovered*, edited by Perry Butler, 119–38. London: SPCK, 1983.
Franzen, August, and John P. Dolan. *A History of the Church*. New York: Herder and Herder, 1969.
Frappell, Leighton. "'Science' in the Service of Orthodoxy: The Early Intellectual Development of Edward Bouverie Pusey." In *Pusey Rediscovered*, edited by Perry Butler, 1–33. London: SPCK, 1983.
Froude, J. A. *Short Studies on Great Subjects*. Fourth series. New York: Scribner's Sons, 1910.
Gallagher, Michael Paul. *Dive Deeper: The Human Poetry of Faith*. London: Darton, Longman and Todd, 2001.

Bibliography

Gilley, Sheridan. "Keble, Froude, Newman, and Pusey." In *The Oxford Handbook of the Oxford Movement*, edited by Stewart J. Brown et al., 97–110. Oxford: Oxford University Press, 2017.

———. "New Light on an Old Scandal: Purcell's Life of Cardinal Manning." In *Opening the Scrolls*, edited by Dominic Aidan Bellenger, 166–98. Bath, UK: Downside Abbey, 1987.

———. *Newman and His Age*. London: Darton, Longman and Todd, 2003.

———. "Newman and the Convert Mind." In *Newman and Conversion*, edited by Ian Ker, 5–20. Notre Dame, IN: University of Notre Dame Press, 1997.

———. "Vulgar Piety and the Brompton Oratory 1815–1860." *Durham University Journal* 43 (1981) 15–19.

Graef, Hilda. *God and Myself: The Spirituality of John Henry Newman*. London: Davies, 1967.

Gray, Robert. *Cardinal Manning*. New York: St. Martin's Press, 1985.

Greenfield, Robert H. "Such a Friend to the Pope." In *Pusey Rediscovered*, edited by Perry Butler, 162–84. London: SPCK, 1983.

Griffin, John R. *John Keble, Saint of Anglicanism*. Macon, GA: Mercer University Press, 1987.

Griffiths, Eric. "Newman: The Foolishness of Preaching." In *Newman After a Hundred Years*, edited by Ian Ker and Alan G. Hill, 63–92. Oxford: Clarendon, 1990.

Hales, Edward E. Y. *The Catholic Church in the Modern World*. Garden City, NY: Doubleday, 1960.

———. *Pio Nono*. New York: Doubleday, 1954.

Härdelin, Alf. "The Eucharist in the Theology of the Nineteenth Century." In *Eucharistic Theology Then and Now*, edited by Ronald E. Clements. London: SPCK, 1968.

———. "The Sacraments in the Tractarian Spiritual Universe." In *Tradition Renewed: The Oxford Movement Conference Papers*, edited by Geoffrey Rowell, 78–95. Allison Park, PA: Pickwick, 1986.

———. *The Tractarian Understanding of the Eucharist*. Uppsala: Acta Universitatis Upsaliensis, 1965.

Hastings, Adrian. *A History of English Christianity 1920–1990*. London: Collins, 1986.

———. "John Henry Newman." In *Key Thinkers in Christianity*, edited by Adrian Hastings et al., 118–24. Oxford: Oxford University Press, 2003.

———. "The Twentieth Century." In *Christianity, Two Thousand Years*, edited by Richard Harries and Henry Mayr-Harting, 218–36. Oxford: Oxford University Press, 2002.

Heft, SM, James L. "From the Pope to the Bishops: Episcopal Authority from Vatican I to Vatican II." In *The Papacy and the Church in the United States*, edited by Bernard Cooke, 55–78. Mahwah, NJ: Paulist, 1989.

Heimann, Mary. *Catholic Devotion in Victorian England*. Oxford: Clarendon, 1995.

Hennessey, James. *American Catholics*. Oxford: Oxford University Press, 1981.

———. *The First Council of the Vatican: The American Experience*. New York: Herder and Herder, 1963.

Hill, Roland. *Lord Acton*. New Haven: Yale University Press, 2000.

Himes, Michael. "The Development of Ecclesiology: Modernity to the Twentieth Century." In *The Gift of the Church*, edited by Peter C. Phan, 45–68. Collegeville, MN: Liturgical, 2000.

Holmes, J. Derek. *The Triumph of the Holy See: A Short History of the Papacy in the Nineteenth Century*. London: Burns and Oates, 1978.

BIBLIOGRAPHY

Honan, Daniel J. "Newman's Poetry." In *A Newman Symposium*, edited by Victor Yanitelli, 92–96. New York: Fordham University Press, 1952.
Howard, Thomas Albert. *The Papacy in the Modern World*. New York: Crossroad, 1981.
———. *The Pope and the Professor*. Oxford: Oxford University Press, 2017.
Hughes, Kevin L. *Church History*. Chicago: Loyola, 2002.
Hughes, Philip. *The Church in Crisis: The Twenty Great Councils*. London: Burns and Oates, 1961.
———. *A Popular History of the Catholic Church*. New York: Macmillan, 1954.
Jasper, David. "Pusey's 'Lectures on Types and Prophecies of the Old Testament.'" In *Pusey Rediscovered*, edited by Perry Butler, 51–70. London: SPCK, 1983.
Jenkins, A. Hilary. "Lyra Apostolica and the Genesis of 'Lead, Kindly Light.'" In *Christliche Heiligkeit als Lehre und Praxis nach John Henry Newman*, edited by G. Biemer and H. Fries, 117–35. Sigmaringensdorf, Germany: Verlag Glock und Lutz, 1988.
Johnson, Maria P. *John Keble: Sermons for the Christian Year*. Grand Rapids: Eerdmans, 2004.
Keble, John. *The Christian Year*. London: Oxford University Press, 1914.
Kelly, John N. D. *The Oxford Dictionary of the Popes*. Oxford: Oxford University Press, 1986.
Kerr, Fergus. "Vatican I and the Papacy: A Proud Appellation." *New Blackfriars* 60 (1979) 164–82.
Ker, Ian. *The Achievement of John Henry Newman*. Notre Dame, IN: University of Notre Dame Press, 1990.
———. *Newman on Vatican II*. Oxford: Oxford University Press, 2014.
Kerr, Ian, and Terrence Merrigan, eds. *The Cambridge Companion to John Henry Newman*. Cambridge: Cambridge University Press, 2009.
Kertzer, David I. *The Kidnapping of Edgardo Mortara*. New York: Knopf, 1997.
———. *The Popes against the Jews*. New York: Knopf, 2001.
Lash, Nicholas. "Modernism, Aggiornamento and the Night Battle." In *Bishops and Writers*, edited by Adrian Hastings, 51–79. Wheathampstead, UK: Clarke, 1977.
———. *Newman on Development*. London: Sheet and Ward, 1975.
———. "On Learning to Be Wise." *Priests and People*, October 2001, 355–59.
Lawlor, F. X. "Infallibility." *New Catholic Encyclopedia*, 7:448–52. Washington, DC: Catholic University of America Press, 2003.
Lease, Gary. *Witness to the Faith: Cardinal Newman on the Teaching Authority of the Church*. Pittsburgh: Duquesne University Press, 1971.
Liddon, H. P. *Life of Edward Bouverie Pusey*. London: Longmans Green, 1893–97.
Lodge, David. "How Far Have We Come?" *The Tablet*, July 26, 2008, 16–17.
McCarren, Gerard H. "Development of Doctrine." In *The Cambridge Companion to John Henry Newman*, edited by Ian Ker and Terrence Merrigan, 118–36. Cambridge: Cambridge University Press, 2009.
McClelland, Vincent A. *Cardinal Manning, His Public Life and Influence 1865–92*. New York: Oxford University Press, 1962.
McCool, SJ, Gerard. *Catholic Theology in the Nineteenth Century*. New York: Seabury, 1977.
McPartlan, Paul. "Go Forth, Christian Soul." *One in Christ* 34 (1998) 247–57.
Macquarrie, John. *Stubborn Theological Questions*. London: SCM, 2003.
———. *Two Worlds Are Ours: An Introduction to Christian Mysticism*. London: SCM, 2004.

Bibliography

Meredith, Anthony. *The Theology of Tradition*. Notre Dame, IN: Fides, 1971.

Messori, Vittorio. *Kidnapped by the Vatican? The Unpublished Memoirs of Edgardo Mortara*. San Francisco: Ignatius, 2017.

Michaels, Anne. *Fugitive Pieces*. London: Bloomsbury, 1998.

Middleton, R. D. "The Vicar of St. Mary's." In *John Henry Newman: Centenary Essays*, 125–40. London: Burns, Oates and Washbourne, 1945.

Mozley, Anne, ed. *Letters and Correspondence of John Henry Newman during His Life in the English Church*. London: Longmans Green, 1891.

Mulcahy, D. G. "Personal Influence, Discipline and Liberal Education in Cardinal Newman's Idea of a University." In *Newman Studien XI*, edited by Heinrich Fries et al., 150–58. Heroldsberg bei Nürnberg: Glock und Lutz, 1980.

Murray, Paul D. "Receptive Ecumenism and Catholic Learning—Establishing the Agenda." In *Receptive Ecumenism and the Call to Catholic Learning*, edited by Paul D. Murray, 5–25. Oxford: Oxford University Press, 2008.

Murray, Placid. *Newman the Oratorian*. Dublin: Gill and Macmillan, 1969.

Newman, John Henry. *An Essay on the Development of Christian Doctrine*. Edited with an introduction by J. M. Cameron. Harmondsworth, UK: Penguin, 1989.

———. *Historical Sketches*, Vol. 2. London: Dent, 1906.

———. *The Idea of a University*. Edited by Ian Ker. Oxford: Oxford University Press, 1976.

———. Lecture 12, "Ecclesiastical History No Prejudice to the Apostolicity of the Church." In *Certain Difficulties Felt by Anglicans in Catholic Teaching*, Vol. 1, 363–400. London: Pickering, 1876.

———. *Parochial and Plain Sermons*. 2 vols. London: Longmans Green, 1891.

———. *Sermons on Subjects of the Day*. New Impression. London: Longmans Green, 1910.

Nicholl, Donald. *Holiness*. London: Darton, Longman and Todd, 1981.

Nockles, Peter. "Foreword." In *Edward Caswall, Newman's Brother and Friend*, by Nancy M. de Flon, ix–xii. Leominster, UK: Gracewing, 2005.

———. "The Oxford Movement: Historical Background, 1718–1833," In *Tradition Renewed: The Oxford Movement Conference Papers*, edited by Geoffrey Rowell, 24–50. Allison Park, PA: Pickwick, 1986.

O'Carroll, Ciaran. "Pius IX: Pastor and Prince." In *The Papacy Since 1500*, edited by James Corkery and Thomas Worcester, 125–42. Cambridge: Cambridge University Press, 2010.

O'Connell, Marvin R. *Critics on Trial: An Introduction to the Catholic Modernist Crisis*. Washington, DC: Catholic Press, 1994.

———. *The Oxford Conspirators: A History of the Oxford Movement 1833–1845*. London: Macmillan, 1969.

O'Donoghue, Noel Dermot. *The Holy Mountain*. Wilmington, DE: Glazier, 1983.

O'Donohue, John. *Anam Chara*. New York: HarperCollins, 1997.

O'Faoláin, Seán. *Newman's Way*. New York: The Devin-Adair Co., 1952.

O'Gara, Margaret. *Triumph in Defeat: Vatican I and the French Minority Bishops*. Washington, DC: Catholic University of America Press, 1988.

Olsen, Glenn W. *Beginning at Jerusalem: Five Reflections on the History of the Church*. San Francisco: Ignatius, 2004.

O'Malley, SJ, John W. "The Beatification of Pope Pius IX." *America*, August 26–September 2, 2000, 10.

Bibliography

———. *Catholic History for Today's Church*. New York: Rowman and Littlefield, 2015.
———. *A History of the Popes*. New York: Rowman and Littlefield, 2010.
———. *Vatican I: The Council and the Making of the Ultramontane Church*. Cambridge: The Belknap Press of Harvard University Press, 2018.
———. *What Happened at Vatican II*. Cambridge: The Belknap Press of Harvard University Press, 2008.
Pereiro, James. *Cardinal Manning, An Intellectual Biography*. Oxford: Clarendon, 1998.
Pipher, Mary. *Letters to a Young Therapist*. New York: Basic, 2003.
Przywara, Erich, ed. *The Heart of Newman*. San Francisco: Ignatius, 1997.
Purcell, E. R. *Life of Cardinal Manning*. 2 vols. London: Macmillan, 1896.
Pusey, Edward Bouverie. *Presence of Christ in the Holy Eucharist*. Los Angeles: Hard, 2015.
———. *Sermons during the Season from Advent to Whitsuntide*. London: Forgotten, 2016.
Quinn, John R. *Revered and Reviled: A Re-Examination of Vatican Council I*. New York: Crossroad, 2017.
Rahner, Karl. *Theological Investigations*, Vol. 23. New York: Crossroad, 1992.
Robinson, Denis. "Preaching." In *The Cambridge Companion to John Henry Newman*, edited by Ian Ker and Terrence Merrigan, 241–54. Cambridge: Cambridge University Press, 2009.
Rowell, Geoffrey. "The Ecclesiology of the Oxford Movement." In *The Oxford Handbook of the Oxford Movement*, edited by Stewart J. Brown et al., 216–30. Oxford: Oxford University Press, 2017.
———. "John Keble: A Bi-Centenary Sermon." In *The English Religious Tradition and the Genius of Anglicanism*, edited by Geoffrey Rowell, 243–49. Nashville: Abingdon, 1992.
———. "The Roots of Newman's 'Scriptural Holiness': Some Formative Influences on Newman's Spirituality." In *Newman Studien X*, edited by Heinrich Fries and Werner Becker, 13–20. Heroldsberg bei Nürnberg, Germany: Glock und Lutz, 1978.
———, ed. *Tradition Renewed: The Oxford Movement Papers*. Allison Park, PA: Pickwick, 1986.
———. *The Vision Glorious: Themes and Personalities of the Catholic Revival in Anglicanism*. Oxford: Oxford University Press, 1983.
Rutler, George W. "Newman, John Henry." In *Concise Encyclopedia of Preaching*, edited by William H. Willimon and Richard Lischer, 344–46. Louisville, KY: John Knox, 1995.
Schultenover, David G. *A View from Rome*. New York: Fordham University Press, 1993.
Sharp, Richard. "New Perspectives on the High Church Tradition: Historical Background, 1730–1780." In *Tradition Renewed: The Oxford Movement Conference Papers*, edited by Geoffrey Rowell, 4–23. Allison Park, PA: Pickwick, 1986.
Sharrock, Roger. "Newman's Poetry." In *Newman After a Hundred Years*, edited by Ian Ker and Alan G. Hill, 43–62. Oxford: Clarendon, 1990.
Strachey, Lytton. *Eminent Victorians*. Garden City, NY: Doubleday, 1918.
Strange, Roderick. *Newman 101*. Notre Dame, IN: Christian Classics, 2008.
———. "Reflections on a Controversy: Newman and Pusey's Eirenicon." In *Pusey Rediscovered*, edited by Perry Butler, 332–48. London: SPCK, 1983.
———. "'A Strange Providence': Newman's Illness in Sicily." *Louvain Studies* 15 (1990) 151–65.
Strong, Rowan, and Carol Englehardt Herringer, eds. *Edward Bouverie Pusey and the Oxford Movement*. London: Anthem, 2014.

Bibliography

Sugg, Joyce. *Snapdragon: The Story of John Henry Newman.* Huntington, IN: Our Sunday Visitor, 1982.

———. *Ever Yours Affly, John Henry Newman and His Female Circle.* Leominster, UK: Gracewing, 1996.

Sweeney, Garrett. "The Forgotten Council." In *Bishops and Writers*, edited by Adrian Hastings, 161–78. Wheathampstead, UK: Clark, 1977.

Tanner, SJ, Norman P., ed. *Documents of the Ecumenical Councils*, vol. I–II. New York: Georgetown University Press, 1990.

Trevor, Meriol. *Newman: Light in Winter.* London: Macmillan, 1962.

———. *Newman's Journey.* Glasgow: Collins, 1974.

———. "Preface." In *Ever Yours Affly, John Henry Newman and His Female Circle*, by Joyce Sugg, n.p. Leominster, UK: Gracewing, 1996.

Tristram, Henry. *John Henry Newman, Autobiographical Writings.* New York: Sheed and Ward, 1956.

Turner, Frank M. *John Henry Newman: The Challenge to Evangelical Religion.* New Haven: Yale University Press, 2002.

Vidler, Alec R. *The Church in an Age of Revolution.* Rev. ed. Harmondsworth, UK: Penguin, 1974.

Von Arx, Jeffrey, ed. *Varieties of Ultramontanism.* Washington, DC: Catholic University of America Press, 1998.

Wilder, Amos. *Theopoetic: Theology and the Religious Imagination.* Philadelphia: Fortress, 1976.

Wilks, Michael. *Wyclif: Political Ideas and Practice.* Oxford: Oxbow, 2000.

Willey, Basil. *More Nineteenth Century Studies.* New York: Harper and Row, 1966.

Williams, Rowan. "Introduction." In John Henry Newman, *The Arians of the Fourth Century*, xix–xlvii. Notre Dame, IN: University of Notre Dame Press, 2001.

———. *Open to Judgment.* London: Darton, Longman and Todd, 1994.

Wilson, A. N. *The Victorians.* London: Norton, 2003.

www.ingramcontent.com/pod-product-compliance
Lightning Source LLC
Chambersburg PA
CBHW031432150426
43191CB00006B/484